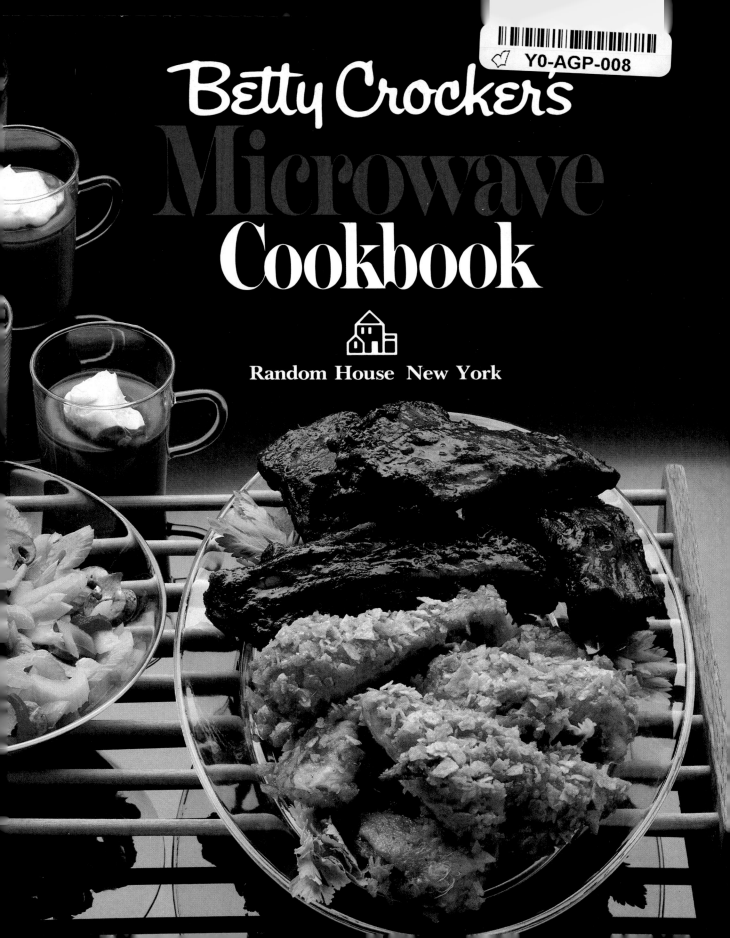

Betty Crocker's
Microwave
Cookbook

Random House New York

FOREWORD

In this era of microwaves, home cooking has been transformed. Clean, cool, safe, convenient and time-and-work saving — microwaving is an established part of today's lifestyle.

Every day of testing and research in the Betty Crocker Kitchens brings new discoveries, techniques and success tips that promise even greater microwave skill for the future. Here, then, is a collection of recipes that explore the marvelous capabilities of microwaving and adapt them to today's living.

This book is the product of the combined efforts of many people. Beginning in the Betty Crocker Kitchens, the recipes were developed, using a variety of microwaves of differing wattage. They were evaluated by a panel of home economists for flavor, texture and appearance as well as for speed and ease of preparation. Finally, hundreds of the recipes were tested by a cross-country microwave panel of home testers in their own kitchens.

The recipes were all designed for best use of the microwave — to save time and produce excellent finished products. For maximum results, some take advantage of complementary cooking, using both the microwave and conventional oven. You'll find recipes organized as you would plan a meal — in chapters on Main Dishes, Vegetables, Breads, Desserts, Appetizers and Snacks. The beautiful color photographs show you just how the finished foods will look.

Look for inspiration to the Menus Chapter for both family and entertaining occasions. The menus are complete with timetables so that all dishes can come to the table at once. Or try the Plan-Ahead recipes for families who eat on different time schedules, and take advantage of do-ahead tips that coordinate freezer and refrigerator with microwave.

Now, read in the introduction about microwave safety and principles, power settings and what they mean and basic techniques. With these facts and the easy "how to do it" tips, you will be ready to enjoy microwaving success to the fullest.

Betty Crocker

Copyright © 1981 by General Mills, Inc., Minneapolis, Minnesota

All rights reserved under International and Pan-American Copyright Conventions. Published in the United States by Random House, Inc., New York, and simultaneously in Canada by Random House of Canada Limited, Toronto.

Library of Congress Cataloging in Publication Data   Crocker, Betty. Betty Crocker's Microwave Cookbook

Includes index.   1. Microwave Cookery.   I. Title.   II. Title: Microwave Cookbook.
TX832.C75   641.5′882   81-40249   ISBN 0-394-51764-4   AACR2

Manufactured in the United States of America   B98765

Betty Crocker's
Microwave
Cookbook

CONTENTS

*Pictured on page 2: Stuffed Tomatoes, Spiced Mocha Drink, Currant-Glazed Ribs,
Garlic Chip Chicken, Celery with Mushrooms, Sweet-Sour Meatballs*

INTRODUCTION

How Microwaves Work

Invisible Light Waves . . .
There's nothing mysterious about microwaves, even though they can't be seen. They are simply a form of radiant energy, much like radio and television waves. They are emitted by all objects in the world — from plants to humans to the kitchen sink.

Uncontained, microwaves spread out in every direction. Their energy diminishes rapidly, like the heat from a little birthday candle. In fact, at a distance of 10 inches from their source of energy, they contain only 1/100 as much energy as they do at a distance of 1 inch.

Generated In Your Oven . . .
Microwaves for cooking are produced by the magnetron tube which converts household electricity into microwaves which *bounce off* the *metal* walls of the microwave. They *pass through* *nonmetal* materials such as glass, paper, plastics and wood, and *are absorbed by* food which contains *moisture.*

Cook With Friction Heat . . .
The microwaves agitate and vibrate the moisture molecules in foods at a speed of about 2½ billion times a second, which causes friction, which in turn heats and cooks the food. Microwaves only penetrate 1 inch into the food from top, sides and bottom, so the rest of the cooking is done by conduction of heat into the food. The hot food heats the container as well, so potholders may be necessary.

Which Stops Automatically . . .
When the set time has elapsed or when you open the door of your microwave, the magnetron turns off and microwaves are no longer produced — similar to your radio or television set, which no longer receive signals when the station has signed off.

And Is Safe To Use . . .
The microwave is one of the safest appliances in the home. According to government reports, after more than a quarter of a century of in-home use, the microwave has yet to result in a single documented instance of injury related to microwave exposure. Strict limits on the level of energy emitted have been established by the government to assure the safety of microwave cooking.

With Proper Operation . . .
Like other cooking appliances, the microwave must be operated properly in order to provide safe usage. Be sure to follow the manufacturer's instructions for operation and cleaning.

But Not Yet Standardized.
Although microwaves operate the same way, they are at the stage conventional ovens were many years ago. *All microwave units are not the same!* They differ from each other in:
1. Wattage (see Testing for This Book on page 8).
2. Power setting descriptions.
3. Cooking patterns, even within brands.

Moreover, cooking time may vary with peak and low loads of electric power from your area going into the microwave. Therefore, you will want to adjust recipes to the workings of your own microwave:
1. Check for doneness at minimum cooking time given in the recipe.
2. Add more cooking time after doneness test only if necessary.
3. Give less or more attention (stirring, rotating or elevating) depending on your microwave's cooking pattern.

Microwaving Techniques

Cover Tightly. To speed heating. Use lid or plastic wrap with 1 corner or edge turned back to prevent splitting.

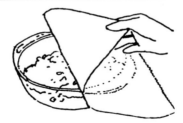

Cover Loosely. To prevent spattering and/or hold in the heat. Use waxed paper or lid slightly ajar.

Stir. To help food cook more quickly. Stir from outside to center to distribute heat; food heats faster on outside.

Rotate. To even cooking for foods which cannot be stirred, such as cakes. Rotate ¼ or ½ turn, as directed in recipes.

Arrange. To take advantage of microwave patterns. Arrange cupcakes, muffins, potatoes, or appetizers in circle.

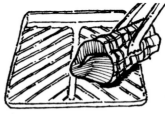

Turn Over. To even cooking from top to bottom for foods such as roasts, whole chickens and meat rolls.

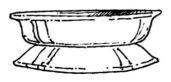

Elevate. To assure doneness on the bottom. Place food on inverted dish so bottom center can absorb microwaves.

Coat. To give color, crispness and flavor. Some foods (such as chicken or fish) and some utensils (such as bundt dishes) are coated.

Pierce. To prevent bursting. Egg yolks and some vegetables (such as whole potatoes, sweet potatoes or squash) are pierced before cooking.

Reheat. To heat evenly, spread food out, add sauce or gravy and cover. Place food needing the most cooking at outside of the plate.

Reheat. To avoid overcooking, place porous food needing least heating (such as roll or muffin) in center or add it later for a brief cooking time.

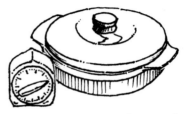

Let Stand. To complete cooking and develop the flavor. Standing time is required for some but not all foods (see individual recipes).

Microwave Cooking Principles

Microwaving involves many of the same principles as conventional cooking, but because the cooking time is accelerated, these principles are even more important.

Density. Porous foods such as breads and cakes absorb microwaves quickly and so cook quickly, while more dense foods such as potatoes, casseroles and roasts absorb microwaves less quickly, so require longer cooking.

Height. Microwave energy usually enters the cavity from the top, resulting in faster cooking there. If the food is close to the microwave source, it may need turning over for even cooking.

Moisture. Food containing moisture usually microwaves well, since microwaves are attracted by moisture. Microwaves also like foods containing sugar and fat. Foods such as cooked roast beef heat best if moisture such as gravy is added or they are covered.

Quantity. There are always the same number of microwaves present. If only one potato is being cooked, all the microwaves are concentrated on that one item. If four potatoes are microwaved, the same number of microwaves must be shared by the four potatoes. Consequently, more food equals more time. This means that for large quantities, microwaving may not be as efficient as conventional baking.

Shape. Evenly shaped foods — round or doughnut shaped — microwave best. Containers that are ring-shaped or round will allow foods (cakes, casseroles, custards) to cook evenly. Unevenly shaped foods are more difficult to cook evenly — they require more attention (rearranging or turning over) during cooking.

Size. Small pieces of foods will cook faster than large pieces. It is important to have cut-up or shaped foods such as vegetables and meatballs in uniform sizes for even microwave cooking.

Standing Time. Standing or carry-over cooking is important in microwaving. Foods continue cooking after removal from the microwave. Note the doneness test specified and check the food at minimum time. The amount of standing time is indicated in each recipe where it is important.

Temperature of Food Before Microwaving. Microwave timing is affected by the starting temperature of the food. The colder the food, the longer it will take to heat or cook. Recipe testing for this book was done with foods taken directly from their normal storage areas — refrigerator (milk, meats, eggs), freezer (frozen vegetables), cupboard shelf (flour, canned goods).

Testing for This Book

These recipes were tested in the Betty Crocker Kitchens using countertop microwaves with 625 to 700 watts. **If your microwave has a rating of 400 to 500 watts, cooking times must be lengthened.** During testing, only the variable power settings described on page 9 were used.

Other features (combination microwave/conventional oven, convection cooking) and accessories (browning grill, meat rack, temperature probe, memory feature) vary among manufacturers. Consult your use and care booklet for guidelines if you have these special features.

Microwave Power Settings

Most recipes in this book are microwaved at high (100%) settings, but certain foods require lower power settings for best results, so some recipes were tested using one or more of the settings below:

Power Level Settings	Percent of High Settings	Power Output at Settings - Watts
		Can be
High	100%	550 (+ or − 50)
Medium-High	70%	385 (+ or − 40)
Medium	50%	275 (+ or − 30)
Medium-Low	30%	165 (+ or − 20)
Low	10%	55 (+ or − 15)

If your microwave does not have settings that match the chart, check your use and care booklet, or with your manufacturer to learn what percent of power your settings are.

Defrosting or thawing instructions were not given in this book because manufacturers vary in the percent of power they indicate for defrosting their products.

IMPORTANT!

Use the power setting first given in the recipe unless a change is indicated.

Foods Not Recommended for Microwaving

The recipes in this book save time over conventional cooking and have acceptable appearance, texture and flavor. However, certain recipes were not included:

Angel, sponge, chiffon cakes: Hot, dry air is needed to set their structure.

Crisply fried foods: Surface cooking is needed for browning and crispness.

Deep-fried foods: Fat may spatter and temperature cannot be kept constant.

Dried beans or peas: Timesaving is only an advantage for reheating cooked beans.

Eggs in shells or whole peeled, cooked eggs: They can burst during microwaving.

Crusty breads, French toast: Only reheating is recommended.

Hash-browned potatoes: Surface cooking is needed for crisp, brown crust.

Home canning: Surface cooking needed to maintain safe internal temperature.

Pancakes, crepes: Surface cooking is necessary. To reheat in microwave, see page 275.

Pasta: Timesaving no advantage. To reheat in microwave, see page 244.

Popcorn: Too dry to microwave unless corn is designed for microwaving or popped in a microwave popper. Microwaving popcorn in a paper bag could cause a fire.

Popovers: Hot, dry air is needed to set the structure. Popovers reheat well (page 109).

Regular rice: No time saved over conventional cooking when cooked alone.

Steaks, broiled or fried: Conventional method needed to brown and cook evenly.

Turkey (15 pounds or over): More attention is needed than for conventional cooking.

Microwave Utensils

Use nonmetal utensils: glassware, paper, plasticware, dishwasher-safe plastic containers, ceramic plates and casseroles containing no metals, and china with no metal trim.

Look for microwave- and dishwasher-safe utensils that are lightweight, with handles that can be gripped with potholders and shapes that store and stack easily. If utensils are resistant to conventional heat, they can be used for complementary cooking.

Avoid metal utensils: they are not suitable for microwaving because arcing (causing a flash as in welding) can occur. Some manufacturers suggest using small pieces of aluminum foil to "shield" areas of foods that might be cooking too quickly (for example, while defrosting, wing tips of a chicken may begin to cook or corners of bar cookies may have a tendency to overcook.) Follow your microwave manufacturer's directions in regard to using aluminum foil or foil-lined containers.

Materials Ideal for Microwaving
Check your kitchen for microwave utensils!

To test utensils for microwave use, place the utensil in question in the microwave beside 1 cup cool water in a glass measure. Microwave uncovered on high (100%) 1 minute. If the water is warm and the dish is cool, the dish can be used for microwaving. However, if the water stayed at the same temperature and the dish feels warm, it should not be used for microwaving.

Ceramic, stoneware and pottery are safe for microwaving if there are no traces of metals in the clay-like composition. If you are in doubt, test the utensils (above).

China can be used for microwaving if recommended by the manufacturer. Often this information appears on the dishes, the label or a leaflet packed with them.

Glassware is well suited to microwave cooking and heating. Use oven-tempered glass, because cooked food does become hot and that heat is transferred to the utensil.

Paper is good for brief reheating. Paper towels designated as microwavable are excellent for reheating rolls or muffins or for absorbing grease. For cooking, durable paper board containers are available in many shapes and sizes. **Caution:** avoid color-printed paper towels (color may run) or recycled paper products (they may contain tiny metal fragments). Unless plastic coated, red or green paper plates may fade color onto the food.

Reusable plastic containers (dishwasher-safe) can also be used for quick reheating, but not for cooking or heating of foods such as chili or spaghetti sauce. Very hot food can stain, distort and melt the plastic.

Plastic cooking pouches that contain (or are used for) frozen vegetables and entrées can withstand high temperatures and be used in your microwave. Be sure to make a slit in the pouch to allow for the escape of steam.

Plastic microwave cookware is available in many microwave-compatible shapes and sizes. These plastics vary in quality, design, durability and price. When buying plastic cookware, read the package information telling which foods can be cooked in the utensil. Some plastics do not withstand high fat- and high sugar-content foods, as the high temperatures distort the cookware. Recommendation by manufacturer as to where the cookware should be placed in a dishwasher is also a clue — placement on lower rack suggests higher durability.

For dual use (microwave and conventional), check the plastic manufacturer's directions. **Caution:** Plastic cookware should never be used for range-top cooking, broiling, or with a browning unit.

Wicker baskets, wooden spoons and bread boards without metal parts can be used in the microwave for short periods of time.

Microwaving Tips

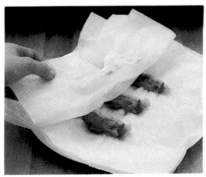

TIMETABLE	
Slices	**Minutes**
1 to 2	¾ to 2
3	2¼ to 3
4	3 to 4
5	3¾ to 5
6	4 to 6

Cooking Bacon. Microwave on high (100%) on plate lined with 2 paper towels. Cover with paper towel before microwaving. To save bacon fat, place bacon on rack and cover with paper towel.

Heating Syrup. Microwave uncovered on high (100%) 45 to 60 seconds for ½ cup, 2 to 2½ minutes for 1 cup.

TIMETABLE	
Tablespoons	**Seconds**
1 to 2	15 to 30
3 to 4	30 to 45
Cups	
⅓ to ½	45 to 60
⅔ to 1	60 to 90

Melting Margarine or Butter. Microwave either one uncovered on high (100%) in custard cup, measuring cup or casserole. To brown margarine or butter, increase timing slightly and watch carefully until it changes to a light brown color.

Softening Brown Sugar. Cover tightly. Microwave on high (100%), checking every 30 seconds, until softened.

TIMETABLE	
Tablespoons	**Seconds**
1 to 3	15 to 30
Cups	
¼ to 1	30 to 45

Softening Margarine or Butter. For easy spreading or mixing, microwave margarine or butter uncovered on serving dish on medium-low (30%) until softened.

Boiling Water. Microwave 1 cup hot water on high (100%) to boiling, 2 to 3 minutes.

Microwaving Tips, continued

TIMETABLE	
Amount	**Minutes**
¼ cup + margarine	1½ to 3
½ cup + margarine	2½ to 4

Toasting Almonds. Add 1 teaspoon margarine for both amounts of almonds. Microwave slivered or sliced almonds uncovered on high (100%), stirring every 30 seconds, until almonds are crisp and light brown. Watch carefully!

Toasting Coconut. Cook on high (100%) 1½ minutes for ½ cup, 2½ minutes for 1 cup. Stir every 30 seconds. Watch carefully!

TIMETABLE	
Amount	**Minutes**
1 cup + margarine	2 to 2½
2 cups + margarine	3 to 4

Toasting Soft Bread Crumbs. Toss 1 cup crumbs with 1 teaspoon melted margarine, 2 cups crumbs with 1 tablespoon margarine. Microwave uncovered on high (100%), stirring every 30 seconds for 1 cup and every minute for 2 cups. (1 cup crumbs equals about 2 slices bread.)

Melting Chocolate Squares. Microwave 1 or 2 squares uncovered on medium (50%) 3 to 4 minutes, stirring after 2½ minutes.

TIMETABLE	
Amount	**Minutes**
14 ounces + 2 tablespoons water	3 to 4
7 ounces + 1 tablespoon water	1½ to 2½

Melting Caramels. Microwave caramels and water uncovered on high (100%), stirring 1 package (14 ounces, 48 caramels) every minute and ½ package every 30 seconds. Stir caramels after microwaving for smooth consistency.

Melting Chocolate Chips. Microwave ½ to 1 cup chips on medium (50%) 3 to 4½ minutes. Stir until smooth.

Microwaving Tips, continued

TIMETABLE	
Amount	**Minutes**
2 cups	½ to 1
4 cups	1 to 2

Crisping Snacks. Microwave pretzels, corn chips, potato chips or popcorn uncovered on high (100%) in napkin-lined basket. (Be sure there is no metal on basket.) Stir and let stand 5 minutes, all except popcorn. Popcorn is best served hot.

Warming Liquor for Flaming (page 203). Microwave uncovered on high (100%) until warm, 15 seconds for ¼ cup, 30 seconds for ½ cup.

TIMETABLE	
Amount	**Seconds**
3 ounces	30 to 45
8 ounces	60 to 90

Softening Cream Cheese. Remove foil wrapper from 3-ounce or 8-ounce package of cream cheese and microwave uncovered in bowl or pie plate on medium (50%) until softened. Cheese will hold its shape while it softens.

Heating Dampened Finger Towels. Microwave uncovered on high (100%) 1 to 2 minutes for 2 to 6 towels.

Microwaving Oysters to Open

1. **Soak** and scrub the oysters in their shells in cold water; arrange 6 at a time with hinges toward outside on paper towel-lined plate.

2. **Cover** tightly; microwave on high (100%) until shells open slightly, 1 to 1½ minutes. Remove oysters as they start to open.

3. **Open** by holding oyster with hinge toward you; insert knife between shells near hinge; open. Run knife around to cut muscle.

Rib Roast with Golden Potatoes

6 to 8 servings

Brush 3- to 4-pound beef rib roast (2 or 3 ribs) with bottled teriyaki sauce. Place fat side down on microwave rack in baking dish. Microwave uncovered on medium-low (30%) 20 minutes; turn roast fat side up. (Prop with custard cup if necessary.) Microwave until meat thermometer registers 135°, 20 to 30 minutes longer. Cover roast with aluminum foil; let stand 15 minutes. (Roast will continue to cook while it stands.) To serve au jus, spoon beef juices over carved beef. Serve with Golden Potatoes (below.)

Golden Potatoes
Make thin crosswise cuts almost through 6 medium potatoes. Arrange in circle on 12-inch plate. Drizzle with ¼ cup melted margarine or butter (page 11) and sprinkle with paprika. Cover tightly and microwave on high (100%) 6 minutes; turn potatoes over, brush with margarine and sprinkle with additional paprika. Cover and microwave until tender, 6 to 8 minutes longer.

Microwaving Beef Roasts

An ideal roast for microwaving, as described by the National Livestock and Meat Board, is a tender cut, boneless preferred, in a compact, uniform shape, weighing 3 to 5 pounds. Microwaving techniques in this book are based on what works well with each roast, but here are some general suggestions:

1. **Choose a high quality roast** of even shape (not irregular). Choices include: boneless top round, sirloin tip, rump or rib-eye roast and bone-in rib roast (small end).
2. **Tenderize less tender roasts** with a marinade or commercial tenderizer.
3. **Place** roast on rack deep enough to keep meat above its juices. Do not add water.
4. **Cover loosely (if at all)** so the meat will not be steamed.
5. **Use low (30%) or medium (50%) power** to prevent shrinkage and retain juiciness, tenderness, flavor and appearance.
6. **Use brush-ons** (sauces) or microwave browning shake-ons to enhance color and add flavor.
7. **Turn roast** over after about ½ the time. Start fat side down (or with chicken, breast side down).
8. **Use a microwave thermometer** or temperature probe inserted horizontally *during* cooking, or conventional thermometer *after* cooking.
9. **Add a standing time** of 10 to 20 minutes with meat covered with aluminum foil to even the cooking. (Allow for internal temperature to rise as meat stands.)

For pot roasts and other less tender cuts of beef, see page 22.

Pictured on previous page: Chicken with Stuffing and Giblet Gravy, Pear Chutney, Gingered Pot Roast, Curried Tuna with Rice

Rib Roast with Golden Potatoes

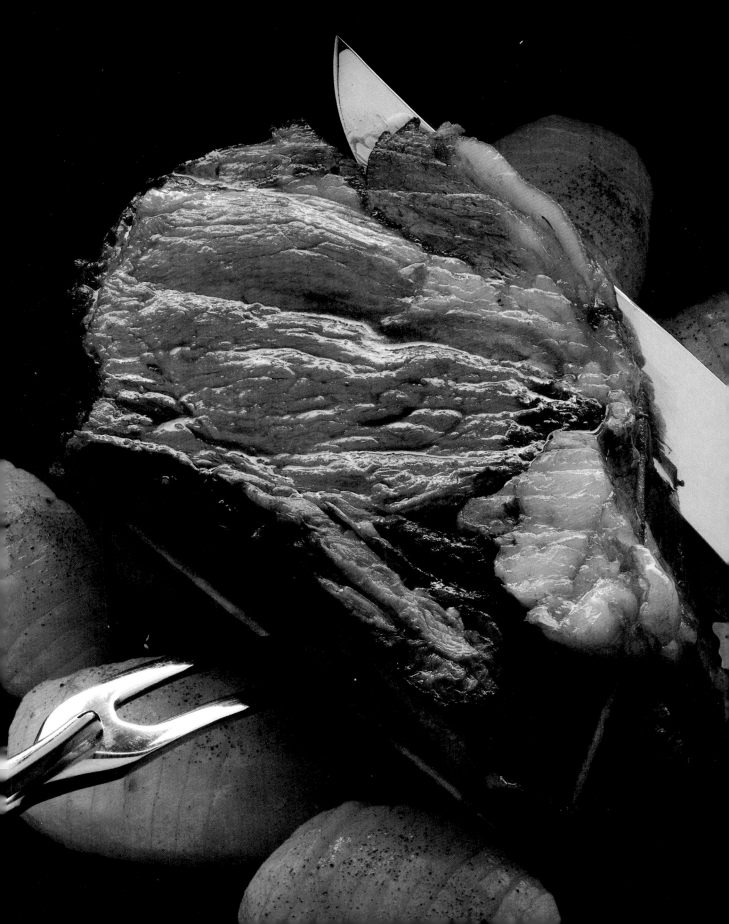

Beer-Garlic Roast Beef

10 to 12 servings

4 - *pound beef top round roast*
¾ *cup beer or apple cider*
2 *tablespoons vegetable oil*
2 *cloves garlic, finely chopped*
½ *teaspoon salt*
⅛ *teaspoon pepper*

2 *teaspoons instant beef bouillon*

¼ *cup cold water*
2 *tablespoons all-purpose flour*

1. Pierce beef roast thoroughly with fork. Place beef in deep glass bowl. Mix beer, oil, garlic, salt and pepper; pour over beef. Cover and refrigerate, turning occasionally, at least 1 hour.

2. Sprinkle roast with beef bouillon. Place beef fat side down on microwave rack in baking dish. (Prop with custard cup if necessary.) Reserve marinade. Cover roast with waxed paper and microwave on medium-low (30%) 35 minutes; turn roast fat side up. Cover and microwave until meat thermometer registers 150°, 25 to 35 minutes longer. Cover roast with aluminum foil and let stand 15 minutes. (Roast will continue to cook while it stands.)

3. Pour drippings into 4-cup measure; skim off fat. Add reserved marinade and enough water, if necessary, to make 1 cup. Shake water and flour in tightly covered container; stir gradually into marinade. Microwave uncovered on high (100%), stirring every minute, until thickened, 2 to 3 minutes. Serve gravy with beef.

Beer-Garlic Roast Beef

Gingered Pot Roast (pictured on page 14)

About 8 servings

1 cup water
1 cup dried apricot halves
 (about 4 ounces)
1 teaspoon salt
1 teaspoon bottled brown bouquet
 sauce
1 teaspoon water
½ teaspoon ground ginger
¼ teaspoon pepper
4 - pound beef cross-rib pot roast
1½ cups chopped onion
 (about 3 medium)
2 cloves garlic, finely chopped
½ cup hot water

1 can (6 ounces) pitted ripe
 olives, drained
2 cups sliced mushrooms
 (about 6 ounces)

2 tablespoons cornstarch
¼ cup cold water

1. Pour 1 cup water over apricots; reserve. Mix salt, bouquet sauce, 1 teaspoon water, the ginger and pepper; brush over beef. Place beef in 3-quart casserole. Add onion, garlic and ½ cup hot water. Cover tightly and microwave on high (100%) 10 minutes.

2. Microwave on medium-low (30%) 20 minutes; turn roast over. Cover tightly and microwave 35 minutes longer.

3. Drain apricots. Add apricots, olives and mushrooms to beef. Cover tightly and microwave on medium-low (30%) until beef is tender, 35 to 45 minutes. Remove roast to platter; keep warm.

4. Pour 2 cups broth into 4-cup measure. Mix cornstarch and ¼ cup water; stir into broth. Microwave uncovered on high (100%), stirring every minute, until thickened and boiling, 2½ to 3½ minutes. Serve gravy with roast.

Corned Beef Brisket

10 servings

3 - pound corned beef boneless brisket
1 clove garlic, cut into 5 or 6
 slivers
½ cup sweet red wine
½ cup water

1. Make 5 or 6 evenly spaced slits about ½ inch deep in brisket; insert garlic sliver into each. Place brisket in 3-quart casserole. Pour wine and water over brisket. Cover tightly and microwave on medium-low (30%), turning meat over every 30 minutes, until tender, 1¾ to 2 hours. Thinly slice brisket diagonally across grain.

Reuben Sandwiches

4 sandwiches

⅓ cup mayonnaise or salad dressing
1 tablespoon chili sauce
8 slices rye bread (toasted if desired)
4 slices cooked corned beef
4 slices Swiss cheese
1 can (8 ounces) sauerkraut,
 well-drained

Mix mayonnaise and chili sauce; spread over each slice bread. Arrange corned beef, cheese and sauerkraut on 4 slices bread; top with remaining bread slices. Arrange sandwiches in circle on paper towel-lined 12-inch plate. Cover with paper towel and microwave on high (100%) 1 minute; rotate plate ½ turn. Microwave until cheese is melted and filling is hot, 1 to 2 minutes longer.

Savory Tostadas

6 servings

1	*tablespoon margarine or butter*
1	*teaspoon cornstarch*
½	*cup chopped green pepper (about 1 small)*
¼	*cup chopped onion (about 1 small)*
1	*clove garlic, finely chopped*
1½	*teaspoons chili powder*
⅛	*teaspoon ground cloves*
2	*cups bite-size pieces cooked beef*
1	*cup chopped tomato (about 1 medium)*
3	*tablespoons raisins*
½	*teaspoon salt*
6	*tostada shells*
1	*cup shredded lettuce*
1	*cup shredded Cheddar cheese (about 4 ounces)*

1. Place margarine in 1½-quart casserole. Microwave uncovered on high (100%) until melted, 15 to 30 seconds; stir in cornstarch.

2. Stir in green pepper, onion, garlic, chili powder and cloves. Cover tightly and microwave on high (100%) until vegetables are hot, 2 to 3 minutes.

3. Stir in beef, tomato, raisins and salt. Cover tightly and microwave on high (100%) until beef and raisins are hot, 3 to 4 minutes.

4. Place 1 tostada shell on each of 6 plates. Spoon about ½ cup beef mixture onto each tostada. Sprinkle with lettuce and cheese.

Beef with Olive Biscuits

4 to 6 servings

1 package (9 ounces) frozen cut
   green beans
¼ cup chopped onion
   (about 1 small)
1 tablespoon vegetable oil

2 cups bite-size pieces cooked beef
1 cup beef gravy*
¼ cup water
1 tablespoon finely chopped green
   chilies

Olive Drop Biscuits (below)
Paprika

1. Place beans, onion and oil in 2-quart casserole. Cover tightly and microwave on high (100%) 2 minutes; stir. Cover and microwave until hot, 2 minutes longer.

2. Stir in beef, gravy, water and chilies. Cover tightly and microwave on high (100%) 5 minutes; stir. Cover and microwave until hot and bubbly, 5 to 7 minutes longer; stir.

3. Prepare Olive Drop Biscuits; drop dough by 12 tablespoonfuls around edge of dish. Sprinkle with paprika. Microwave uncovered on high (100%) 3 minutes; rotate casserole ½ turn. Microwave until biscuits are no longer doughy, 2 to 4 minutes longer. Cover loosely; let stand 5 minutes. (Biscuits will continue to cook while they stand.)

* 1 envelope (⅝ ounce) gravy mix and 1 cup water can be substituted for the gravy. Prepare as directed.

Olive Drop Biscuits
⅓ cup shortening
1¾ cups all-purpose flour
2½ teaspoons baking powder
½ teaspoon salt
1 cup milk
⅓ cup chopped pimiento-stuffed
   olives

Cut shortening into flour, baking powder and salt with pastry blender until mixture resembles fine crumbs. Stir in milk and olives until soft dough forms (dough will be sticky).

Beef-Zucchini Casserole

4 servings

1 cup uncooked macaroni
   (about 4 ounces)
1 cup water

½ cup milk
1 tablespoon all-purpose flour
½ teaspoon dry mustard
2 cups sliced zucchini
   (about 3 small)
1 cup shredded Cheddar cheese
   (about 4 ounces)
1 jar (2½ ounces) dried beef,
   cut up

1. Place macaroni and water in 2-quart casserole. Cover tightly and microwave on high (100%) to boiling, 4 to 5 minutes. Let stand 5 minutes. (Macaroni will continue to cook and absorb most of water while it stands.)

2. Stir in milk, flour and mustard. Fold in zucchini, cheese and dried beef. Cover tightly and microwave on high (100%) 4 minutes; stir. Cover and microwave until mixture is bubbly and macaroni is tender, 3 to 4 minutes longer.

Steak with Refried Beans

6 *to* 8 *servings*

1½ - *pound beef round steak, ½ inch thick*
1 *envelope (about 1 ounce) instant meat marinade*
¼ *cup catsup*
1 *tablespoon Worcestershire sauce*
6 *drops red pepper sauce*

1 *can (16 ounces) refried beans*
1 *can (4 ounces) whole green chilies, cut into strips*
Corn chips

1. Cut beef into serving pieces. Prepare instant meat marinade as directed on envelope except — stir in catsup, Worcestershire sauce and red pepper sauce. Marinate steak as directed on envelope, using baking dish, 12 × 7½ × 2 inches.

2. Cover steak tightly and microwave on medium-high (70%) 10 minutes; rearrange pieces. Cover and microwave on medium-low (30%) until beef is tender, 18 to 22 minutes longer.

3. Place beans in 1-quart casserole. Cover tightly and microwave on high (100%) 2 minutes; stir. Cover and microwave until hot, 1 to 2 minutes longer. Top each serving of steak with strip of green chili and large spoonful of beans. Serve with corn chips.

Mushroom Steaks

4 *servings*

1 *teaspoon bottled brown bouquet sauce*
1 *tablespoon water*
4 *beef cubed steaks (3 to 4 ounces each)*
½ *teaspoon salt*
¼ *teaspoon lemon pepper*
1 *can (4 ounces) sliced mushrooms, drained*
¼ *cup chopped green pepper*
¼ *cup chopped onion (about 1 small)*
2 *tablespoons dry white or red wine*

Mix bouquet sauce and water; brush both sides of beef cubed steaks. Arrange steaks in baking dish, 8 × 8 × 2 inches. Sprinkle with salt and lemon pepper. Top with mushrooms, green pepper and onion; drizzle with wine. Cover with waxed paper and microwave on high (100%) 5 minutes; rotate baking dish ½ turn. Microwave until steaks are tender and no longer pink, 4 to 6 minutes longer. Let stand 5 minutes. Serve with hot cooked rice, noodles or potatoes if desired.

Microwaving Less Tender Cuts of Beef

Pot roasts, round steaks and other less tender meat cuts need different techniques from roasts: cover tightly, add liquid, use full (100%) power for a short time, then lower power. The steaming and simmering cooks the meat to fork-tenderness, but does not provide a crisp surface, since the cooking is essentially moist heat. Using an acid food such as tomatoes, pineapple, vinegar or wine helps tenderize the meat. Coverings such as gravies, sauces, vegetables or cheese can enhance the appearance.

A tenderized (or tender) steak browned by broiling or grilling can be covered loosely and microwave-reheated — yet still retain the same flavor.

Beef-Wine Spaghetti

Beef-Wine Spaghetti

8 *servings*

2 *pounds beef for stew, cut into ½-inch pieces*
1 *jar (32 ounces) spaghetti sauce*
½ *cup dry red wine*
1 *envelope (about 1½ ounces) onion soup mix*

8 *cups hot cooked spaghetti*
 Grated Parmesan cheese

Mix all ingredients except spaghetti and cheese in 3-quart casserole. Cover tightly and microwave on high (100%) 15 minutes; stir. Cover and microwave on medium-low (30%), stirring every 30 minutes, until tender, 1¼ to 1½ hours. Spoon sauce over hot spaghetti. Sprinkle with cheese.

Chunky Chili Con Carne

6 servings

1   *pound beef for stew, cut into ½-inch pieces*
½   *cup chopped green pepper (about 1 small)*
½   *cup chopped onion (about 1 medium)*
2   *cloves garlic, finely chopped*
1   *teaspoon bottled brown bouquet sauce*

2   *cans (15½ ounces each) kidney beans*
1   *can (8 ounces) stewed tomatoes*
1   *can (8 ounces) tomato sauce*
2   *tablespoons chili powder*
1   *tablespoon all-purpose flour*
1   *teaspoon salt*

1. Mix beef, green pepper, onion, garlic and brown bouquet sauce in 3-quart casserole. Cover tightly and microwave on high (100%) 5 minutes; stir. Cover and microwave until beef is no longer pink, 3 to 5 minutes longer.

2. Stir in beans, tomatoes (with liquid), tomato sauce, chili powder, flour and salt. Cover tightly and microwave on medium-low (30%) 35 minutes; stir. Cover and microwave until beef is tender, 35 to 45 minutes longer. Let stand 10 minutes.

Beer Stew

5 or 6 servings

4   *slices bacon, cut into ½-inch pieces*

1½ - *pound beef boneless round steak, cut into 1-inch pieces*
4   *medium onions, sliced*
1   *clove garlic, finely chopped*

1   *can (12 ounces) beer*
⅓   *cup all-purpose flour*
1   *tablespoon packed brown sugar*
2   *teaspoons bottled brown bouquet sauce*
1½ *teaspoons salt*
½   *teaspoon dried thyme leaves*
¼   *teaspoon pepper*

1   *tablespoon vinegar*
   Snipped parsley
3½ *to 4½ cups hot cooked noodles*

1. Place bacon in 3-quart casserole. Cover with paper towel and microwave on high (100%) 2 minutes; stir. Cover and microwave until crisp, 3 to 4 minutes longer; drain on paper towel. Pour off fat; return 2 tablespoons fat to casserole.

2. Stir in beef, onions and garlic. Cover tightly and microwave on high (100%) 6 minutes; stir. Cover and microwave until meat is no longer pink, 5 to 7 minutes longer.

3. Stir in beer, flour, brown sugar, bouquet sauce, salt, thyme and pepper. Cover tightly and microwave on medium-low (30%) 30 minutes; stir. Cover and microwave until beef is tender, 25 to 35 minutes longer. Stir in vinegar; sprinkle with bacon and parsley. Serve with hot cooked noodles.

Barbecued Meatloaf

6 *servings*

1½ *pounds ground beef*
1 *cup soft bread crumbs*
    (about 2 slices bread)
1 *cup milk*
1 *egg*
¼ *cup chopped onion*
    (about 1 small)
¼ *cup chopped green pepper*
1 *tablespoon Worcestershire sauce*
1 *teaspoon salt*
½ *teaspoon dry mustard*
¼ *teaspoon pepper*
¼ *teaspoon ground sage*
3 *tablespoons barbecue sauce*

Mix all ingredients except barbecue sauce. Spread mixture evenly in loaf dish, 9 × 5 × 3 inches. Spread barbecue sauce over meat mixture. Cover with waxed paper and microwave on medium-high (70%) 12 minutes; rotate loaf dish ½ turn. Microwave until center is no longer pink, 13 to 16 minutes longer. Remove to serving platter; cover and let stand 5 minutes. Top with additional barbecue sauce if desired.

Mexican-Style Meatloaf: Substitute 1 to 2 tablespoons chopped green chilies for the green pepper and 2 tablespoons taco sauce for the barbecue sauce. Arrange 3 slices processed American cheese on meatloaf before standing time. Serve with chopped tomatoes, shredded lettuce and taco sauce if desired.

Barbecued Meatloaf

Spoon Burgers (pictured at right)   4 or 5 sandwiches

1   pound ground beef
½   cup chopped onion
⅓   cup chopped celery
¼   cup chopped green pepper

⅓   cup barbecue sauce
½   teaspoon salt
4   to 6 drops red pepper sauce
4   or 5 wiener buns

1. Crumble ground beef into 2-quart casserole; add onion, celery and green pepper. Cover loosely and microwave on high (100%) 3 minutes; break up and stir. Cover and microwave until very little pink remains in beef, 3 to 4 minutes longer; drain.

2. Stir in remaining ingredients except buns. Cover tightly and microwave on high (100%) until hot, 3 to 5 minutes; stir. Fill buns with beef mixture.

Pizza Burgers (pictured at right)   6 servings

1   can (8 ounces) tomato sauce
1   pound ground beef
½   cup dry bread crumbs
½   teaspoon dried oregano leaves
¼   teaspoon salt

1   cup shredded Cheddar or
        Monterey Jack cheese
        (about 4 ounces)
3   English muffins, cut into halves
        and toasted

1. Reserve ½ cup tomato sauce. Mix remaining tomato sauce, the ground beef, bread crumbs, oregano and salt. Divide mixture into 6 parts; pat each into 4-inch circle about ½ inch thick. Pinch edge of each circle to make stand-up rim. Arrange on microwave rack in baking dish or in circle on 12-inch plate. Spread reserved sauce over patties. Cover loosely and microwave on high (100%) 5 minutes; rotate baking dish ½ turn. Microwave until edges are brown and firm, 4 to 7 minutes longer.

2. Sprinkle each patty with cheese. Microwave uncovered on high (100%) until cheese begins to melt, about 1 minute. Serve on toasted muffin halves. Garnish with snipped parsley if desired.

Bacon Burgers (pictured at right)   5 servings

5   slices bacon, cut into halves

1   pound ground beef
1   egg
¼   cup finely chopped green pepper
¼   cup finely chopped onion
¼   cup dry bread crumbs
2   tablespoons lemon juice
½   teaspoon salt
½   teaspoon instant beef bouillon
5   hamburger buns, split
        and toasted

1. Place bacon on microwave rack in baking dish. Cover with paper towel and microwave on high (100%) until nearly crisp, 3 to 5 minutes; drain.

2. Mix remaining ingredients except hamburger buns; shape into 5 patties, each about ¾ inch thick. Criss-cross 2 half-slices bacon on each patty. Arrange patties on microwave rack in baking dish. Cover with paper towel and microwave on high (100%) 3 minutes; rotate baking dish ½ turn. Microwave until patties are almost done, about 2 minutes longer. Let stand 3 minutes. Serve in hamburger buns.

Sweet-Sour Meatballs (pictured on page 2)

4 *servings*

Basic Meatballs *(page 223)*

1. Prepare and microwave Basic Meatballs.

½ cup packed brown sugar
1 tablespoon cornstarch
1 can (13¼ ounces) pineapple
  tidbits or chunks
⅓ cup vinegar
1 tablespoon soy sauce

2. Mix brown sugar and cornstarch in 2-quart casserole. Stir in pineapple (with syrup), vinegar and soy sauce. Microwave uncovered on high (100%) 2 minutes; stir. Microwave until mixture thickens and boils, 3 to 4 minutes longer.

1 small green pepper, cut into
  ½-inch pieces

3. Add cooked meatballs and green pepper. Cover tightly and microwave on high (100%) until pepper is crisp-tender, 3 to 4 minutes.

Meatballs in Wine Sauce

4 *servings*

1 pound ground beef
1 can (8 ounces) water chestnuts,
  chopped
½ cup dry bread crumbs
¼ cup chopped onion
  (about 1 small)
¼ cup water
1 egg
1 small clove garlic, finely chopped
½ teaspoon salt
½ teaspoon Worcestershire sauce
⅛ teaspoon pepper

1. Mix all ingredients except Wine Sauce. Shape mixture by teaspoonfuls into 1-inch balls. Arrange in baking dish, 12 × 7½ × 2 inches. Cover loosely and microwave on high (100%), rearranging meatballs every 3 minutes, until no longer pink inside, 7 to 10 minutes. Let stand 3 minutes. Transfer meatballs to serving dish with slotted spoon; keep warm.

2. Prepare Wine Sauce. Pour hot Wine Sauce over meatballs; gently stir to coat. Garnish with snipped parsley if desired.

Wine Sauce *(below)*

Wine Sauce

3 tablespoons cornstarch
¼ cup water
1 can (10½ ounces) condensed
  beef broth
⅓ cup dry red wine
1 tablespoon soy sauce

Mix cornstarch and water in 4-cup measure; gradually stir in remaining ingredients. Microwave uncovered on high (100%), stirring every minute, to boiling, 3 to 4 minutes.

Cooking and Draining Ground Beef

An easy way to microwave and drain crumbled ground beef at the same time is to put the beef in a microwaveproof colander and put the colander in a casserole. Cover loosely and microwave as the recipe directs. While the ground beef cooks, the fat will drain through.

Beef-Olive Tacos

Beef-Olive Tacos

4 *to* 6 *servings*

1	*pound ground beef*
½	*cup chopped onion*
	(about 1 medium)
1	*clove garlic, finely chopped*
½	*cup chopped green pepper*
	(about 1 small)
¼	*cup raisins*
1	*teaspoon salt*
¼	*teaspoon ground cinnamon*
¾	*cup chopped tomato*
¼	*cup slivered almonds, toasted*
	(page 12)
¼	*cup sliced pimiento-stuffed olives*
8	*to 12 taco shells*

1. Crumble ground beef into 2-quart casserole; add onion and garlic. Cover loosely and microwave on high (100%) 3 minutes; break up and stir. Cover and microwave until very little pink remains in beef, 2 to 3 minutes longer; drain.

2. Add green pepper, raisins, salt and cinnamon. Cover tightly and microwave on high (100%) until hot, 4 to 6 minutes.

3. Stir tomato, almonds and olives into beef mixture. Serve in taco shells. Garnish with sour cream and lime wedges if desired.

Beef-Corn Pie

4 servings

3/4 pound ground beef
2 tablespoons chopped onion
1 small clove garlic, finely chopped

1 can (8 ounces) whole tomatoes, drained (reserve 1/2 cup liquid)
1 can (8 ounces) whole kernel corn, drained
12 pitted ripe olives, sliced
1 1/2 to 2 1/2 teaspoons chili powder
1/2 teaspoon salt

1 egg
1/2 cup yellow cornmeal
1/2 cup shredded Cheddar cheese
Paprika

1. Crumble ground beef into 1 1/2-quart casserole; add onion and garlic. Cover loosely and microwave on high (100%) 2 minutes; break up and stir. Cover and microwave until very little pink remains in beef, 2 to 3 minutes longer; drain.

2. Stir in tomatoes, corn, olives, chili powder and salt. Cover tightly and microwave on high (100%) until hot and bubbly, 4 to 6 minutes; stir.

3. Beat egg; stir in cornmeal and reserved tomato liquid. Pour over meat mixture; sprinkle with cheese and paprika. Microwave uncovered on high (100%) until topping is no longer doughy, 3 to 6 minutes.

Beef-Corn Pie

Hamburger Tostada Salads

6 servings

Guacamole Dressing (below)

1 *pound ground beef*

½ *cup water*
1 *package (1¼ ounces) taco seasoning mix*
1 *can (15½ ounces) red kidney beans, drained*
¾ *teaspoon salt*
¼ *to ½ teaspoon chili powder*

6 *tostada shells*
6 *cups shredded lettuce*
1 *cup shredded Cheddar cheese*
3 *cups chopped tomatoes (about 3 medium)*

Guacamole Dressing
1 *medium avocado*
¼ *cup finely chopped onion*
2 *tablespoons chopped green chilies*
1½ *teaspoons vinegar*
½ *teaspoon salt*
¼ *teaspoon pepper*
  Mayonnaise or salad dressing

1. Prepare Guacamole Dressing.

2. Crumble ground beef into 2-quart casserole. Cover loosely and microwave on high (100%) 3 minutes; break up and stir. Cover and microwave until very little pink remains, 2 to 3 minutes longer; drain.

3. Stir in water, seasoning mix, beans, salt and chili powder. Cover tightly and microwave on high (100%) 3 minutes; stir. Cover and microwave to boiling, 3 to 4 minutes longer.

4. Place 1 tostada on each of 6 plates; sprinkle with lettuce. Spoon about ½ cup beef mixture over lettuce; sprinkle with cheese. Top with tomatoes and serve with dressing.

Mash avocado; beat in onion, chilies, vinegar, salt and pepper until creamy. Spoon dressing into dish. Spread with thin layer of mayonnaise to prevent discoloration. Cover and refrigerate. Stir gently just before serving.

Curried Beef

4 servings

1 *pound ground beef*
¾ *cup chopped onion*
1 *cup diced potatoes*

1 *cup hot water*
½ *cup chopped green pepper (about 1 small)*
¼ *cup shredded coconut*
2 *tablespoons catsup*
2 *to 3 teaspoons curry powder*
1 *teaspoon salt*
¾ *teaspoon ground turmeric*
¼ *teaspoon ground ginger*
1 *stick cinnamon*
2 *cups hot cooked rice*
  Pear Chutney (page 43)

1. Crumble ground beef into 2-quart casserole; add onion and potatoes. Cover loosely and microwave on high (100%) 4 minutes; break up and stir. Cover and microwave until very little pink remains in beef, 3 to 4 minutes longer; drain.

2. Stir in remaining ingredients except rice and chutney. Cover tightly and microwave on high (100%) 5 minutes; stir. Cover and microwave until vegetables are tender, 5 to 7 minutes longer. Serve with rice and Pear Chutney.

Stuffed Green Peppers

6 *servings*

¾ *cup hot water*
⅓ *cup cracked wheat (bulgur)*
¼ *cup chopped onion*
     (about 1 small)
1 *teaspoon instant beef bouillon*
1 *teaspoon salt*
⅛ *teaspoon garlic powder*

6 *medium green peppers*
1 *pound ground beef*
1 *can (15 ounces) tomato sauce*
¾ *cup shredded Cheddar cheese*

1. Mix water, cracked wheat, onion, bouillon, salt and garlic powder in 2-quart casserole. Cover tightly and microwave on high (100%) to boiling, 6 to 8 minutes; stir. Cover and let stand until water is absorbed, about 10 minutes.

2. Cut thin slice from stem end of each pepper. Remove seeds and membranes; rinse. Arrange peppers cut sides up in circle in 9- or 10-inch pie plate. Stir the uncooked ground beef and 1 cup of the tomato sauce into cracked wheat mixture. Stuff each pepper with about ½ cup mixture. Pour remaining sauce over peppers. Cover tightly and microwave on high (100%) 7 minutes; rotate pie plate ¼ turn. Microwave until meat mixture is done, 5 to 7 minutes longer. Sprinkle peppers with shredded cheese; let stand 5 minutes.

Microwave cracked wheat mixture to boiling.

Let stand until water is absorbed, about 10 minutes.

Place prepared peppers cut sides up in pie plate.

Add uncooked beef and 1 cup tomato sauce to mixture.

Stuff each green pepper with about ½ cup of filling.

Add remaining sauce. Microwave; top with cheese.

Dilled Beef and Mushrooms

4 servings

1 *pound ground beef*
½ *cup chopped onion*
    (about 1 medium)
1 *clove garlic, finely chopped*

1 *can (10¾ ounces) condensed*
    cream of mushroom soup
2 *jars (4½ ounces each) sliced*
    mushrooms (reserve ⅓
    cup liquid)
2 *tablespoons all-purpose flour*
1 *teaspoon dried dill weed*
½ *teaspoon salt*
¼ *teaspoon pepper*

1 *cup dairy sour cream*
2 *or 3 cups chow mein noodles*
2 *tablespoons snipped parsley*

1. Crumble ground beef into 2-quart casserole; add onion and garlic. Cover loosely and microwave on high (100%) 3 minutes; break up and stir. Cover and microwave until very little pink remains in beef, 2 to 3 minutes longer; drain.

2. Stir in soup, mushrooms, reserved liquid, flour, dill weed, salt and pepper. Cover tightly and microwave on high (100%) 5 minutes; stir. Cover and microwave until hot and bubbly, 3 to 5 minutes longer.

3. Stir in sour cream and serve over chow mein noodles. Sprinkle with snipped parsley.

Beef with Cracked Wheat (Bulgur)

4 servings

1 *pound ground beef*
½ *cup chopped onion*
    (about 1 medium)
1 *small clove garlic, finely*
    chopped

1½ *cups water*
½ *cup uncooked cracked wheat*
2 *tablespoons snipped parsley*
1 *teaspoon instant beef bouillon*
½ *teaspoon salt*
¼ *teaspoon dried oregano leaves*
¼ *teaspoon pepper*

¼ *cup Parmesan cheese*
1 *cup chopped tomato*
    (about 1 medium)

1. Crumble ground beef into 1½-quart casserole; add onion and garlic. Cover loosely and microwave on high (100%) 3 minutes; break up and stir. Cover and microwave until very little pink remains in beef, 2 to 3 minutes longer; drain.

2. Stir in remaining ingredients except cheese and tomato. Cover tightly and microwave on high (100%) until cracked wheat is tender and water is absorbed, 14 to 16 minutes.

3. Stir in cheese and tomato. Cover and let stand 1 minute. Sprinkle with Parmesan cheese. Garnish with snipped parsley if desired.

Lasagne

6 to 8 servings

1 pound ground beef

1 can (15½ ounces) spaghetti sauce
1 can (8 ounces) tomato sauce
1 tablespoon dried parsley flakes
1 teaspoon dried oregano leaves

1 carton (16 ounces) creamed
    cottage cheese
¼ cup grated Parmesan cheese
1 egg
1 tablespoon dried parsley flakes
1 teaspoon dried basil leaves

8 uncooked lasagne noodles
2 cups shredded mozzarella cheese
    (about 8 ounces)
3 tablespoons grated Parmesan
    cheese

1. Crumble beef into 1½-quart casserole. Cover loosely and microwave on high (100%) 3 minutes; break up and stir. Cover and microwave until very little pink remains, 2 to 3 minutes longer; drain.

2. Stir in spaghetti sauce, tomato sauce, 1 tablespoon parsley and oregano. Cover tightly and microwave on high (100%) to boiling, 3 to 4 minutes.

3. Mix cottage cheese, ¼ cup Parmesan cheese, the egg, 1 tablespoon parsley flakes and the basil.

4. Spread 1⅓ cups meat sauce in baking dish, 12 × 7½ × 2 inches. Overlap 4 lasagne noodles on sauce. Add 1 cup cheese filling and 1 cup mozzarella cheese (reserve 1 cup mozzarella cheese for top after cooking). Repeat layers with 1⅓ cups meat sauce, remaining noodles and cheese filling. Top with remaining meat sauce. Cover tightly and microwave on high (100%) 10 minutes; rotate baking dish ½ turn. Microwave on medium (50%) until noodles are tender, 22 to 28 minutes longer. Sprinkle with remaining mozzarella cheese and 3 tablespoons Parmesan cheese. Cover and let stand 10 minutes.

Spaghetti with Italian Sauce

4 servings

1 pound ground beef
⅓ cup chopped onion
3 tablespoons finely chopped green
    pepper
1 large clove garlic, finely chopped

1 can (15 ounces) tomato sauce
1 can (4 ounces) mushroom stems
    and pieces, drained
½ cup dry red wine
1 teaspoon salt
¼ teaspoon pepper
¼ teaspoon dried basil leaves

3 cups hot cooked spaghetti

1. Crumble ground beef into 2-quart casserole; add onion, green pepper and garlic. Cover loosely and microwave on high (100%) 3 minutes; break up and stir. Cover and microwave until very little pink remains in beef, 3 to 4 minutes longer; drain.

2. Stir in tomato sauce, mushrooms, wine, salt, pepper and basil. Cover tightly and microwave on high (100%) 6 minutes; stir. Cover and microwave until hot and bubbly, 5 to 7 minutes longer.

3. Pour meat sauce over hot spaghetti. Serve with grated Parmesan cheese if desired.

Hominy with Beef Sauce

4 *to* 6 *servings*

1 *pound ground beef*
⅓ *cup chopped onion*
1 *clove garlic, finely chopped*

1 *tablespoon all-purpose flour*
1 *can (28 ounces) tomatoes*
⅓ *cup sliced pimiento-stuffed olives*
1 *teaspoon salt*
1 *teaspoon dried oregano leaves*
¼ *teaspoon red pepper sauce*

2 *cans (20 ounces each) hominy, drained*
¼ *cup margarine or butter*

1. Crumble ground beef into 2-quart casserole; add onion and garlic. Cover loosely and microwave on high (100%) 3 minutes; break up and stir. Cover and microwave until very little pink remains in beef, 2 to 3 minutes longer; drain.

2. Sprinkle beef with flour. Stir in tomatoes (with liquid), olives, salt, oregano and pepper sauce; break up tomatoes with fork. Cover tightly and microwave on high (100%) 4 minutes; stir. Cover and microwave to boiling, 4 to 6 minutes longer.

3. Place hominy and margarine in 1½-quart casserole. Cover tightly and microwave on high (100%) 2 minutes; stir. Cover and microwave until hominy is hot, 1 to 3 minutes longer; stir. Pour beef sauce over hominy.

Hominy with Beef Sauce

Lentil-Hamburger Soup

6 *servings* (1½ *cups each*)

1   *pound ground beef*
¾   *cup ⅛-inch slices carrot*
        (about 1 large)
½   *cup chopped onion (about*
        1 medium)
1   *clove garlic, finely chopped*

2   *cups hot water*
1   *can (16 ounces) stewed tomatoes*
1   *can (4 ounces) mushroom stems*
        and pieces
¾   *cup uncooked dried lentils*
½   *cup sliced celery (about 1*
        medium stalk)
2   *tablespoons dried parsley flakes*
2   *teaspoons salt*
1   *teaspoon instant beef bouillon*
1   *teaspoon Worcestershire sauce*
¼   *teaspoon pepper*
1   *bay leaf*

1   *cup hot water*

1. Crumble ground beef into 3-quart casserole; add carrot, onion and garlic. Cover loosely and microwave on high (100%) 4 minutes; break up and stir. Cover and microwave until very little pink remains in beef, 3 to 4 minutes longer; drain.

2. Stir in 2 cups hot water, stewed tomatoes (with liquid), mushrooms (with liquid) and remaining ingredients except 1 cup hot water. Cover tightly and microwave on high (100%), stirring every 6 minutes, until vegetables are tender, 24 to 28 minutes.

3. Stir in 1 cup hot water. Cover tightly and microwave on high (100%) until bubbly, 3 to 5 minutes. Serve with crusty French bread if desired.

Two-Bean Chili Soup

6 servings (1⅓ cups each)

1 *pound ground beef*
½ *cup finely chopped onion*
　　(about 1 medium)
½ *cup finely chopped green pepper*
　　(about 1 small)
1 *clove garlic, finely chopped*

1 *can (16 ounces) whole tomatoes*
1 *can (15½ ounces) kidney beans*
1 *can (8½ ounces) lima beans,*
　　drained
1 *can (8 ounces) tomato sauce*
⅓ *cup dry red wine*
2 *tablespoons Worcestershire sauce*
2 *to 3 teaspoons chili powder*
½ *teaspoon pepper*
¼ *teaspoon salt*
¼ *teaspoon ground cumin*

1. Crumble ground beef into 3-quart casserole; add onion, green pepper and garlic. Cover loosely and microwave on high (100%) 3 minutes; break up and stir. Cover and microwave until very little pink remains in beef, 3 to 4 minutes longer; drain.

2. Stir in tomatoes; break up with fork. Stir in kidney beans (with liquid) and remaining ingredients. Cover tightly and microwave on high (100%) 10 minutes; stir. Cover and microwave until hot and bubbly, 8 to 10 minutes longer.

Vegetable-Beef Soup

4 servings (about 1½ cups each)

1 *pound ground beef*
½ *cup chopped onion*
　　(about 1 medium)

⅔ *cup chopped carrot*
　　(about 1 large)
⅔ *cup chopped celery*
⅔ *cup ½-inch pieces potato*
¼ *cup water*
1½ *teaspoons salt*
1 *teaspoon bottled brown bouquet*
　　sauce
¼ *teaspoon pepper*
⅛ *teaspoon dried basil leaves*
1 *bay leaf*

1¾ *cups hot water*
1 *can (16 ounces) whole tomatoes*

1. Crumble ground beef into 3-quart casserole; add onion. Cover loosely and microwave on high (100%) 3 minutes; break up and stir. Cover and microwave until very little pink remains in beef, 2 to 3 minutes longer; drain.

2. Stir in remaining ingredients except 1¾ cups water and tomatoes. Cover tightly and microwave on high (100%) 5 minutes; stir. Cover and microwave until vegetables are tender, 4 to 6 minutes longer.

3. Stir water and tomatoes (with liquid) into beef mixture; break up tomatoes with fork. Cover tightly and microwave on high (100%) 5 minutes; stir. Cover and microwave to boiling, 4 to 6 minutes longer.

Pork Tenderloin Hawaiian

4 servings

1 *pork tenderloin (10 to 12 ounces)*
1 *can (8 ounces) pineapple chunks in juice, drained (reserve 2 tablespoons juice)*
2 *tablespoons dry white wine*
1 *tablespoon soy sauce*
1 *tablespoon chili sauce*
¼ *teaspoon salt*
1 *green onion, thinly sliced*
1 *clove garlic, finely chopped*
1 *slice gingerroot, smashed*

3 *tablespoons honey*

2 *teaspoons cornstarch*
1 *tablespoon cold water*
3 *cups hot cooked rice*
   Parsley sprigs

1. Place pork tenderloin in baking dish, 10 × 6 × 2 inches. Mix pineapple chunks, reserved pineapple juice, wine, soy sauce, chili sauce, salt, onion, garlic and gingerroot; pour over pork. Cover and refrigerate 2 hours, turning once.

2. Remove pork to microwave rack in baking dish; reserve marinade. Brush pork with honey. Cover with waxed paper and microwave on medium (50%) 3 minutes. Rotate dish ¼ turn. Microwave 3 minutes longer. Turn pork over; rearrange pork in dish and brush with honey. Cover and microwave, rotating baking dish ¼ turn every 3 minutes, until meat thermometer registers 170°, 5 to 9 minutes. Remove to serving plate.

3. Mix cornstarch and water; stir into marinade. Cover tightly and microwave on high (100%) until thickened and boiling, 2 to 3 minutes. To serve, cut pork diagonally into ¼-inch slices. Serve pork and pineapple sauce over rice.

Herbed Pork Roast

10 to 14 servings

4 - *pound pork boneless top loin roast*
1 *clove garlic, cut into halves*
2 *teaspoons dried sage leaves*
2 *teaspoons dried marjoram leaves*
½ *teaspoon pepper*

Gravy (below)

1. Rub roast with garlic. Mix sage, marjoram and pepper; sprinkle over pork roast. Place roast fat side down on microwave rack in baking dish. Cover with waxed paper and microwave on medium (50%) 10 minutes. Rotate dish ½ turn. Microwave 12 minutes longer. Turn roast fat side up. Cover and microwave, rotating dish ½ turn every 15 minutes, until meat thermometer registers 165°, 22 to 32 minutes. Cover with aluminum foil and let stand 15 minutes. (Roast will continue to cook while standing. Meat thermometer should register 170° in several places. If it does not, continue microwaving until done.)

Pork Gravy
Drain drippings from baking dish, reserving ¼ cup. Pour reserved drippings into 1½-quart casserole. Stir in ¼ cup all-purpose flour and 1¾ cups water or meat juices. Stir in ¼ teaspoon bottled brown bouquet sauce if desired. Microwave uncovered on high (100%) 2 minutes; stir. Microwave, stirring every minute until thickened, 2 to 3 minutes longer. Sprinkle with salt and pepper.

Glazed Ham with Corn Relish (pictured on page 248) 10 *servings*

Corn Relish (below)

3 - *pound fully cooked boneless smoked ham*

⅓ cup orange marmalade
2 tablespoons sweet white wine
1 teaspoon prepared horseradish
    Dash of ground cloves

1. Prepare Corn Relish.

2. Place ham fat side down on microwave rack in baking dish. Cover tightly and microwave on medium (50%) 17 minutes; turn ham fat side up.

3. Cut fat surface of ham in diamond pattern ¼ inch deep. Mix remaining ingredients; spoon over ham. Cover ham tightly and microwave on medium (50%) until meat thermometer registers 135°, 15 to 22 minutes. Cover with aluminum foil; let stand 10 minutes. (Ham will continue to cook while standing.)

Corn Relish

½ cup sugar
⅓ cup vinegar
½ teaspoon salt
½ teaspoon celery seed
¼ teaspoon mustard seed
¼ teaspoon red pepper sauce
1 can (17 ounces) whole kernel corn, drained
2 tablespoons chopped green or red pepper
2 tablespoons chopped celery
1 tablespoon instant minced onion

Mix sugar, vinegar, salt, celery seed, mustard seed and red pepper sauce in 1½-quart casserole. Microwave uncovered on high (100%) to boiling, 2 to 3 minutes; stir. Stir in remaining ingredients. Cover; refrigerate several days to blend flavors.

Pork-Rice Casserole

4 *servings*

1 cup ¼-inch diagonal slices celery (about 2 medium stalks)
½ cup chopped onion
1 tablespoon margarine or butter

2 cups 1-inch pieces cooked pork
1 cup uncooked instant rice
1 cup hot water
2 tablespoons soy sauce
1 teaspoon instant chicken bouillon
1 cup chopped green pepper

1. Place celery, onion and margarine in 2-quart casserole. Cover tightly and microwave on high (100%) 2 minutes; stir. Cover and microwave until celery is crisp-tender, 2 to 3 minutes longer.

2. Stir in pork, rice, water, soy sauce and bouillon. Cover tightly and microwave on high (100%) 4 minutes; stir. Cover and microwave until water is absorbed, 4 to 6 minutes longer. Stir in green pepper. Cover and let stand 5 minutes.

Pork with Chinese Vegetables

Pork with Chinese Vegetables

4 servings

1   can (16 ounces) Chinese vege-
     tables, rinsed and drained
1½ cups ¾-inch pieces cooked pork
1½ cups pork or beef gravy
1   cup ¼-inch diagonal slices
     celery (about 2 medium
     stalks)
1   can (4½ ounces) sliced
     mushrooms, drained
1   jar (2 ounces) sliced pimiento,
     drained
2   teaspoons soy sauce

Mix all ingredients in 2-quart casserole. Cover tightly and microwave on high (100%) 6 minutes; stir. Cover and microwave until hot and bubbly, 5 to 7 minutes longer. Serve over chow mein noodles if desired.

Ham with Beans and Pineapple

5 servings

1 cup *½-inch pieces fully cooked smoked ham*
1 can *(15½ ounces) butter beans, drained*
1 can *(16 ounces) baked beans in molasses sauce*
1 can *(8½ ounces) lima beans, drained*
¼ cup *chopped onion*
1 teaspoon *prepared mustard*
1 can *(8 ounces) pineapple chunks in juice, drained*

Mix ham with all ingredients except pineapple in 2-quart casserole. Cover tightly and microwave on high (100%) 5 minutes; stir. Cover and microwave until hot and bubbly, 5 to 7 minutes longer. Top with pineapple chunks.

Ham with Scalloped Corn

2 servings

1 can *(8 ounces) cream-style corn*
2 tablespoons *chopped green pepper*
1 tablespoon *margarine or butter*
1 teaspoon *instant minced onion*

1 egg, *beaten*
½ cup *diced fully cooked smoked ham*
¼ cup *shredded Cheddar cheese*
¼ teaspoon *salt*
½ cup *crushed crackers*

1. Stir corn, green pepper, margarine and onion in 1-quart casserole. Cover tightly and microwave on high (100%) until corn is hot, 1½ to 3 minutes; stir.

2. Quickly stir in egg; mix in ham, cheese, salt and ½ of cracker crumbs. Cover loosely and microwave on medium-high (70%) 2 minutes; stir. Sprinkle with remaining cracker crumbs. Cover and microwave until center is set, 4 to 6 minutes longer. Sprinkle with paprika if desired.

Ham-Rye Sandwiches

4 open-face sandwiches

2½ cups *sliced mushrooms*
1 small *onion, sliced*
1 clove *garlic, finely chopped*
1 tablespoon *margarine or butter*

4 thin *slices fully cooked smoked ham*
4 slices *dark rye bread, toasted*
8 thin *tomato slices*
4 slices *Cheddar cheese*

1. Place mushrooms, onion, garlic and margarine in 1½-quart casserole. Cover tightly and microwave on high (100%) 2 minutes; stir. Cover and microwave until onion is tender, 2 to 3 minutes longer.

2. Place 1 ham slice on each toast slice. Spoon about ¼ of mushroom mixture onto ham. Top each sandwich with 2 tomato slices and 1 cheese slice. Arrange sandwiches in circle on paper towel-lined 12-inch plate. Microwave uncovered on high (100%) 1 minute; rotate plate ½ turn. Microwave until cheese is melted and filling is hot, ½ to 1 minute longer.

Curried Ham Slice with Pear Chutney

4 servings

Pear Chutney (below)

1 fully cooked smoked ham slice,
    1 inch thick (about
    1 pound)

1 tablespoon margarine or butter,
    melted (page 11)
1 tablespoon lemon juice
1 teaspoon curry powder
¼ teaspoon dry mustard

Pear Chutney
1½ cups sliced pears (about
    2 medium)
½ cup sugar
⅓ cup vinegar
3 tablespoons raisins
1 to 2 tablespoons cut-up
    crystallized ginger
1 tablespoon finely chopped green
    pepper
    Dash of salt
3 whole cloves
3 whole allspice
1 three-inch cinnamon stick

1. Prepare Pear Chutney.

2. Slash diagonally outer edge of fat of ham slice at 1-inch intervals to prevent curling. Place ham slice in baking dish, 12 × 7½ × 2 inches.

3. Mix margarine, lemon juice, curry powder and mustard. Brush ½ of mixture over ham. Cover with waxed paper and microwave on medium-high (70%) 4 minutes. Turn ham over; brush with remaining sauce. Cover and microwave until hot, 4 to 6 minutes longer. Serve with Pear Chutney.

Mix all ingredients in 1½-quart casserole. Cover tightly and microwave on high (100%) 5 minutes; stir. Cover and microwave until pears are transparent, 5 to 7 minutes longer. Refrigerate until chilled. Cover and store in refrigerator no longer than 2 weeks.

Curried Ham Slice with Pear Chutney

Orange-Spiced Pork Chops

4 servings

4 *pork loin chops, about ½ inch thick*
½ *teaspoon salt*
1 *small onion, thinly sliced*
   Grated peel of 1 large orange
   Juice of 1 large orange
¼ *cup medium red wine*
2 *tablespoons packed brown sugar*
¼ *teaspoon ground cloves*
1 *small clove garlic, finely chopped*
1 *small orange, thinly sliced*

2 *teaspoons cornstarch*
1 *tablespoon cold water*

1. Arrange pork chops with narrow ends toward center in baking dish, 8 × 8 × 2 inches. Sprinkle pork with salt; arrange onion slices on pork. Mix orange peel, orange juice, wine, brown sugar, cloves and garlic; pour over pork. Cover tightly and microwave on medium (50%) 5 minutes; rotate baking dish ¼ turn. Microwave 5 minutes longer. Arrange orange slices on pork; rotate baking dish ½ turn. Cover and microwave, rotating baking dish ¼ turn every 5 minutes, until pork is done (170° on meat thermometer), 12 to 15 minutes.

2. Remove pork chops to serving platter. Cover with aluminum foil and keep warm. Pour 1 cup of juices from baking dish into 2-cup measure. Mix cornstarch and water; stir into juice. Cover loosely and microwave on high (100%) until thickened and boiling, 1 to 2 minutes. Serve on a mixture of white and wild rice if desired. Spoon sauce over pork chops.

Pineapple Pork Steaks

4 servings

4 *pork blade steaks, about ½ inch thick*
1 *teaspoon instant beef bouillon*

2 *cups soft bread cubes (about 4 slices bread)*
1 *can (8 ounces) pineapple chunks in juice, drained*
½ *cup chopped celery (about 1 medium stalk)*
¼ *cup chopped onion (about 1 small)*
3 *tablespoons margarine, melted (page 11)*
½ *teaspoon salt*
¼ *teaspoon ground sage*
⅛ *teaspoon ground cinnamon*

1. Arrange pork steaks with meaty edges toward edge on microwave rack in baking dish, 12 × 7½ × 2 inches. Cover tightly and microwave on medium (50%) 15 minutes, rotating baking dish ¼ turn every 5 minutes; drain. Rearrange pork in dish; sprinkle with bouillon.

2. Toss remaining ingredients; spoon bread cube mixture evenly over each pork steak. Cover tightly and microwave on medium (50%), rotating baking dish ¼ turn every 5 minutes, until pork is done (170° on meat thermometer), 15 to 20 minutes. Let stand 5 minutes.

Orange-Spiced Pork Chops

Currant-Glazed Ribs (pictured on page 2) *4 servings*

3 *pounds fresh pork spareribs,*
   cut into serving pieces

½ *cup chili sauce*
½ *cup currant jelly*
2 *tablespoons soy sauce*

1. Arrange pork spareribs meaty sides up in 3-quart casserole. Cover loosely and microwave on medium (50%), rearranging every 3 minutes, until no pink remains, 27 to 29 minutes; drain and rearrange.

2. Mix chili sauce, currant jelly and soy sauce in 2-cup measure. Cover loosely and microwave on high (100%) to boiling, 2 to 3 minutes; stir.

3. Pour sauce over ribs. Cover tightly and microwave on medium (50%), rearranging every 15 minutes, until meat separates from bones, 45 to 50 minutes.

Dilled Pork Hocks with Sauerkraut *4 servings*

3 *pounds smoked pork hocks*
3 *cups hot water*
1 *small onion, sliced*

2 *cans (16 ounces each)*
   sauerkraut, drained
1 *cup hot water*
1½ *teaspoons dried dill weed*
½ *teaspoon celery seed*
1 *medium red apple, cut into*
   eighths

1. Place pork hocks, 3 cups hot water and onion in 3-quart casserole. Cover tightly and microwave on medium (50%) 25 minutes, rearranging every 10 minutes; turn pork over. Cover and microwave 25 minutes longer; drain.

2. Add sauerkraut, 1 cup hot water, the dill weed and celery seed to pork. Cover tightly and microwave on medium (50%) 15 minutes, rearranging every 5 minutes; stir in apple. Cover and microwave until pork is tender, 20 to 25 minutes. Let stand 5 minutes.

Microwaving Pork

All pork (except fully-cooked smoked pork) must be cooked until well done. (Meat thermometer should register 170° throughout.) If microwaving a pork roast or chops, check several places with a meat thermometer and cook longer if necessary. If you are microwaving pork pieces, check several pieces for doneness. To help even out cooking, follow individual recipes which call for rearranging pork, stirring mixtures, rotating baking dish and standing times. When microwaving fully-cooked pork (such as ham, Polish sausage and cooked luncheon meat) do not use a substitute. If you do, microwaving times and methods will not be correct.

Pepper Pork with Noodles

6 servings

1½   *pounds pork boneless shoulder*
  3   *medium onions, sliced*

1½   *teaspoons salt*
  ½   *teaspoon paprika*
  ¼   *teaspoon pepper*
  ⅛   *to ¼ teaspoon crushed red*
         peppers

  ¾   *teaspoon cornstarch*
  1   *tablespoon cold water*
  1   *cup chopped tomato*
         (about 1 medium)

  1   *medium green pepper, cut*
         into strips
  ⅓   *cup shredded Cheddar cheese*
  4   *cups hot cooked noodles*

1. Cut pork into ½-inch slices; cut slices into ½-inch strips. (For ease in cutting, partially freeze pork about 1 hour.) Mix pork and onions in 3-quart casserole. Cover tightly and microwave on medium (50%), stirring every 3 minutes, until pork is no longer pink, 12 to 14 minutes; drain.

2. Stir in salt, paprika, pepper and red peppers. Cover tightly and microwave on medium (50%) 12 minutes, stirring every 3 minutes. Mix cornstarch and water; stir into pork. Add tomato. Cover and microwave, stirring every 3 minutes, until pork is tender, 12 to 14 minutes longer.

3. Stir in green pepper. Cover and let stand 5 minutes. Sprinkle with cheese; serve with noodles.

Pepper Pork with Noodles

Pork and Carrots with Spaghetti

Pork and Carrots with Spaghetti

4 servings

1	*pound pork boneless shoulder, cut into ¾-inch pieces*
1½	*cups ¼-inch slices carrots (about 3 medium)*
½	*cup chopped onion (about 1 medium)*
2	*cloves garlic, finely chopped*
1	*tablespoon water*
¾	*cup water*
1	*teaspoon instant chicken bouillon*
¾	*teaspoon dried basil leaves*
½	*teaspoon salt*
½	*teaspoon bottled brown bouquet sauce*
¼	*teaspoon pepper*
1	*tablespoon cornstarch*
2	*tablespoons cold water*
2	*tablespoons margarine or butter*
¼	*cup grated Parmesan cheese*
3	*cups hot cooked spaghetti*

1. Mix pork, carrots, onion, garlic and 1 tablespoon water in 2-quart casserole. Cover tightly and microwave on medium (50%), stirring every 3 minutes, until pork is no longer pink and vegetables are crisp-tender, 9 to 11 minutes.

2. Stir in ¾ cup water, the bouillon, basil, salt, bouquet sauce and pepper. Cover tightly and microwave on medium (50%), stirring every 3 minutes, until pork is tender, 27 to 29 minutes.

3. Mix cornstarch and 2 tablespoons water; stir into meat mixture. Cover tightly and microwave on high (100%) until thickened and boiling, 1½ to 2 minutes.

4. Stir margarine and cheese into cooked spaghetti. Serve pork and vegetables over spaghetti.

Pork Paprika with Sauerkraut

4 servings

1 *pound pork boneless shoulder,*
cut into 1-inch pieces
½ *cup chopped onion (about*
1 medium)
1 *small clove garlic, finely chopped*

1 *can (16 ounces) sauerkraut,*
drained
½ *cup hot water*
1 *tablespoon all-purpose flour*
1 *tablespoon paprika*
1 *teaspoon instant chicken bouillon*
½ *teaspoon caraway seed*
½ *teaspoon salt*

½ *cup dairy sour cream*
Snipped parsley
3 *cups hot cooked noodles*

1. Mix pork, onion and garlic in 2-quart casserole. Cover tightly and microwave on medium (50%), stirring every 3 minutes, until pork is no longer pink and onion is tender, 11 to 13 minutes.

2. Stir in remaining ingredients except sour cream, parsley and noodles. Cover tightly and microwave on medium (50%), stirring every 3 minutes, until pork is tender, 27 to 29 minutes.

3. Stir in sour cream. Cover and let stand 5 minutes. Sprinkle with parsley and serve over hot noodles.

Burritos with Cheese

4 servings

1 *pound bulk pork sausage*

1 *cup coarsely chopped tomato*
(about 1 medium)
1 *tablespoon chili powder*
1 *tablespoon lemon juice*
1 *clove garlic, finely chopped*
½ *teaspoon salt*
¼ *teaspoon ground allspice*

8 *six-inch flour tortillas*
1 *can (16 ounces) refried beans*
1 *cup shredded Cheddar cheese*
(about 4 ounces)

1. Crumble pork sausage into 2-quart casserole. Cover loosely and microwave on high (100%) 3 minutes; break up and stir. Cover and microwave until very little pink remains, 3 to 4 minutes longer; drain.

2. Stir in tomato, chili powder, lemon juice, garlic, salt and allspice. Cover tightly and microwave on high (100%) to boiling, 3 to 5 minutes; stir.

3. Wrap 4 tortillas in damp cloth or paper towel and microwave on high (100%) until softened, 1 to 2 minutes (keep tortillas covered while working with filling). Spread about ¼ cup refried beans over each tortilla. Spoon about ⅓ cup sausage mixture on center of each tortilla; sprinkle with 2 tablespoons cheese. Fold up bottom of tortillas. Fold sides over and roll from bottom. Arrange seam sides down in baking dish, 12 × 7½ × 2 inches. Repeat with remaining tortillas. Cover loosely and microwave until hot, 7 to 9 minutes.

Savory Sausage

4 servings

1   *teaspoon instant beef bouillon*
¼   *cup hot water*
½   *cup dry white wine*
1   *tablespoon prepared mustard*
¼   *teaspoon ground ginger*
1   *cup raisins*
1   *pound fully cooked smoked
        Polish sausage, diagonally
        sliced into 1-inch pieces*

1   *tablespoon cornstarch*
¼   *cup dry white wine*

3   *cups hot cooked rice*

1. Dissolve bouillon in hot water in 1½-quart casserole. Stir in ½ cup wine, the mustard, ginger, raisins and sausage; turn sausage to coat. Cover tightly and microwave on medium-high (70%) 3 minutes; stir. Cover and microwave 3 minutes longer.

2. Mix cornstarch and ¼ cup wine. Stir into sausage mixture. Cover tightly and microwave on medium-high (70%) until thickened and hot, 3 to 4 minutes. Serve with hot cooked rice.

Franks with Bacon, Beans and Biscuits

4 servings

8   *slices bacon, cut into ½-inch
        pieces*
1   *cup finely chopped onion
        (about 1 large)*

1   *pound frankfurters, diagonally
        sliced into 1-inch pieces*
1   *can (16 ounces) lima beans,
        drained*
1   *can (16 ounces) tomatoes, cut up*
2   *tablespoons chopped green pepper*
1   *tablespoon buttermilk baking mix*
½   *teaspoon salt*
⅛   *teaspoon pepper*

Cornmeal Drop Biscuits (below)

Cornmeal Drop Biscuits
¾   *cup buttermilk baking mix*
½   *cup shredded Cheddar cheese
        (about 2 ounces)*
¼   *cup yellow cornmeal*
¼   *cup milk*
2   *tablespoons chopped green pepper*
2   *teaspoons vegetable oil*
1   *teaspoon sugar*
⅛   *teaspoon salt*

1. Place bacon and onion in 2-quart casserole. Cover loosely and microwave on high (100%) 4 minutes; stir. Cover and microwave until bacon is crisp, 6 to 9 minutes longer; drain.

2. Stir in remaining ingredients except Cornmeal Biscuits. Cover loosely and microwave on high (100%) until mixture is hot, 3 to 5 minutes; stir.

3. Prepare Cornmeal Biscuits. Drop dough by 6 tablespoonfuls around edge of dish. Microwave uncovered on high (100%) 2 minutes; rotate casserole ¼ turn. Microwave until biscuits are no longer doughy, 3 to 4 minutes longer.

Mix ingredients until blended. (Dough will be stiff.)

Filled Franks in Buns

4 sandwiches

Microwave 4 strips bacon (page 11). Split 4 frankfurters lengthwise, not cutting completely through. Place 1 of the Fillings (below) in each cut. Place bacon and frankfurters in weiner buns. Wrap each bun in napkin or paper towel. Arrange in circle in microwave. Microwave on high (100%) until hot, 1 minute 45 seconds to 2 minutes.

Fillings
Thin dill pickle slices, thin cheese slices, hot dog relish, potato salad, well-drained sauerkraut, pineapple spear, mixture of equal amounts chopped dill pickle and chopped onion.

Macaroni and Cheese with Franks

4 servings

1   cup uncooked macaroni
        (about 4 ounces)
1   cup water

½   cup milk
1   tablespoon flour
½   teaspoon dry mustard
⅛   teaspoon salt
4   frankfurters, cut into 1-inch
        pieces
1   cup shredded Cheddar cheese
        or 1 cup cubed process cheese
        spread loaf (about 4 ounces)

1. Place macaroni and water in 2-quart casserole. Cover tightly and microwave on high (100%) to boiling, 4 to 5 minutes. Let stand 5 minutes.

2. Stir in milk, flour, mustard and salt; add frankfurters and cheese. Cover tightly and microwave on high (100%) 4 minutes; stir. Cover and microwave until mixture is bubbly and macaroni is tender, 3 to 5 minutes longer.

Covering Foods During Microwaving

"Cover tightly" means that moisture and steam should be retained. The tightest cover is a lid that matches a casserole. For odd-shaped dishes, cover with plastic wrap but turn back a small edge. Without this "vent", the plastic might split.

"Cover loosely" means that a certain amount of moisture and steam should escape (to prevent sogginess, such as in breads or steaming as in roasts). Cover with a lid slightly ajar, waxed paper, a paper towel or napkin.

When a specific *kind* of loose cover (such as waxed paper) is recommended, it is listed for a definite reason (such as a food sticking to a paper towel, but not to waxed paper).

"Microwave uncovered" is recommended when the food heats quickly, and needs drying rather than steam or moisture, and will not pop or spatter.

The covering for standing time is usually the same type of cover given in the recipe.

Pork Loaf with Apple Rings

4 servings

1 *can (12 ounces) pork luncheon meat*
2 *teaspoons prepared mustard*
4 *spiced red apple rings*,
    cut into halves
2 *tablespoons packed brown sugar*

Cut pork luncheon meat slightly more than halfway through loaf into 8 sections. Place pork in 1-quart casserole. Spread ½ teaspoon mustard between every other cut. Insert ½ slice apple ring in each cut; top with remaining ½ slice apple ring. Insert whole cloves in apple rings if desired. Sprinkle brown sugar over pork. Cover tightly and microwave on high (100%) until pork is hot, 5 to 7 minutes. Let stand 3 minutes.

* Four canned pineapple rings can be substituted for the apple rings.

Spread alternate cuts in pork luncheon loaf with ½ teaspoon prepared mustard.

Place ½ apple ring in each cut; insert whole cloves in apples if desired.

Sprinkle with brown sugar; microwave, let stand 3 minutes and serve.

Roast Lamb with Apple-Mint Glaze

10 to 12 servings

3½ - *pound lamb boneless shoulder roast*

Bottled brown bouquet sauce

½ *cup mint-flavored apple jelly*
1 *clove garlic, finely chopped*

1. Place lamb roast fat side down on microwave rack in baking dish. Brush with brown bouquet sauce. Cover with waxed paper and microwave on medium (50%) 17 minutes.

2. Turn lamb over and rotate baking dish ½ turn. Brush lamb with bouquet sauce. Microwave until meat thermometer registers 160°, 18 to 23 minutes. Brush with sauce, cover and let stand 10 minutes. (Lamb will continue to cook while it stands.)

3. Mix mint-flavored apple jelly and garlic in 1-cup measure. Microwave uncovered on high (100%) until jelly is melted, 1 to 2 minutes. Serve with lamb.

Note: It may be neccessary to trim some of the fat surrounding roast before cooking.

Lamb with Lemon Sauce

2 servings

2 *tablespoons margarine or butter*

2 *tablespoons all-purpose flour*
1 *teaspoon instant chicken bouillon*
1 *teaspoon dried dill weed*
⅔ *cup water*
3 *tablespoons lemon juice*

2 *cups bite-size pieces lamb*
   Paprika

1. Place margarine in 1½-quart casserole. Microwave uncovered on high (100%) until margarine is melted, 15 to 30 seconds.

2. Stir in flour, bouillon and dill weed. Stir in water and lemon juice. Microwave uncovered on high (100%), stirring every minute, until thickened, about 2 minutes.

3. Add meat, stirring to coat. Cover tightly and microwave on high (100%) until meat is hot, 2 to 4 minutes; stir. Sprinkle with paprika.

Braised Lamb Shanks with Buttermilk Gravy

4 servings

4 *lamb shanks (about 12 ounces each)*
1 *cup buttermilk*
2 *tablespoons instant minced onion*
1 *teaspoon salt*
1 *teaspoon paprika*
¾ *teaspoon ground ginger*
¾ *teaspoon ground coriander*
½ *teaspoon celery seed*
½ *teaspoon pepper*

3 *tablespoons cold water*
2 *tablespoons all-purpose flour*

1. Arrange lamb shanks in 3-quart casserole. Mix remaining ingredients except water and flour; pour over lamb. Cover tightly and microwave on medium-high (70%) 20 minutes.

2. Turn lamb over. Cover and microwave on medium-low (30%) until tender, 45 to 55 minutes. Remove lamb to platter; keep warm.

3. Skim fat from buttermilk mixture in casserole. Shake water and flour in tightly covered container; stir into buttermilk. Microwave uncovered on high (100%), stirring every minute, until thickened, 1 to 3 minutes. Pour gravy over lamb shanks.

Some Glass and Plastic Cookware for Microwaving

Utensils	Dimensions	Use (Measuring, Mixing, Cooking)
Baking Dishes	12 × 7 × 1½, 8 × 8 × 2, or 8 × 1½-inch round	Chicken, fish, roasts, lasagne, vegetables, cookies, cakes
Bundt dishes	10, 12, 16 cups	Cakes, coffee cakes, breads
Casseroles	1 to 3 quarts	Main dishes, vegetables, fruits
Custard cups	6, 10 ounces	Leftovers, casseroles, eggs, muffins
Liquid measures	1, 2, 4, 8 cups	Sauces, puddings, beverages
Muffin ring		Cupcakes, muffins, eggs
Microwave rack		Roasts, hamburgers, appetizers
Pie plates	9, 10 inches	Main dishes, pies, appetizers
Ring dishes	5 to 10 cups	Cakes, coffee cakes, custards

Veal with Sour Cream

4 *servings*

½ cup chopped onion (about 1
    medium)
1 tablespoon margarine or butter
1 teaspoon instant beef bouillon
1 can (4 ounces) mushroom stems
    and pieces, drained
⅓ cup hot water
2 teaspoons grated lemon peel
½ teaspoon paprika
¼ teaspoon dried dill weed
⅛ teaspoon pepper

1 - pound veal shoulder steak, ½ to
    ¾ inch thick, cut into
    serving pieces

1 tablespoon plus 1 teaspoon
    cornstarch
2 tablespoons cold water
½ cup dairy sour cream

1. Place onion and margarine in 4-cup measure. Microwave uncovered on high (100%) until onion is crisp-tender, 2 to 3 minutes. Stir in bouillon, mushrooms, ⅓ cup hot water, the lemon peel, paprika, dill weed and pepper.

2. Arrange veal in baking dish, 8 × 8 × 2 inches. Pour onion mixture over veal. Cover tightly and microwave on medium (50%) 10 minutes; rotate baking dish ½ turn. Microwave until veal is done, 10 to 13 minutes longer.

3. Remove veal to warm platter. Mix cornstarch and water; gradually stir into onion mixture. Stir in sour cream. Microwave uncovered on medium-high (70%), stirring every minute, until thickened, 2 to 3 minutes. Pour over veal. Garnish with parsley sprigs if desired.

Beer Barbecued Turkey Drumsticks

6 servings

1 *package (about 2½ pounds)*
   frozen turkey drumsticks,
   defrosted
1 *cup barbecue sauce*
½ *cup beer*
¼ *teaspoon salt*
⅛ *teapsoon pepper*

Spiced peaches

1. Arrange turkey drumsticks in baking dish, 10 × 6 × 1½ inches. Mix barbecue sauce, beer, salt and pepper. Pour over drumsticks. Cover tightly and microwave on high (100%) 10 minutes.

2. Turn drumsticks over. Cover tightly and microwave on medium (50%) 25 minutes; turn drumsticks again. Cover and microwave until meat feels very soft when pressed between fingers, 25 to 40 minutes longer. Remove drumsticks to platter; skim off fat. Serve drumsticks with sauce and spiced peaches.

Poached Turkey Breast

About 6 cups cut-up turkey

1. Place defrosted frozen turkey breast (about 5 pounds) skin side down in baking dish, 12 × 7½ × 2 inches. Sprinkle with salt and white pepper. Add 1 cup water. Cover tightly and microwave on high (100%) 10 minutes.

2. Microwave on medium (50%) 25 minutes; turn turkey breast over. Cover and microwave until meat thermometer registers 185°, 20 to 30 minutes longer. Remove turkey from broth; refrigerate at least 1 hour but no longer than 2 days. Slice and serve, or remove meat from bones and skin and cut up for use in salads and other recipes calling for leftover turkey.

Microwaving Poultry for Leftovers

Whole chicken and chicken and turkey breasts can be microwaved, cut up or sliced, and used in casseroles, hot sandwiches or pies which are also microwaved with speed and ease. You can cool the cooked poultry and use it right away. Or wrap, label and freeze it no longer than 1 month. When microwaving casseroles containing leftover poultry (or cooked meats) push the pieces under the other ingredients or into the sauce. Covering and stirring from outside to inside will help casseroles cook quickly and evenly.

Beer Barbecued Turkey Drumsticks

Turkey Stuffing Casserole

6 servings

⅓ cup margarine or butter
3 cups herb-seasoned stuffing mix
¼ cup water

1 can (10¾ ounces) condensed
cream of mushroom soup
1 package (10 ounces) frozen
green peas
⅓ cup milk
2 teaspoons instant minced onion

2 cups coarsely cut-up cooked turkey
or chicken
2 tablespoons chopped pimiento
Cranberry Relish (page 251)

1. Place margarine in round baking dish, 8 × 1½ inches. Cover loosely and microwave on high (100%) until melted, 45 to 60 seconds. Add stuffing and water; toss to coat stuffing. Remove 1 cup stuffing. Spread remaining mixture evenly in baking dish.

2. Mix soup, peas, milk and onion in 1½-quart casserole. Cover tightly and microwave on high (100%) 3 minutes; stir. Cover and microwave until hot and bubbly, 3 to 4 minutes longer.

3. Stir in turkey and pimiento. Spread mixture over stuffing in baking dish. Sprinkle with reserved stuffing mixture. Microwave uncovered on high (100%) until hot and bubbly, 7 to 9 minutes. Serve with Cranberry Relish and any remaining stuffing.

Turkey Stuffing Casserole

Chicken with Stuffing and Giblet Gravy

6 or 7 servings

Cooked Giblets (below)

½ *cup chopped celery (about 1
      medium stalk)*
¼ *cup finely chopped onion
      (about 1 small)*
⅓ *cup margarine or butter*
3 *cups soft bread cubes (about 1½
      slices bread)*
⅓ *cup raisins*
½ *teaspoon dried sage*
½ *teaspoon dried thyme leaves*
¼ *teaspoon salt*
⅛ *teaspoon pepper*

3½ - *pound whole broiler-fryer
         chicken*
¼ *cup margarine or butter, melted
      (page 11)*
½ *teaspoon paprika*

Giblet Gravy (below)

1. Prepare Cooked Giblets.

2. Place celery, onion and ⅓ cup margarine in a 2-quart casserole. Microwave uncovered on high (100%) until crisp-tender, 2 to 3 minutes. Add bread cubes, raisins, sage, thyme, salt and pepper; toss.

3. Fill wishbone area of chicken with stuffing first. Fasten neck skin to back with wooden skewer. Lift wing tips up and over back for natural brace. Fill body cavity lightly. (Do not pack — stuffing will expand.) Tie or skewer drumsticks to tail. Mix ¼ cup melted margarine and the paprika; brush ½ of mixture over back of chicken. Place chicken breast side down on microwave rack in baking dish. Cover with waxed paper and microwave on medium-high (70%) 15 minutes. Turn chicken breast side up. Brush with remaining margarine mixture. Cover and microwave until drumstick meat feels soft when pressed between fingers, 13 to 18 minutes longer. Let stand covered 15 minutes. Release drumsticks from tail.

4. Prepare Giblet Gravy. Serve with chicken.

Cooked Giblets

*Gizzard, heart, liver and neck
   from 3½-pound broiler-fryer
   chicken*
1 *cup water*
1 *small onion, cut into fourths*
½ *teaspoon salt*
2 *peppercorns*
2 *whole cloves*
1 *bay leaf*

1. Mix all ingredients in 1-quart casserole. Cover tightly and microwave on medium (50%) 10 minutes; stir. Cover and microwave until tender, 8 to 12 minutes longer. Refrigerate until giblets are cool enough to handle.

2. Remove giblets and neck from broth. Refrigerate neck for later use; coarsely chop giblets.

Giblet Gravy

2 *tablespoons drippings*
2 *tablespoons all-purpose flour*

1 *cup broth from giblets*
   Salt and pepper

1. Place chicken on platter; keep warm while preparing gravy. Pour 2 tablespoons drippings in 4-cup measure. (Measure accurately because too little fat makes gravy lumpy.) Stir in flour. Microwave uncovered on high (100%) until bubbly, about 1 minute.

2. Stir in broth from giblets. Microwave uncovered on high (100%), stirring every minute, until thickened, 2 to 3 minutes. Stir in giblets; sprinkle with salt and pepper. Stir in few drops bottled brown bouquet sauce if desired.

Cooked Stewing Chicken

About 4 cups cooked chicken

4 - *pound stewing chicken, cut up*
   (about 8 pieces)
2 *large onions, sliced*
2 *teaspoons salt*
2 *cups hot water*

1. Cut chicken breast halves into halves. Place chicken, onions and salt in 3-quart casserole; pour water over chicken. Cover tightly and microwave on high (100%) 15 minutes; rearrange chicken.

2. Cover tightly and microwave on medium (50%) 20 minutes; rearrange chicken. Cover and microwave until thickest pieces are done, 20 to 30 minutes longer. Remove chicken from broth. Cover and refrigerate until cool enough to handle, about 15 minutes.

3. Remove meat from bones and skin and cut up for use in salads and other recipes calling for leftover chicken. (Broth can be strained and refrigerated up to 2 days or frozen up to 6 months.)

Poached Chicken Breast

About 1¾ cups cut-up chicken

1. Arrange 2 chicken breast halves (about 1 pound) skin sides up with thickest parts to outside edge in 2-quart casserole or 10-inch plate. Cover tightly and microwave on high (100%) 3 minutes; rotate plate ½ turn. Microwave until chicken is done, 3 to 5 minutes longer. Let stand 5 minutes. Refrigerate until cool enough to handle, about 10 minutes.

2. Slice and serve, or remove meat from bones and skin and cut up for use in salads and other recipes calling for leftover chicken.

Note: For Poached Turkey Breast, see page 57.

Microwaving Chicken Pieces

Chicken pieces can be microwaved quickly and in different ways — with a crisp coating, topped with dumplings, combined with vegetables — with very little attention while in the microwave. Easy sauces, which cover as well as season the chicken, and accompaniments such as chutney (another microwave special) help to accent the delicate flavor.

Because chicken pieces are irregular in shape, they form their own rack. Arrange the pieces meaty sides toward the edge of the dish, cover them (except when coated), and rotate the baking dish as directed in the recipe.

Buying a whole chicken and cutting it up yourself (see page 69) not only saves money but consistently gives pieces of uniform size. Pre-cut packaged chicken will vary as to size and number of pieces; cut the drumsticks from the thighs or cut the breast halves into halves for more even shapes.

Chicken a la King over Biscuits

Chicken a la King over Biscuits

4 servings

1   *can (10¾ ounces) condensed cream of chicken soup*
1   *cup coarsely cut-up cooked chicken or turkey*
1   *can (2 ounces) mushroom stems and pieces, drained*
¼   *cup dry white wine*
1   *tablespoon chopped pimiento*
1   *teaspoon parsley flakes*
⅛   *teaspoon dried marjoram leaves*
    Dash of pepper
    Baking Powder Biscuits (page 164)

Mix all ingredients except Baking Powder Biscuits in 1-quart casserole. Cover tightly and microwave on high (100%) until hot and bubbly, 5 to 7 minutes; stir. Serve over Baking Powder Biscuits.

Chicken Taco Pockets

8 pocket sandwiches

1 *small avocado*
1½ *teaspoons lemon juice*
¼ *teaspoon salt*

2 *cups finely cut-up cooked chicken or turkey*
1 *can (4 ounces) chopped green chilies, drained*
1 *small onion, sliced*
1 *tablespoon vegetable oil*
¾ *teaspoon salt*
1 *package (8 ounces) miniature pocket breads, (8 pockets, about 3½ inches each)*
2 *cups shredded Monterey Jack cheese (about 8 ounces)*
⅓ *cup sliced pimiento-stuffed olives*
1 *cup shredded lettuce*
Dairy sour cream
Taco sauce

1. Cut avocado into halves; cut halves into thin slices. Sprinkle with lemon juice and ¼ teaspoon salt.

2. Mix chicken, chilies, onion, vegetable oil and ¾ teaspoon salt in 1½-quart casserole. Cover tightly and microwave on high (100%) 2 minutes; stir. Cover and microwave until chicken is hot, 2 to 3 minutes longer. Spoon about ¼ cup chicken mixture into each pocket bread. Top with cheese, olives, lettuce and avocado. Serve with sour cream and taco sauce.

Chicken Taco Pockets

Chicken Enchiladas

6 *to* 8 *servings*

2 *cups chopped cooked chicken
     or turkey*
1 *can (3 ounces) chopped green
     chilies, drained*
¾ *cup chopped tomato (about
     1 medium)*
½ *cup chopped onion (about
     1 medium)*
1 *clove garlic, finely chopped*

8 *six-inch flour tortillas*
1 *can (6 ounces) frozen avocado
     dip, defrosted*

½ *cup shredded Cheddar cheese
     (about 2 ounces)*
1 *jar (8 ounces) mild taco sauce*

1. Mix chicken, chilies, tomato, onion and garlic in 1½-quart casserole. Cover tightly and microwave on high (100%) 3 minutes; stir. Cover and microwave until hot, 2 to 3 minutes longer; drain.

2. Wrap 4 tortillas in damp cloth or paper towel and microwave on high (100%) until softened, about 45 seconds. Spread about ¼ cup filling on each tortilla; top with about 1 tablespoon avocado dip. Roll tortilla around filling. Arrange seam sides down in baking dish, 12 × 7½ × 2 inches. Repeat with remaining tortillas.

3. Sprinkle with cheese. Microwave uncovered on high (100%) until enchiladas are hot and cheese is melted, 4 to 6 minutes. Serve with any remaining avocado dip and Warm Taco Sauce.

Warm Taco Sauce: Place taco sauce in 2-cup pitcher. Microwave uncovered on high (100%) until hot, about 1 minute; stir.

Chicken Enchiladas

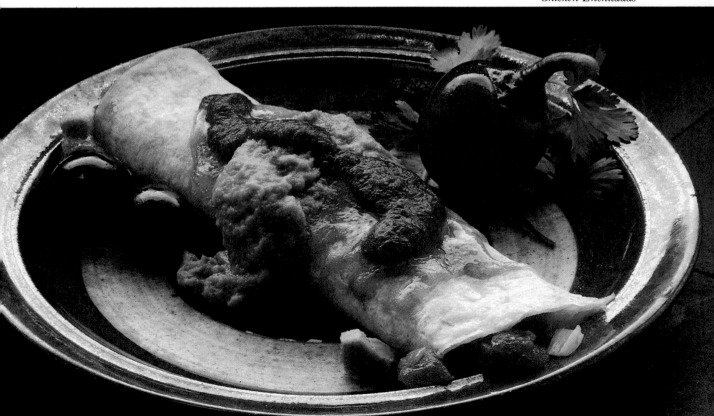

Hot Chicken Salad in Cheese Tarts

6 servings

Tart Shells (page 210)
½ cup finely shredded Cheddar
    cheese (about 2 ounces)

2 cups coarsely cut-up cooked
    chicken or turkey
1 cup thinly sliced celery
2 tablespoons lemon juice
1 tablespoon finely chopped onion
½ teaspoon salt
¼ teaspoon pepper
¾ cup mayonnaise or salad dressing
1 cup halved seedless green grapes
½ cup slivered almonds, toasted
    (page 12)

1. Prepare Tart Shells as directed except — stir cheese into flour mixture before adding water.

2. Toss chicken, celery, lemon juice, onion, salt and pepper in 1½-quart bowl. Mix in mayonnaise. Carefully fold in grapes and ¼ cup almonds. Cover loosely and microwave on medium (50%) 3 minutes; stir. Cover and microwave until hot, 3 to 4 minutes longer. Spoon chicken mixture into tart shells. Sprinkle with remaining almonds.

Chicken-Macaroni Casserole

6 servings

1½ cups uncooked macaroni
    (about 5 ounces)
1 can (10¾ ounces) condensed
    cream of chicken soup
1 cup milk
½ teaspoon salt
½ teaspoon curry powder

1½ cups coarsely cut-up
    cooked chicken or turkey
1 cup shredded Cheddar cheese
1 can (4 ounces) mushroom stems
    and pieces
1 jar (2 ounces) chopped pimiento,
    drained

1. Mix macaroni, soup, milk, salt and curry powder in 2-quart casserole. Cover tightly and microwave on high (100%) 3 minutes; stir. Cover and microwave 3 minutes longer.

2. Stir chicken, cheese, mushrooms (with liquid) and pimiento into macaroni. Cover tightly and microwave on medium-high (70%) 8 minutes; stir. Cover and microwave until hot and bubbly, 7 to 10 minutes longer. Let stand 5 minutes.

Microwaving Main Dish Pastries

Microwaving a pizza crust or cheese-flavored tarts involves a bit of preparation — does this contradict the speedy aspect of microwaving? Not so! These and other recipes bring microwaving beyond shortcuts alone and into the area of special treats. So be adventurous, and reap the rewards: a pizza crust that stays crunchy to the last crumb, piquant holders for a delicious, speedily prepared chicken salad, and more!

Hot Chicken Salad in Cheese Tarts

Chicken with Rice and Bacon

8 *to* 10 *servings*

8 slices bacon, finely chopped

½ cup chopped onion
(about 1 medium)

1 cup chopped green pepper
(about 1 medium)

1 can (28 ounces) whole tomatoes

4 cups ¾-inch pieces cooked
chicken or turkey

1½ cups uncooked instant rice

½ cup hot water

1 teaspoon salt

1 teaspoon ground cumin

½ cup raisins

1. Place bacon in 3-quart casserole. Cover with paper towel and microwave on high (100%) 3 minutes; stir. Cover and microwave until crisp, 2 to 3 minutes longer. Drain on paper towels; reserve.

2. Stir onion and green pepper into bacon fat. Cover tightly and microwave on high (100%) 2 minutes; stir. Cover and microwave until onion is tender, 2 to 3 minutes longer.

3. Stir in tomatoes (with liquid); break up tomatoes with fork. Add chicken, rice, hot water, salt and cumin. Cover tightly and microwave on high (100%) 8 minutes; stir. Cover and microwave until mixture is hot and rice is tender, 7 to 9 minutes longer. Stir in raisins. Cover and let stand 5 minutes. Sprinkle with reserved bacon.

Chicken with Rice and Bacon

Chicken-Fruit Pilaf

6 servings

½ cup chopped onion (about 1 medium)
⅓ cup chopped celery
2 tablespoons margarine or butter

2 cups coarsely cut-up cooked chicken or turkey
1½ cups uncooked instant rice
1½ cups hot water
1 package (8 ounces) mixed dried fruits, cut into fourths
2 tablespoons raisins
2 teaspoons instant chicken bouillon
¾ teaspoon salt
¼ teaspoon ground cinnamon
¼ teaspoon ground thyme
⅛ teaspoon pepper
¼ cup chopped pecans

1. Place onion, celery and margarine in 2-quart casserole. Microwave uncovered on high (100%) until onion is tender, 2 to 3 minutes.

2. Stir in remaining ingredients except pecans. Cover tightly and microwave on high (100%) 5 minutes; stir. Cover and microwave until water is absorbed, 5 to 7 minutes longer; stir in pecans.

Layered Chicken and Broccoli

6 servings

1 package (10 ounces) frozen chopped broccoli, defrosted and drained
1 tablespoon finely chopped onion
1 clove garlic, finely chopped
½ teaspoon salt
Dash of pepper

2 cups coarsely cut-up cooked chicken or turkey
1 can (8 ounces) water chestnuts, sliced

½ cup dairy sour cream
2 tablespoons milk
½ teaspoon salt
1 cup shredded mozzarella cheese (about 4 ounces)
¼ cup grated Parmesan cheese
Paprika

1. Stir broccoli, onion, garlic, salt and pepper in round baking dish, 8 × 1½ inches. Cover tightly and microwave on high (100%) until vegetables are crisp-tender, 3 to 4 minutes; stir.

2. Arrange chicken and water chestnuts evenly on broccoli. Cover with waxed paper and microwave on high (100%) 3 minutes.

3. Mix sour cream, milk and salt; pour evenly over water chestnuts. Sprinkle with cheeses and paprika. Cover with waxed paper and microwave on medium-high (70%) until cheeses are melted, 3 to 5 minutes.

Chicken Pie with Celery Seed Pastry

8 servings

*Celery Seed 9-inch Two-crust
    Pastry (below)*

4   cups coarsely cut-up cooked
        chicken or turkey
1   can (10¾ ounces) condensed
        cream of celery soup
1   can (10¾ ounces) condensed
        cream of mushroom soup
1   can (8¾ ounces) corn, drained
½   cup chopped onion (about
        1 medium)
¼   cup chopped green pepper
1   tablespoon snipped parsley
⅛   teaspoon pepper

1. Prepare pastry.

2. Mix remaining ingredients; turn into pastry-lined pie plate. Cover with top crust that has slits cut in it; seal and flute. Microwave uncovered on medium-high (70%) until filling begins to bubble through slits in crust and pastry looks dry and flaky, 16 to 20 minutes.

3. Transfer pie to conventional oven (do not pre-heat). Bake at 450° until crust is brown and flaky, 10 to 15 minutes. Let stand 15 minutes before cutting.

Celery Seed 9-inch Two-crust Pastry

¾   cup margarine
2   cups all-purpose flour
2   teaspoons celery seed
½   teaspoon salt
4   to 5 tablespoons cold water

1. Cut margarine into flour, celery seed and salt until particles are size of small peas. Sprinkle in water, 1 tablespoon at a time, tossing with fork, until all flour is moistened and pastry almost cleans side of bowl (1 to 2 teaspoons water can be added if necessary).

2. Gather pastry into a ball. Divide into halves; shape into 2 flattened rounds on lightly floured cloth-covered board. Roll each half 2 inches larger than inverted 9-inch pie plate with floured stockinet-covered rolling pin. Fold one half into quarters; unfold and ease into pie plate.

Chicken in Buns

6 sandwiches

1 *cup cut-up cooked chicken or turkey*
1 *cup chopped celery*
1 *tablespoon finely chopped onion*
¼ *teaspoon salt*
⅛ *teaspoon pepper*
 Dash of ground sage
¼ *cup mayonnaise or salad dressing*
6 *hamburger buns, buttered*
6 *slices process American cheese*

Mix all ingredients except buns and cheese. Fill buns with chicken mixture; add cheese. Arrange buns in circle on paper towel-lined 12-inch plate. Microwave uncovered on high (100%) 1 minute; rotate plate ½ turn. Microwave until cheese is melted and filling is hot, 1 to 2 minutes longer.

Cutting Up a Chicken

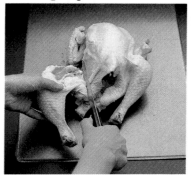

Cut through skin, then through the meat between leg and hip joint. Pull leg out; cut remaining skin and separate leg. Repeat.

Cut drumstick from thigh by cutting ⅛ inch from fat line which runs crosswise between drumstick and thigh. Repeat.

Cut off wing by cutting into wing joint, then rolling the blade to follow around curve of joint. Repeat with second wing.

Cut out backbone by holding body neck end down and cutting through the rib joints along each side of backbone to separate back from breast.

Cut through white cartilage at the "V" of neck. To do this, hold breast skin side down with "V" toward you while cutting.

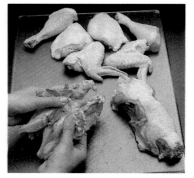

Bend back sides; pop out cartilage. Then draw out bone and cartilage and discard. Cut each breast half into halves.

Curried Chicken with Peach Chutney

6 *or* 7 *servings*

Peach Chutney (below)

3 - *pound broiler-fryer chicken,*
    cut up (about 8 pieces)
1   *cup chopped onion*
    (about 2 medium)
1   *teaspoon instant chicken*
    bouillon

1   *cup dairy sour cream*
2   *teaspoons curry powder*
½   *teaspoon salt*
⅛   *teaspoon ground ginger*
⅛   *teaspoon ground cumin*
    Snipped parsley
3½ *cups hot cooked rice*

1. Prepare Peach Chutney.

2. Cut each chicken breast half into halves. Arrange pieces skin sides up with thickest parts to outside edge in baking dish, 12 × 7½ × 2 inches. Sprinkle with onion and bouillon. Cover with waxed paper and microwave on high (100%) 10 minutes; rotate baking dish ½ turn. Microwave until thickest parts of chicken are done, 6 to 10 minutes longer.

3. Remove chicken to serving dish; keep warm. Pour juices from baking dish into bowl; skim off fat. Return ¼ cup liquid to baking dish; stir in sour cream, curry powder, salt, ginger and cumin. Microwave uncovered on medium (50%), stirring every minute, until hot, 5 to 7 minutes. Spoon sauce over chicken. Top with parsley. Serve with chutney and rice.

Peach Chutney

2   *cups coarsely chopped peaches*
    (about 2 large)
1   *cup raisins*
1   *cup packed brown sugar*
⅓   *cup lemon juice*
1   *jar (2⅞ ounces) crystallized*
    ginger, finely chopped
1   *clove garlic, finely chopped*
½   *teaspoon salt*

Mix all ingredients in 2-quart casserole. Cover tightly and microwave on high (100%) 5 minutes; stir. Cover and microwave until peaches are transparent and chutney is syrupy, 5 to 7 minutes longer. Refrigerate until chilled. Store in refrigerator no longer than 2 weeks.

Garlic Chip Chicken (pictured on page 2)

6 *or* 7 *servings*

¼   *cup margarine or butter, melted*
    (page 11)
½   *teaspoon salt*
¼   *teaspoon instant minced garlic*
⅛   *teaspoon pepper*

3 - *pound broiler-fryer chicken, cut*
    up (about 8 pieces)
2   *cups finely crushed potato chips*
    (about 4 ounces)

1. Place margarine in 9-inch pie plate. Microwave uncovered on high (100%) until melted, 30 to 45 seconds. Sprinkle with salt, garlic and pepper.

2. Cut each chicken breast half into halves. Dip chicken into margarine mixture; coat with crushed potato chips. Arrange pieces skin sides up with thickest parts to outside edge in baking dish, 12 × 7½ × 2 inches. Microwave uncovered on high (100%) 10 minutes; rotate baking dish ½ turn. Microwave until thickest parts of chicken are done, 8 to 12 minutes longer. Let stand 5 minutes.

Italian-Style Chicken

6 or 7 servings

3 - *pound broiler-fryer chicken, cut up (about 8 pieces)*

1 *can (16 ounces) tomatoes*
1 *can (8 ounces) tomato sauce*
1 *cup sliced mushrooms (about 4 ounces)*
½ *cup chopped onion (about 1 medium)*
¼ *cup sliced pitted ripe olives*
2 *cloves garlic, finely chopped*
1 *teaspoon salt*
1 *teaspoon dried oregano leaves*
¼ *teaspoon pepper*
1 *bay leaf*
   Snipped parsley
4 *to 5 cups hot cooked spaghetti*

1. Cut each chicken breast half into halves. Place chicken in 3-quart casserole. Cover tightly and microwave on high (100%) 12 minutes; drain.

2. Mix tomatoes (with liquid) and remaining ingredients except parsley and spaghetti; break up tomatoes with fork. Stir mixture into chicken. Cover tightly and microwave on high (100%) until thickest parts of chicken are done, 14 to 18 minutes. Remove bay leaf. Sprinkle with parsley; serve over spaghetti.

Chicken with Fruit Sauce

6 or 7 servings

2 *tablespoons margarine or butter*
½ *teaspoon salt*
   Paprika

3 - *pound broiler-fryer chicken, cut up (about 8 pieces)*

2 *tablespoons cornstarch*
2 *teaspoons instant chicken bouillon*
¼ *teaspoon ground ginger*
⅓ *cup dry white wine*
1 *can (13½ ounces) pineapple chunks in juice*
1 *jar (4 ounces) mushroom stems and pieces*

1. Place margarine in baking dish, 12 × 7½ × 2 inches. Microwave uncovered on high (100%) until melted, 15 to 30 seconds. Sprinkle margarine with salt and paprika.

2. Cut each chicken breast half into halves. Place chicken in dish, turning to coat with margarine. Arrange pieces skin sides up with thickest parts to outside edge in baking dish. Cover with waxed paper and microwave on high (100%) 10 minutes; rotate baking dish ½ turn. Microwave until thickest parts of chicken are done, 6 to 10 minutes longer.

3. Mix cornstarch, bouillon and ginger in 1½-quart casserole. Stir in wine. Add pineapple (with juice) and mushrooms (with liquid). Cover tightly and microwave on high (100%), stirring every 2 minutes, until thickened, 6 to 7 minutes. Arrange chicken on platter. Spoon hot sauce over chicken.

Chicken with Cauliflower and Peas

6 or 7 servings

3 - *pound broiler-fryer chicken, cut up (about 8 pieces)*
1 *teaspoon salt*
1 *clove garlic, finely chopped*
½ *teaspoon dried basil leaves*
¼ *teaspoon paprika*
1 *medium onion, cut into 8 wedges*

3 *cups 1-inch flowerets cauliflower (about 1 pound)*
1 *package (10 ounces) frozen green peas*
½ *teaspoon salt*
⅛ *teaspoon pepper*

1. Cut each chicken breast half into halves. Arrange pieces skin sides up with thickest parts to outside edge in baking dish, 12 × 7½ × 2 inches. Sprinkle with 1 teaspoon salt, the garlic, basil and paprika. Add onion. Cover tightly and microwave on high (100%) 10 minutes.

2. Add cauliflower and peas; sprinkle with ½ teaspoon salt and the pepper. Rotate baking dish ½ turn. Cover tightly and microwave on high (100%) until thickest parts of chicken are done and vegetables are tender, 10 to 15 minutes. Uncover and let stand 3 minutes.

Chicken with Cauliflower and Peas

Chicken Fricassee with Parsley Dumplings 6 *or* 7 *servings*

3 - *pound broiler-fryer chicken, cut*
      up (about 8 pieces)
      Salt
      Pepper
      Paprika

1   *can (10¾ ounces) condensed*
      cream of chicken soup
1   *cup milk*

      Parsley Dumplings (below)

1. Cut each chicken breast half into halves. Arrange pieces, skin sides up, with meatiest parts to outside edge in baking dish, 12 × 7½ × 2 inches. Sprinkle with salt and pepper. Sprinkle generously with paprika. Cover with waxed paper and microwave on high (100%) 10 minutes. Skim off fat if necessary.

2. Mix soup and milk; spoon over chicken pieces. Rotate baking dish ½ turn. Cover with waxed paper and microwave on high (100%) until thickest parts of chicken are done, 8 to 12 minutes longer.

3. Prepare Parsley Dumplings. Drop by spoonfuls around edge of dish. Microwave uncovered on high (100%) 3 minutes; rotate baking dish ½ turn. Microwave until dumplings are no longer doughy, 3 to 4 minutes longer.

Parsley Dumplings
2   *cups buttermilk baking mix*
⅔   *cup milk*
2   *teaspoons parsley flakes*
¼   *teaspoon poultry seasoning*

Mix all ingredients until soft dough forms.

Orange-Spiced Chicken 6 *or* 7 *servings*

3 - *pound broiler-fryer chicken, cut*
      up (about 8 pieces)
2   *medium onions, sliced*
1½ *teaspoons salt*
1   *teaspoon paprika*
⅛   *teaspoon pepper*
⅔   *cup orange juice*
3   *tablespoons packed brown sugar*
2   *tablespoons vinegar*
½   *teaspoon ground ginger*
¼   *teaspoon ground nutmeg*
½   *cup pimiento-stuffed olives*

1   *tablespoon cornstarch*
1   *tablespoon cold water*
      Orange slices

1. Cut each chicken breast half into halves. Arrange pieces skin sides up with thickest parts to outside edge in baking dish, 12 × 7½ × 2 inches; top with onions. Sprinkle with salt, paprika and pepper. Mix juice, brown sugar, vinegar, ginger and nutmeg; pour over chicken. Cover tightly and microwave on high (100%) 10 minutes. Add olives; rotate baking dish ½ turn. Cover and microwave until thickest parts of chicken are done, 8 to 13 minutes longer.

2. Arrange chicken, onions and olives on platter; keep warm. Pour juices from baking dish into 4-cup measure. Mix cornstarch and water; stir into juices. Microwave uncovered on high (100%), stirring every minute, until slightly thickened, 3 to 4 minutes. Garnish chicken with orange slices; serve with sauce.

Chicken Fricassee with Parsley Dumplings

Speedy Chicken and Seafood

6 *servings*

1 *can (8¼ ounces) pineapple*
   chunks, drained
½ *cup chopped onion*
   (about 1 medium)

2 *cans (10½ ounces each) chicken*
   a la king
1 *can (4½ ounces) deveined*
   medium shrimp, rinsed
   and drained
2 *tablespoons lemon juice*
3 *to 4 cups hot cooked noodles*
   Imitation bacon
   Snipped parsley (if desired)

1. Place pineapple and onion in 1½-quart casserole. Cover tightly and microwave on high (100%) 3 minutes; stir. Cover and microwave until onion is crisp-tender, 2 to 3 minutes longer.

2. Stir in chicken a la king, shrimp and lemon juice. Cover tightly and microwave on high (100%) 3 minutes; stir. Cover and microwave until hot, 2 to 4 minutes longer. Serve over noodles; sprinkle with imitation bacon. Garnish with snipped parsley.

Chicken with Three Vegetables

4 *servings*

1 *can (8 ounces) stewed tomatoes*
¾ *cup water*
½ *cup uncooked regular rice*
¼ *cup chopped onion*
   (about 1 small)
1 *small clove garlic, finely*
   chopped
¾ *teaspoon salt*
⅛ *teaspoon pepper*
1½ *pounds chicken drumsticks and*
   thighs
1 *teaspoon dried oregano leaves*
½ *teaspoon paprika*

1 *package (10 ounces) frozen*
   green peas
¼ *cup chopped green pepper*
3 *tablespoons sliced*
   pimiento-stuffed olives
   Grated Parmesan cheese

1. Mix tomatoes (with liquid), water, rice, onion, garlic, salt and pepper in 2-quart casserole. Arrange chicken pieces skin sides up with thickest parts to outside edge in casserole; sprinkle with oregano and paprika. Cover tightly and microwave on high (100%) 15 minutes.

2. Stir in peas, green pepper and olives. Cover and microwave on high (100%) until thickest parts of chicken are done and vegetables are tender, 10 to 15 minutes. Let stand 5 minutes. Serve with cheese.

Your Microwave Dish-Saver

Try heating food in napkins, paper plates, or paper hot cups, cooking and serving in the same container, measuring and mixing in the same glass measure, and taking leftovers from refrigerator to microwave to table in the same dish. Or reheat an entire microwave meal on a plate that comes to the table. Just one of the many microwave advantages.

Gingered Chicken

Gingered Chicken

8 servings

3   *pounds chicken drumsticks and thighs*
⅓   *cup honey*
⅓   *cup chili sauce*
⅓   *cup soy sauce*
1   *teaspoon ground ginger*
½   *teaspoon salt*
¼   *teaspoon pepper*

1   *tablespoon cornstarch*
2   *tablespoons cold water*

1. Arrange chicken pieces skin sides up with thickest parts to outside edge in baking dish, $12 \times 7\frac{1}{2} \times 2$ inches. Mix remaining ingredients except cornstarch and water; pour over chicken. Cover with waxed paper and microwave on high (100%) 10 minutes. Spoon sauce over chicken; rotate baking dish ½ turn. Cover and microwave until thickest parts of chicken are done, 7 to 11 minutes longer.

2. Remove chicken to platter; keep warm. Skim fat from sauce. Mix cornstarch and water; stir into sauce. Microwave uncovered on high (100%), stirring every minute, until thickened, about 2 minutes. Pour sauce over chicken.

Chicken Livers a la King

6 *servings*

1 *pound chicken livers*
¼ *cup margarine or butter*

1 *can (10¾ ounces) condensed*
    cream of mushroom soup
1 *can (8 ounces) water chestnuts,*
    sliced
2 *tablespoons chopped pimiento*
1 *teaspoon Worcestershire sauce*
¼ *teaspoon salt*
3 *cups chow mein noodles*
    Snipped parsley

1. Cut chicken livers into 1-inch pieces and place in 2-quart casserole. Add margarine. Cover tightly and microwave on high (100%) 2 minutes; stir. Cover tightly and microwave 2 minutes longer.

2. Stir in soup, water chestnuts, pimiento, Worcestershire sauce and salt. Cover tightly and microwave on high (100%) 2 minutes; stir. Cover and microwave until hot and bubbly, 2 to 4 minutes longer. Serve over chow mein noodles. Sprinkle with parsley.

Duckling with Tangy Sauce

4 *servings*

1 *ready-to-cook duckling*
    (4 to 5 pounds)
2 *tablespoons orange juice*
½ *teaspoon bottled brown bouquet*
    sauce

½ *cup orange juice*
¼ *cup orange marmalade*
1 *tablespoon lemon juice*
⅛ *teaspoon ground ginger*
⅛ *teaspoon salt*

2 *teaspoons cornstarch*
1 *tablespoon cold water*
1 *orange, peeled and sectioned*

1. Fasten neck skin of duckling to back with wooden skewers. Lift wing tips up and over back for natural brace. Prick skin with fork. Mix 2 tablespoons orange juice and the bouquet sauce; brush half of mixture over duckling. Place duckling breast side down on microwave rack in baking dish. Cover with waxed paper and microwave on medium-high (70%) 18 minutes; drain. Turn duckling breast side up; brush with remaining juice mixture. Cover and microwave until drumstick meat feels very soft when pressed between fingers, 18 to 23 minutes longer. Cover with aluminum foil and let stand 10 minutes.

2. Mix ½ cup orange juice, the marmalade, lemon juice, ginger and salt in 2-cup measure. Microwave uncovered on high (100%) to boiling, 1 to 2 minutes.

3. Mix cornstarch and water; stir into sauce. Microwave uncovered on medium-high (70%), stirring every minute, until thickened and boiling, 1 to 2 minutes. Stir in orange sections. Brush duckling with orange sauce; serve with remaining sauce.

Cornish Hens with Bacon Stuffing

Cornish Hens with Bacon Stuffing

6 *servings*

Bacon Stuffing (below)

3 *Rock Cornish hens (about 1¼
    pounds each), thawed*
¼ *cup margarine or butter, melted
    (page 11)*
½ *teaspoon paprika*

1. Prepare Bacon Stuffing.

2. Stuff each hen with about ½ cup stuffing. Secure opening with wooden skewers. Fasten neck skin to back with wooden skewer. Tie drumsticks together. Place hens breast sides down on microwave rack in baking dish. Mix margarine and paprika; brush ½ of mixture over hens. Cover with waxed paper and microwave on high (100%) 15 minutes.

3. Turn hens breast sides up and rearrange; brush with remaining margarine mixture. Cover and microwave until done, 15 to 20 minutes longer. To serve, cut hens with kitchen scissors, cutting through the breast and along backbone from tail to neck. Serve with dressing.

Bacon Stuffing

6 *slices bacon, cut into ½-inch
    pieces*

½ *cup chopped onion
    (about 1 medium)*
⅓ *cup margarine or butter*
1¾ *cups soft bread cubes*
½ *cup chopped celery with leaves
    (about 1 medium stalk)*
2 *tablespoons snipped parsley*
½ *teaspoon poultry seasoning*
⅛ *teaspoon pepper*

1. Place bacon in 2-quart casserole. Cover with paper towel and microwave on high (100%) 3 minutes; stir. Cover and microwave until crisp, 3 to 4 minutes longer; drain on paper towel. Pour off fat; return 2 tablespoons fat to casserole.

2. Add onion to bacon fat. Cover tightly and microwave on high (100%) until onion is tender, 3 to 4 minutes. Add margarine; stir until melted. Add remaining ingredients; toss.

Fluffy Eggs with Broccoli

4 *to* 6 *servings*

1   *package (10 ounces) frozen chopped broccoli*

9   *eggs*
½   *cup shredded Cheddar cheese (about 2 ounces)*
2   *tablespoons instant minced onion*
2   *tablespoons milk*
1   *teaspoon salt*
½   *teaspoon dried basil leaves*
¼   *teaspoon garlic powder*
4   *tomatoes, cut in halves*

1. Place broccoli in baking dish, 10 × 6 × 1½ inches. Cover tightly and microwave on high (100%) 4 minutes; break up and stir. Cover and microwave until crisp-tender, 2 to 3 minutes longer; drain well.

2. Beat eggs; stir in cheese, onion, milk, salt, basil and garlic powder. Pour over broccoli. Elevate baking dish on inverted dinner plate in microwave. Cover loosely and microwave on medium-high (70%) 5 minutes; push cooked edges to center. Microwave until center is almost set, 4 to 6 minutes longer. Arrange tomatoes on top.

Eggs in Hash Nests

6 *servings*

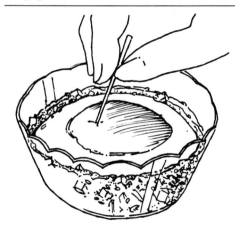

1. Divide 1 can (15 ounces) corned beef hash among 6 six-ounce custard cups. Press hash against bottom and side of each cup. Arrange cups in circle on 12-inch plate. Microwave uncovered on high (100%) until hot, 2½ to 3½ minutes.

2. Break an egg on hash in each dish; pierce yolk with wooden pick. Cover tightly and microwave on medium-high (70%) 3 minutes; rotate plate ½ turn. Microwave until eggs are almost set, removing custard cups as eggs are done, 1 to 3 minutes longer. Let stand 3 minutes. (Eggs will continue to cook while standing.) Season with salt and pepper.

Microwaving Eggs

Eggs should never be microwaved in their shells! Pressure will build up within the membrane of the yolk, which cooks faster because of its fat content and causes the egg to explode.

However, conventionally hard-cooked eggs can be sliced and added to a hot cheese or cream sauce (pages 84 and 85).

To poach or steam whole shelled eggs in the microwave, first pierce the yolk with a wooden pick. Microwave covered at a lower setting and cover tightly to even the heat distribution.

Scrambled eggs eliminate the problem of uneven cooking and are fluffy and light. They do require stirring, just as conventionally scrambled eggs do. Be careful to note doneness tests and standing times for eggs — they become rubbery if they are overcooked.

Fluffy Eggs with Broccoli

Puffy Scrambled Eggs

2 servings

4 *eggs*
¼ *cup milk*
¼ *teaspoon salt*
   Dash of pepper

Beat all ingredients with fork in 1-quart casserole. If desired, stir in ¼ cup shredded cheese, crumbled cooked bacon, chopped fully-cooked ham, snipped chives or green onions or chopped canned mushrooms. Cover tightly and microwave on high (100%), stirring every minute, until eggs are puffy and set but still moist, 3 to 4 minutes. Stir before serving.

Note: Recipe can be doubled. Increase microwave time to 6 to 8 minutes, stirring every 2 minutes.

Puffy Scrambled Eggs

Scrambled Eggs in Bologna Cups

4 servings

4 slices bologna, about 4 inches
   in diameter
3 eggs
3 tablespoons half-and-half
¼ teaspoon salt
   Dash of pepper
1 jar (2½ ounces) sliced
   mushrooms, drained
1 tablespoon finely chopped green
   pepper

½ cup shredded Cheddar cheese

1. Place each bologna slice in 6-ounce custard cup or coffee mug. Arrange cups in circle on dinner plate. Beat eggs, half-and-half, salt and pepper in 4-cup measure. Mix in mushrooms and green pepper. Microwave uncovered on medium (50%) until hot, 1 to 2 minutes.

2. Stir in shredded cheese. Divide mixture among bologna cups. Cover loosely and microwave on medium (50%) 3 minutes; rotate plate ½ turn. Microwave until egg mixture is almost set, 1 to 3 minutes longer. Let stand 5 minutes. (Eggs will continue to cook while standing.)

Chili-Cheese Eggs

6 to 8 servings

2 cups shredded Cheddar cheese
   (about 8 ounces)
1 can (4 ounces) chopped green
   chilies, drained
2 cups shredded Monterey Jack
   cheese (about 8 ounces)

3 eggs
⅓ cup all-purpose flour
½ teaspoon salt
2 cans (5⅓ ounces each)
   evaporated milk

1 can (8 ounces) tomato sauce
   (if desired)

1. Layer Cheddar cheese, chilies and Monterey Jack cheese in baking dish, 8 × 8 × 2 inches.

2. Beat eggs, flour, salt and milk in 4-cup measure. Microwave uncovered on medium (50%), stirring with fork every minute, until hot, 4 to 5 minutes.

3. Quickly pour egg mixture evenly over cheese. Elevate baking dish on inverted dinner plate in microwave. Cover loosely and microwave on medium (50%), rotating baking dish ½ turn every 5 minutes, until center is set, 15 to 17 minutes.

4. Pour tomato sauce into small bowl. Microwave uncovered on high (100%) until hot, 1 to 2 minutes. Serve with eggs.

Microwaving Cheese

Cheese becomes tough and rubbery if it is overcooked, so it is sometimes microwaved at a lower power setting, added at the end of a recipe, or just cooked for a very short time.

Packaged shredded natural cheese is especially good as a microwave timesaver and garnish. Process cheese blends readily with other ingredients in soups, sandwiches, and sauces (as for macaroni and cheese). Grated Parmesan cheese is used as a flavorful ingredient and/or topping. Cheese generally goes hand-in-hand with eggs to provide thrifty as well as complete animal protein in dishes combined with macaroni, dried beans, rice and bread.

Chinese-Style Casserole

4 *to* 6 *servings*

Sauce (below)

1 *can (16 ounces) bean sprouts,
  rinsed and drained*
1 *can (8 ounces) sliced water
  chestnuts, drained*
½ *cup chopped green pepper
  (about 1 small)*
¼ *cup chopped onion
  (about 1 small)*

6 *eggs, beaten*
1 *tablespoon chopped pimiento*
¾ *teaspoon salt*

Sauce
⅔ *cup water*
3 *tablespoons soy sauce*
1 *tablespoon cornstarch*
1 *teaspoon sugar*
1 *teaspoon vinegar*

1. Prepare Sauce.

2. Mix bean sprouts, water chestnuts, green pepper and onion in 1½-quart casserole. Cover tightly and microwave on high (100%) 3 minutes; stir. Cover and microwave until vegetables are hot, 2 to 3 minutes longer; drain.

3. Stir in eggs, pimiento and salt. Cover tightly and microwave on high (100%) 2 minutes; stir. Cover and microwave until eggs are set but still moist, 1½ to 4 minutes longer. Spoon Sauce over each serving.

Mix all ingredients in 2-cup measure. Microwave uncovered on high (100%), stirring every minute, until mixture boils and thickens, 3 to 4 minutes.

Eggs in Cheese Sauce

4 *servings*

2 *tablespoons margarine or butter*
3 *tablespoons all-purpose flour*
1 *teaspoon instant chicken bouillon*
⅛ *teaspoon pepper*

1 *cup water*
½ *cup milk*

½ *cup shredded Cheddar cheese
  (about 2 ounces)*
¼ *teaspoon Worcestershire sauce*

6 *hard-cooked eggs*

¼ *cup dry bread crumbs*
¼ *cup grated Parmesan cheese*
1 *tablespoon margarine or butter,
  melted (page 11)*
4 *English muffins, split and toasted*

1. Place margarine in 1½-quart casserole. Microwave uncovered on high (100%) until melted, 15 to 30 seconds. Stir in flour, bouillon and pepper.

2. Gradually stir in water and milk. Microwave uncovered on high (100%), stirring every minute, until thickened, 3 to 5 minutes.

3. Stir in Cheddar cheese and Worcestershire sauce. Microwave uncovered on high (100%) until cheese is melted, 2 to 3 minutes.

4. Cut peeled eggs lengthwise into halves. Arrange eggs around edge of round baking dish, 8 × 1½ inches. Pour cheese sauce over eggs. Cover with waxed paper and microwave on medium (50%) 6 to 8 minutes.

5. Mix bread crumbs, Parmesan cheese and margarine; sprinkle over eggs. Serve on English muffins. Garnish with parsley if desired.

Creamed Eggs Over Cheese Bread

6 *servings*

Prepare Cheese Bread (left) and Creamed Eggs (below). Serve Creamed Eggs over Cheese Bread.

Cheese Bread

2 *tablespoons yellow cornmeal*
¼ *teaspoon paprika*
1 *egg*
1 *cup milk*
¼ *cup vegetable oil*
1 *cup all-purpose flour*
1 *cup whole wheat flour*
1 *cup shredded sharp Cheddar cheese (about 4 ounces)*
2 *tablespoons sugar*
3 *teaspoons baking powder*
½ *teaspoon salt*
½ *teaspoon onion salt*
¼ *teaspoon poultry seasoning*

Mix cornmeal and paprika. Generously grease 6-cup ring mold; coat with cornmeal mixture. Beat egg; stir in milk and oil. Stir in flours, cheese, sugar, baking powder, salt, onion salt and poultry seasoning just until flour is moistened. (Batter will be lumpy.) Spoon into ring dish. Microwave uncovered on medium-high (70%) 4 minutes; rotate ring mold ½ turn. Microwave until no longer doughy, 3 to 5 minutes longer. Let stand 5 minutes. Invert onto plate. Slice and top with Creamed Eggs.

Creamed Eggs

1 *package (10 ounces) frozen green peas*
1 *can (10¾ ounces) condensed cream of chicken soup*

3 *hard-cooked eggs, sliced*
¼ *cup sliced pimiento-stuffed olives*
2 *tablespoons finely chopped onion*
⅛ *teaspoon poultry seasoning*

1. Mix peas and soup in 1½-quart casserole. Cover tightly and microwave on high (100%) 3 minutes; stir. Cover and microwave until hot and bubbly, 2 to 3 minutes longer.

2. Fold in eggs, olives, onion and poultry seasoning. Cover tightly and microwave on medium-high (70%) until hot and bubbly, 4 to 6 minutes. If a thinner consistency is desired, stir in 2 tablespoons milk.

Cheese Bread is made from a seasoned whole wheat muffin batter in a ring-shaped dish.

Eggs hard-cooked conventionally are added with peas and olives to a micro-waved sauce.

Cheese Bread is inverted onto a plate and sliced, then each serving topped with creamed eggs.

Macaroni Pie with Easy Mushroom Sauce

Macaroni Pie with Easy Mushroom Sauce
5 servings

⅓   cup dry bread crumbs
2   tablespoons grated Parmesan
        cheese
2   tablespoons margarine or butter

1   package (7 ounces) macaroni
        rings, cooked and drained
1   cup creamed cottage cheese
¾   cup shredded sharp Cheddar
        cheese (about 3 ounces)
2   eggs, slightly beaten
½   teaspoon salt
⅛   teaspoon pepper

        Easy Mushroom Sauce (below)

Easy Mushroom Sauce
1   can (10¾ ounces) condensed cream
        of mushroom soup
1   can (2 ounces) mushroom stems and
        pieces, drained
¼   cup milk
1   tablespoon margarine or butter
1   teaspoon instant minced onion
⅛   teaspoon Worcestershire sauce

1. Mix bread crumbs, Parmesan cheese and margarine in 2-cup measure. Microwave uncovered on high (100%), stirring every 30 seconds, until light brown, 1½ to 2 minutes; reserve.

2. Mix hot macaroni, cottage cheese, Cheddar cheese, eggs, salt and pepper. Turn into greased 9-inch pie plate. Cover with waxed paper and microwave on medium (50%) 8 minutes.

3. Sprinkle crumbs over pie. Microwave uncovered on medium (50%) until center is almost set, 8 to 10 minutes. Let stand 10 minutes. Serve with Easy Mushroom Sauce.

Mix all ingredients in 4-cup measure. Microwave uncovered on high (100%), stirring every minute, until hot and bubbly, 3 to 4 minutes.

Cheese-Tomato Pie in Rice Crust

6 servings

2 *cups hot cooked regular rice*
1 *tablespoon snipped chives*
1 *egg white*
3 *tablespoons grated Parmesan cheese*

1 *package (2½ ounces) smoked sliced beef, cut into small pieces*
⅓ *cup finely chopped onion*
1 *cup shredded mozzarella or Monterey Jack cheese (about 4 ounces)*
3 *eggs plus 1 egg yolk*
1 *can (13 ounces) evaporated milk*
½ *teaspoon salt*
¼ *teaspoon dried sage leaves*
4 *drops red pepper sauce*

6 *tomato slices*
Grated Parmesan cheese
Snipped chives

1. Mix rice, chives and egg white with fork. Spread evenly over bottom and halfway up side of 10-inch pie plate (do not leave any holes). Sprinkle with 3 tablespoons Parmesan cheese. Microwave uncovered on high (100%) 2 minutes.

2. Sprinkle beef, onion and mozzarella cheese over rice crust. Beat eggs, egg yolk, milk, salt, sage and pepper sauce in 4-cup measure. Microwave uncovered on medium-high (70%), stirring every minute, until hot, 4 minutes.

3. Pour carefully into crust. Elevate pie plate on inverted dinner plate in microwave. Cover with waxed paper and microwave on medium-high (70%) 5 minutes; rotate pie plate ½ turn. Microwave until center is almost set, 6 to 9 minutes longer. Top with tomato slices; sprinkle with Parmesan cheese and chives. Cover and let stand 10 minutes. (Center will continue to cook while standing.)

Vegetable-Cheese Pizza Pie (pictured at right)

1 pizza pie

9   *inch One-crust Pastry (page 206)*
¼   *cup yellow cornmeal*
1   *tablespoon yellow cornmeal*

1   *can (8 ounces) tomato sauce*
1   *teaspoon dried oregano leaves*
1   *clove garlic, finely chopped*
6   *drops red pepper sauce*

2   *cups shredded mozzarella cheese
     (about 8 ounces)*
1   *can (8 ounces) mushroom stems
     and pieces, drained*
¼   *cup finely chopped onion
     (about 1 small)*
¼   *cup finely chopped green pepper*
2   *tablespoons grated Parmesan
     cheese*

1. Prepare 9-inch One-crust Pastry as directed except — stir in ¼ cup cornmeal with the flour, and roll into 12-inch circle. Sprinkle 12-inch plate with 1 tablespoon cornmeal. Place pastry on cornmeal; pinch edge of pastry to make a stand-up rim about ½ inch high. Elevate plate on inverted dinner plate in microwave. Microwave uncovered on high (100%) 5 minutes; rotate plate ½ turn. Microwave until crust is dry and flaky, 2 to 4 minutes longer.

2. Mix tomato sauce, oregano, garlic and pepper sauce. Cover tightly and microwave on high (100%) until hot, about 2 minutes. Spread sauce over pizza crust. Sprinkle with 1 cup of the mozzarella cheese, the mushrooms, onion, green pepper, remaining mozzarella cheese and Parmesan cheese. Microwave uncovered on high (100%) until topping is hot and cheese is bubbly, 3 to 5 minutes.

Beef Pizza Pie: Substitute ½ pound ground beef for 1 cup of the shredded cheese. Omit mushrooms. Crumble beef into 1-quart casserole. Cover loosely and microwave on high (100%) 2 minutes; break up and stir. Cover and microwave until very little pink remains, 1 to 2 minutes longer; drain. Sprinkle ground beef over sauce on pizza crust; sprinkle with onion, green pepper, mozzarella and Parmesan cheeses. Microwave as directed.

Macaroni and Cheese

4 to 6 servings

2   *cups uncooked macaroni
     (about 8 ounces)*
2   *cups hot water*
⅓   *cup margarine or butter*
¼   *cup chopped onion*
¾   *teaspoon salt*
¼   *teaspoon pepper*
¼   *teaspoon dry mustard*

1¼ *cups milk*
8   *ounces process American cheese
     loaf, cut into cubes*
⅓   *cup all-purpose flour*

1. Mix macaroni, water, margarine, onion, salt, pepper and mustard in 2-quart casserole. Cover tightly; microwave on high (100%) 5 minutes; stir.

2. Cover tightly and microwave on medium (50%) to boiling, 4 to 6 minutes.

3. Stir in remaining ingredients. Cover tightly and microwave on high (100%), stirring every 4 minutes, until mixture is bubbly and macaroni is tender, 10 to 12 minutes.

Spinach-Cheese Pie

6 servings

1 *package (10 ounces) frozen chopped spinach*
⅓ *cup sliced green onions*
2 *tablespoons margarine or butter*
2 *teaspoons instant chicken bouillon*
¼ *teaspoon pepper*
Dash of anise seed (if desired)

1 *package (11 ounces) pie crust mix*

3 *eggs, beaten*
1½ *cups creamed cottage cheese*
2 *tablespoons grated Parmesan cheese*
1 *teaspoon water*

1. Place spinach in 2-quart casserole. Cover tightly and microwave on high (100%) 4 minutes; break up and stir. Cover and microwave until spinach is hot, 1 to 2 minutes longer; drain. Stir in onions, margarine, bouillon, pepper and anise seed.

2. Prepare pastry for 9-inch Two-crust Pie as directed on package.

3. Reserve 1 tablespoon of the eggs. Stir remaining eggs, the cottage cheese and Parmesan cheese into spinach mixture. Turn into pastry-lined pie plate. Cover with top crust that has slits cut in it; seal and flute. Mix water and reserved egg; brush over pastry. Microwave uncovered on medium-high (70%) 6 minutes; rotate pie plate ½ turn. Microwave until filling is hot and pastry looks dry and flaky, 6 to 8 minutes longer.

4. Transfer pie to conventional oven (do not preheat). Bake at 450° until crust is brown and flaky, about 15 minutes.

Spinach-Cheese Pie

Cheesy Sandwiches

4 servings

Margarine or butter, softened
(page 11)
4 slices square sandwich bread
1½ cups shredded process American
cheese (about 6 ounces)

2 eggs
1 can (5⅓ ounces) evaporated
milk
⅓ cup milk
2 tablespoons margarine or butter,
melted (page 11)
½ teaspoon salt
½ teaspoon dry mustard
¼ teaspoon paprika
Dash of red pepper

1. Spread margarine over 1 side of each slice bread. Arrange bread slices, buttered sides down, in baking dish, 8 × 8 × 2 inches. Sprinkle with cheese.

2. Beat eggs in 4-cup measure; mix in remaining ingredients. Microwave uncovered on medium-high (70%), stirring every minute, until mixture is hot, 3 to 4 minutes.

3. Pour egg mixture evenly over cheese. Elevate baking dish on inverted dinner plate in microwave. Cover with waxed paper and microwave on medium (50%) 8 minutes; rotate baking dish ½ turn. Microwave until center is set, 8 to 11 minutes longer. Let stand 10 minutes.

Potato Soup with Cheese

4 servings (about 1 cup each)

2 cups finely chopped potatoes
(about 2 medium)
1 cup chopped onion
(about 1 large)
½ cup hot water
2 teaspoons instant chicken bouillon

8 ounces process cheese spread loaf,
cut up
1 cup hot water
¼ cup imitation bacon

1. Place potatoes, onion, ½ cup hot water and the chicken bouillon in 2-quart casserole. Cover tightly and microwave on high (100%) 3 minutes; stir. Cover and microwave until potatoes are tender, 3 to 5 minutes longer.

2. Place potato mixture in blender container; add cheese and 1 cup hot water. Cover and blend on high speed until uniform consistency, about 45 seconds. Pour soup into casserole. Cover tightly and microwave on high (100%) until hot, 1 to 2 minutes. Stir in small amount of hot water for thinner consistency if desired. Sprinkle each serving with 1 tablespoon imitation bacon. Garnish with snipped parsley if desired.

Microwaving Soups

When microwaving vegetable soups, be sure that cut-up vegetables are the same size. Start with hot water (providing water is an ingredient). Small amounts of soups microwave well uncovered. For large amounts, cover tightly to speed the cooking. Since soup flavors mellow in standing and reheating is so easy in a microwave, soup is an excellent do-ahead food. It can be reheated in bowls, mugs, or the container in which it was microwaved. To crisp crackers to go with your soup, follow directions for Crisping Snacks, page 13.

Swiss Cheese-Veggie Sandwiches

6 open-face sandwiches

1   cup shredded Swiss cheese
      (about 4 ounces)
1   cup shredded zucchini or carrots
      (about 1 small)
½   cup chopped tomato
      (about 1 medium)
½   cup thinly sliced small
      cauliflowerets
2   tablespoons mayonnaise or salad
      dressing
½   teaspoon salt
½   teaspoon dried dill weed
      (if desired)
3   English muffins, cut into halves
      and toasted

Mix cheese, zucchini, tomato, cauliflower, mayonnaise, salt and dill weed; spread evenly over muffin halves. Arrange on microwave rack in baking dish. Microwave uncovered on high (100%) until hot and bubbly, 3 to 4 minutes.

Rice-Cheese-Chili Medley

6 servings

1   cup dairy sour cream
1   can (4 ounces) chopped green
      chilies, drained
1   tablespoon dried parsley
3   cups hot cooked white or brown
      rice
12 ounces Monterey Jack cheese,
      cut into strips

½   cup shredded Cheddar cheese
2   tablespoons slivered almonds,
      toasted *(page 12)*

1. Mix sour cream and chilies. Stir parsley into rice. Layer 1 cup of the rice, half the sour cream mixture and half the cheese strips in 1½-quart casserole; repeat. Cover with remaining rice. Cover tightly and microwave on medium-high (70%) 4 minutes; rotate casserole ½ turn. Microwave until hot and bubbly, 4 to 6 minutes longer.

2. Sprinkle with Cheddar cheese and almonds. Cover and let stand until cheese is melted, about 3 minutes.

Microwaving Sandwiches

Hot microwaved sandwiches can be delicious! For added crispness, toast the bread or English muffins first or use crunchy ingredients in the filling. Microwaving can steam the bread (or toast) as it heats, so be sure to microwave on a rack, napkin or paper towel. This allows the moisture to escape and prevents a soggy sandwich.

Since sandwich fillings heat more slowly than the porous bread, frozen bread can be used with a refrigerated filling. If you keep wiener buns in the freezer and franks in the refrigerator, put a cold frank in a frozen bun, wrap a napkin around the roll and microwave about 1 minute. You'll have a warm, tender bun and hot meat inside.

Vegetarian Spaghetti

6 *servings*

4   cups ¼-inch slices zucchini
      (about 1 pound)
1   can (28 ounces) whole tomatoes
1   can (12 ounces) tomato paste
1   can (4 ounces) mushroom stems
      and pieces, drained
½   cup dry red wine
½   cup finely chopped onion
      (about 1 medium)
1   clove garlic, finely chopped
2   teaspoons dried parsley flakes
2   teaspoons dried oregano leaves
2   teaspoons sugar
1   teaspoon salt
6   cups hot cooked spaghetti
1   cup shredded mozzarella cheese
      (about 4 ounces)
⅓   cup grated Parmesan cheese

Mix zucchini and tomatoes (with liquid). Break up tomatoes with fork. Stir in remaining ingredients except spaghetti and cheeses in 3-quart casserole. Cover tightly and microwave on high (100%) 8 minutes; stir. Cover and microwave until zucchini is tender and mixture is bubbly, 8 to 12 minutes longer. Serve sauce over hot spaghetti; sprinkle with cheeses.

Mushroom-Cheese Rarebit

4 *servings*

¼   cup margarine or butter
¼   cup all-purpose flour
½   teaspoon salt
¼   teaspoon pepper
¼   teaspoon dry mustard
¼   teaspoon Worcestershire sauce

1   can (4½ ounces) mushroom stems
      and pieces, drained
      (reserve liquid)
    Milk

½   cup beer or medium white wine
2   cups shredded Cheddar cheese
      (about 8 ounces)
1   jar (2 ounces) chopped pimiento,
      drained
    Toast, Baking Powder Biscuits
      (page 164), toasted English
      muffins or hot cooked potatoes
      (page 153)

1. Place margarine in 1½-quart casserole. Microwave uncovered on high (100%) until melted, 30 to 45 seconds. Stir in flour, salt, pepper, mustard and Worcestershire sauce.

2. Add enough milk to mushroom liquid to equal 1 cup. Gradually stir into flour mixture. Microwave uncovered on high (100%), stirring every minute, to boiling, 2 to 3 minutes.

3. Add beer; stir in cheese, mushrooms and pimiento. Microwave uncovered on high (100%), stirring every minute, until mixture is hot and cheese is melted, 3 to 4 minutes. Serve over toast.

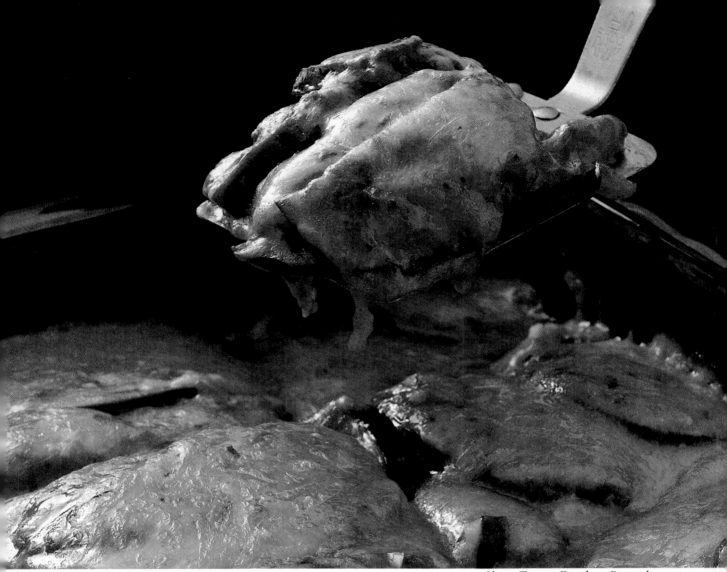

Cheese-Tomato-Eggplant Casserole

Cheese-Tomato-Eggplant Casserole

4 or 5 servings

1 *can (15 ounces) tomato sauce*
1 *medium eggplant (about 1½ pounds)*
⅓ *cup grated Parmesan cheese*
½ *teaspoon dried oregano leaves*
1 *clove garlic, finely chopped*

2 *cups shredded Cheddar cheese (about 8 ounces)*

1. Pour ½ cup of the tomato sauce into baking dish, 12 × 7½ × 2 inches. Cut eggplant into halves lengthwise; cut crosswise into ¼-inch slices. Layer one-third of eggplant and ⅓ cup tomato sauce in baking dish. Repeat layers twice. Sprinkle with Parmesan cheese, oregano and garlic. Cover tightly and microwave on high (100%) 6 minutes; rotate baking dish ½ turn. Microwave until tender when pierced in center with fork, 4 to 7 minutes longer.

2. Sprinkle eggplant with Cheddar cheese; rotate baking dish ½ turn. Microwave uncovered on medium-high (70%) until hot and bubbly and cheese is melted, 2 to 4 minutes. Let stand 5 minutes.

Fish with Asparagus and Hollandaise (left)   5 or 6 servings

1   *package (10 ounces) frozen asparagus spears*

1   *pound fresh or frozen (defrosted) fish fillets, cut into serving pieces*
    Salt and pepper
    Paprika
1   *tablespoon margarine or butter*

    Hollandaise Sauce (page 220)

1. Place block of asparagus in baking dish, 12 × 7½ × 2 inches. Cover tightly and microwave on high (100%) 3 minutes; drain. Arrange asparagus spears lengthwise (tips in center) in center of dish. Cover tightly and microwave 3 minutes longer.

2. Arrange fish with thickest parts to outside edge in 9-inch pie plate. Sprinkle with salt, pepper and paprika; dot with margarine. Cover tightly and microwave on high (100%) 3 minutes; drain.

3. Arrange fish on both ends of asparagus. Cover tightly and microwave until fish flakes easily with fork, 3 to 4 minutes; keep warm.

4. Prepare Hollandaise Sauce. Pour sauce over fish and asparagus.

Fish with Zucchini and Red Sauce (left)   5 or 6 servings

1   *pound fresh or frozen (defrosted) fish fillets, cut into serving pieces*
½   *teaspoon salt*

    Tomato-Chili Sauce (below)
2   *tablespoons grated Parmesan cheese*
2   *small zucchini, cut crosswise into ¼-inch slices (about ½ pound)*
¼   *teaspoon garlic salt*
¼   *cup coarsely shredded carrot*

Tomato-Chili Sauce
1   *cup chili sauce*
2   *teaspoons prepared horseradish*
2   *teaspoons lemon juice*
¼   *teaspoon Worcestershire sauce*
⅛   *teaspoon salt*

1. Arrange fish with thickest parts to outside edge in 9-inch pie plate; sprinkle with salt. Cover tightly and microwave on high (100%) 3 minutes; drain.

2. Prepare Tomato-Chili Sauce. Spread 1 tablespoon of the sauce over each piece of fish; sprinkle with 1 tablespoon of the cheese. Arrange zucchini slices on fish; sprinkle with garlic salt and remaining cheese. Cover tightly and microwave on high (100%) until fish flakes easily with fork, 3 to 4 minutes. Top with shredded carrot and serve with remaining Tomato-Chili Sauce.

Mix all ingredients in 2-cup measure. Microwave uncovered on high (100%) until hot, 1 to 2 minutes; stir before serving.

Fish with Asparagus and Hollandaise   Fish with Zucchini and Red Sauce

Fish Fillets with Curry Sauce

5 or 6 servings

1	*pound fresh or frozen (defrosted) fish fillets, cut into serving pieces*
2	*tablespoons lemon juice*
¼	*teaspoon salt*
¼	*teaspoon paprika*
	Curry Sauce (below)
	Snipped parsley
	Chopped salted peanuts (if desired)

1. Arrange fish with thickest parts to outside edge in baking dish, 12 × 7½ × 2 inches. Drizzle with lemon juice; sprinkle with salt and paprika. Cover tightly and microwave on high (100%) 3 minutes; rotate baking dish ½ turn. Microwave until fish flakes easily with fork, 2 to 4 minutes longer. Let stand 3 minutes. Remove to platter; keep warm.

2. Prepare Curry Sauce. Pour sauce over fish. Sprinkle with parsley and peanuts.

Curry Sauce

1	*tablespoon margarine or butter*
1	*tablespoon all-purpose flour*
⅛	*teaspoon salt*
⅛	*teaspoon curry powder*
	Dash of pepper
½	*cup milk*

1. Place margarine in 2-cup measure. Microwave uncovered on high (100%) until margarine is melted, 15 to 30 seconds.

2. Stir in flour, salt, curry powder and pepper. Gradually stir in milk. Microwave uncovered on high (100%), stirring every minute, until thickened, 2 to 3 minutes.

Fish Fillets with Shrimp Sauce

Fish Fillets with Shrimp Sauce

5 or 6 *servings*

1   *pound fresh or frozen (defrosted)*
      fish fillets, cut into
      serving pieces
1   *tablespoon lemon juice*
½   *teaspoon salt*
⅛   *teaspoon pepper*

      Shrimp Sauce (below)
2½ *to 3 cups hot cooked macaroni*
      shells

1. Arrange fish with thickest parts to outside edge in baking dish, 12 × 7½ × 2 inches. Sprinkle with lemon juice, salt and pepper. Cover tightly and microwave on high (100%) 3 minutes; rotate baking dish ½ turn. Microwave until fish flakes easily with fork, 2 to 4 minutes longer. Remove fish to platter; keep warm.

2. Prepare Shrimp Sauce. Pour fish and sauce over hot macaroni. Garnish with cucumber slices or parsley, if desired.

Shrimp Sauce
2   *tablespoons margarine or butter*
1   *tablespoon all-purpose flour*
1   *cup milk*

1   *egg yolk, slightly beaten*
1   *can (4½ ounces) shrimp, rinsed*
      and drained
⅓   *cup finely chopped cucumber*
⅛   *teaspoon chili powder*
      Dash of pepper

1. Place margarine in 4-cup measure. Microwave uncovered on high (100%) until melted, 15 to 30 seconds. Stir in flour and milk. Microwave, stirring every minute, until thickened, 2 to 3 minutes.

2. Stir at least half the hot mixture into the egg yolk. Blend egg mixture into remaining hot mixture. Stir in remaining ingredients. Microwave uncovered on medium (50%) 2 minutes; stir. Microwave until hot, 1 to 2 minutes longer.

Fish with Broccoli and Cheese Sauce

5 *or* 6 *servings*

2 *tablespoons margarine or butter*
2 *tablespoons all-purpose flour*
1 *teaspoon instant chicken bouillon*
  Dash of ground nutmeg
  Dash of red pepper
1 *cup milk*
⅔ *cup shredded Cheddar cheese*

1 *package (10 ounces) frozen chopped broccoli, defrosted and well drained*
1 *tablespoon lemon juice*
1 *pound fresh or frozen (defrosted) fish fillets, cut into serving pieces*
½ *teaspoon salt*
2 *tablespoons grated Parmesan cheese*
  Paprika

1. Place margarine in 4-cup measure. Microwave uncovered on high (100%) until melted, 15 to 30 seconds. Stir in flour, bouillon, nutmeg and red pepper; stir in milk. Microwave uncovered, stirring every minute, until sauce is thickened, 3 to 4 minutes. Stir in cheese.

2. Spread broccoli in baking dish, 8 × 8 × 2 inches; sprinkle with lemon juice. Arrange fish on broccoli with thickest parts to outside edge; sprinkle with salt. Spread sauce over fish and broccoli. Cover with waxed paper and microwave on high (100%) 4 minutes; rotate baking dish ½ turn. Microwave until fish flakes easily with fork, 3 to 5 minutes longer. Let stand 3 minutes. Sprinkle top with Parmesan cheese and paprika.

Stir shredded Cheddar cheese into hot white sauce.

Spread chopped broccoli in baking dish; add lemon juice.

Arrange fish on broccoli with thickest parts out; add salt.

Spread cheese sauce on fish and broccoli in baking dish.

Microwave until fish flakes easily with fork.

Let stand 3 minutes; sprinkle with cheese and paprika.

Fish Fillets with Grapes (pictured on page 253)   5 or 6 servings

2 green onions (with tops), finely chopped
1 pound fresh or frozen (defrosted) sole fillets, cut into serving pieces
½ teaspoon salt
⅛ teaspoon pepper
⅓ cup dry white wine
2 teaspoons lemon juice

1 tablespoon margarine or butter
1 tablespoon all-purpose flour
2 tablespoons milk
2 tablespoons dry white wine
1 cup seedless green grapes or 1 can (8 ounces) green grapes, drained

1. Sprinkle green onions in 9-inch pie plate. Sprinkle fish with salt and pepper. Fold fillets in half; arrange in circle on onions with folded sides to outside edge in pie plate. Add ⅓ cup wine and the lemon juice. Cover tightly and microwave on high (100%) 3 minutes; rotate pie plate ½ turn. Microwave until fish flakes easily with fork, 2 to 4 minutes longer. Remove fish to platter; keep warm. Reserve liquid.

2. Place 1 tablespoon margarine in 4-cup measure. Microwave uncovered on high (100%) until melted, 15 to 30 seconds. Stir in flour; add milk, 2 tablespoons wine and the liquid from fish. Microwave uncovered, stirring every minute until thickened, 3 to 4 minutes; stir in grapes. Spoon sauce over fish. Sprinkle with paprika if desired.

Note: Recipe can be doubled. Use baking dish, 12 × 7½ × 2 inches. Increase first cooking time in step 1 to 4 minutes; rotate dish ½ turn. Microwave 3 to 5 minutes longer.

Fish Fillets with Peppers   5 or 6 servings

1 pound fresh or frozen (defrosted) fish fillets, cut into ½-inch pieces
½ cup lime juice

3 tablespoons chopped onion
1 small clove garlic, finely chopped
1 tablespoon vegetable oil

1 medium tomato, chopped
⅓ cup chopped red pepper
⅓ cup chopped green pepper
¾ teaspoon salt
2 drops red pepper sauce
1 tablespoon cornstarch
¼ cup orange juice
3 cups hot cooked rice

1. Place fish in shallow glass or plastic dish. Pour lime juice on fish. Cover and refrigerate at least 1 hour, spooning juice onto fish occasionally.

2. Mix onion, garlic and vegetable oil in 2-quart casserole. Cover tightly and microwave on high (100%) until onion is tender, 1 to 2 minutes.

3. Drain fish; stir fish, tomato, red and green pepper, salt and pepper sauce into onion mixture. Mix cornstarch and orange juice; stir into mixture. Cover tightly and microwave on high (100%) 4 minutes; stir. Cover and microwave until fish flakes easily with fork, 3 to 5 minutes longer. Serve over hot rice.

Fish with Vegetables and Olives

5 or 6 servings

1 *pound fresh or frozen (defrosted) fish fillets, cut into serving pieces*
1 *teaspoon salt*
¼ *teaspoon pepper*
¼ *teaspoon paprika*
1 *green pepper, cut into rings*
1 *small onion, thinly sliced*
2 *tablespoons lemon juice*
1 *small clove garlic, finely chopped*

1 *medium tomato, sliced*
¼ *cup sliced pitted ripe olives*

1. Arrange fish with thickest parts to outside edge in baking dish, 8 × 8 × 2 inches. Sprinkle with salt, pepper and paprika. Top with green pepper rings and onion slices. Mix lemon juice and garlic; pour over peppers and onions. Cover tightly and microwave on high (100%) 3 minutes.

2. Top with tomato slices and sprinkle with olives. Rotate baking dish ½ turn. Cover tightly and microwave on high (100%) until fish flakes easily with fork, 4 to 6 minutes. Let stand 3 minutes. Garnish with lemon wedges if desired.

Breaded Lemon Fish Fillets

5 or 6 servings

½ *cup crushed round crackers (20)*
¼ *teaspoon salt*
⅛ *teaspoon white pepper*
¼ *cup margarine, melted (page 11)*
2 *tablespoons lemon juice*
1 *pound fresh or frozen (defrosted) fish fillets, cut into serving pieces*
 Paprika

Reserve 2 tablespoons cracker crumbs. Mix remaining crumbs with salt and pepper. Mix margarine and lemon juice. Dip fish into margarine mixture, then into cracker crumbs. Arrange fish with thickest parts to outside edge on microwave rack in baking dish. Sprinkle with paprika. Microwave uncovered on high (100%) 2 minutes; rotate baking dish ½ turn. Microwave until fish flakes easily with fork, 2 to 4 minutes longer. Sprinkle with reserved cracker crumbs. Garnish with lemon slices if desired.

Vegetable-Fish Chowder

5 or 6 servings

1½ *cups coarsely shredded cabbage*
1 *can (8 ounces) tomato sauce*
1 *cup hot water*
⅔ *cup thinly sliced carrot*
1 *small onion, thinly sliced*
1½ *teaspoons salt*
¼ *to ½ teaspoon red pepper*

1 *pound fresh or frozen (defrosted) fish fillets, cut into pieces*
1 *package (10 ounces) frozen cut okra*
1 *cup hot water*
¾ *cup uncooked instant rice*

1. Mix cabbage, tomato sauce, 1 cup hot water, the carrot, onion, salt and red pepper in 3-quart casserole. Cover tightly and microwave on high (100%) 4 minutes; stir. Cover and microwave until carrots are crisp-tender, 3 to 4 minutes longer.

2. Stir in remaining ingredients. Cover tightly and microwave on high (100%) 6 minutes; stir. Cover and microwave until fish flakes easily with fork and vegetables are tender, 4 to 7 minutes longer.

Parmesan Fish with Mushrooms

5 or 6 servings

4 *ounces mushrooms, sliced*
¼ *cup chopped onion*
    (about 1 small)
1 *tablespoon margarine or butter*

1 *pound fresh or frozen (defrosted)*
    fish fillets, cut into
    serving pieces
½ *teaspoon salt*
⅛ *teaspoon pepper*

½ *cup dairy sour cream*
3 *tablespoons grated Parmesan*
    cheese
2 *tablespoons dry bread crumbs*
    Paprika
    Snipped parsley

1. Place mushrooms, chopped onion and margarine in 1-quart casserole. Cover tightly and microwave on high (100%) until onion is crisp-tender, about 2 minutes; stir.

2. Arrange fish with thickest parts to outside edge in baking dish, 12 × 7½ × 2 inches. Spoon mushroom mixture over fish; sprinkle with salt and pepper. Cover with waxed paper and microwave on high (100%) 3 minutes.

3. Mix sour cream and cheese; spread over mushroom mixture. Sprinkle with bread crumbs. Microwave uncovered on high (100% until fish flakes easily with fork, 3 to 5 minutes. Sprinkle with paprika and snipped parsley.

Parmesan Fish with Mushrooms

Halibut Steaks with Wine

3 or 4 servings

1 package (12 ounces) fresh or frozen (defrosted) halibut steaks
2 tablespoons dry white wine
¼ teaspoon salt
¼ teaspoon dried oregano leaves

1 tablespoon dry bread crumbs
1 tablespoon grated Parmesan cheese
1 tablespoon margarine or butter, melted (page 11)
1 green onion (with top), finely chopped

1. Arrange fish with thickest parts to outside edge in baking dish, 10 × 6 × 2 inches. Sprinkle with wine, salt and oregano. Cover tightly and microwave on high (100%) 3 minutes; drain.

2. Sprinkle fish with bread crumbs and cheese; drizzle with margarine. Rotate baking dish ½ turn. Microwave uncovered on high (100%) until small ends of fish flake easily with fork, 2 to 4 minutes. Let stand 3 minutes. (Fish will continue to cook while standing.) Remove fish to platter. Sprinkle with onion.

Halibut Steaks with Olive Sauce

6 servings

1½ pounds fresh or 2 packages (12 ounces each) frozen (defrosted) halibut steaks
¼ cup lemon juice
¼ cup water
3 tablespoons soy sauce
1 teaspoon ground ginger
1 teaspoon grated lemon peel
½ teaspoon garlic powder

Lemon wedges
Parsley
Olive Sauce (below) or 1 package (8 ounces) frozen avocado dip, defrosted

1. Place fish in shallow glass or plastic dish. Mix lemon juice, water, soy sauce, ginger, lemon peel and garlic powder; pour over fish. Cover and refrigerate at least 1 hour, spoon liquid over fish occasionally.

2. Arrange steaks in circle with thickest parts to outside edge on 12-inch plate; reserve marinade. Cover tightly and microwave on high (100%) 4 minutes; brush with marinade and rotate plate ½ turn. Cover and microwave until small ends of fish flake easily with fork, 3 to 5 minutes longer. Let stand 3 minutes. (Fish will continue to cook while standing.) Serve with lemon wedges, parsley and Olive Sauce.

Olive Sauce
¼ cup mayonnaise or salad dressing
¼ cup dairy sour cream
¼ cup chopped pimiento-stuffed olives
1 tablespoon lemon juice

Mix all ingredients.

Hot Tuna Salads in Avocado Shells

Hot Tuna Salads in Avocado Shells

6 servings

1   *cup thin slices celery (about* 2
      medium stalks)
1   *can (6½ ounces) tuna, drained*
⅓   *cup mayonnaise or salad dressing*
1   *jar (2 ounces) sliced pimiento,
      drained*
½   *teaspoon chili powder*
3   *avocados*

½   *cup shredded Cheddar or taco-
      seasoned cheese (about 2
      ounces)*

1. Mix celery, tuna, mayonnaise, pimiento and chili powder. Cut each avocado lengthwise into halves; remove pit. Cut thin layer from bottom of each half to prevent tipping if necessary.

2. Arrange avocados cut sides up in circle with narrow ends to center on 12-inch plate. Spoon about ¼ cup tuna mixture onto each avocado half, spreading to cover entire cut surface. Cover with waxed paper and microwave on high (100%) 3 minutes. Sprinkle with cheese; rotate plate ½ turn. Microwave uncovered until tuna mixture is hot and cheese is melted, 3 to 5 minutes longer.

Curried Tuna with Rice (pictured on page 14)

6 *servings*

3   *hard-cooked eggs*

¼   *cup margarine or butter*
2   *green onions (with tops) thinly
        sliced*
2   *teaspoons curry powder*

3   *cups hot cooked rice*
1   *can (12½ ounces) tuna, drained*
½   *teaspoon salt*
¼   *teaspoon ground ginger*
⅛   *teaspoon garlic powder*
⅛   *teaspoon red pepper*
1   *tablespoon snipped parsley
        Pear Chutney (page 43)*

1. Separate cooked egg yolks from whites. Press yolks through sieve and chop whites; reserve.

2. Place margarine, onions and curry powder in 2-quart casserole. Cover tightly and microwave on high (100%) until margarine is melted, 1 to 2 minutes.

3. Stir in rice, tuna, salt, ginger, garlic powder, red pepper and reserved egg whites. Cover tightly and microwave on high (100%) until tuna is hot, 3 to 5 minutes. Sprinkle tuna mixture with reserved egg yolks and parsley. Serve with chutney.

Tuna, Eggs and Cheese

6 *servings*

2   *tablespoons margarine or butter*
1   *can (6½ ounces) tuna, drained*

9   *eggs*
½   *cup milk*
¾   *teaspoon salt*
½   *teaspoon dried dill weed*
¼   *teaspoon white pepper*

1   *package (3 ounces) cream cheese,
        cut into ¼-inch slices
        Paprika
        Buttered Bread Crumbs (below)*

1. Place margarine in round baking dish, 8 × 1½ inches. Microwave uncovered on high (100%) until margarine is melted, 15 to 30 seconds. Sprinkle tuna over margarine.

2. Beat eggs, milk, salt, dill weed and pepper; pour over tuna. Elevate on inverted dinner plate in microwave. Microwave uncovered on high (100%) 5 minutes; push outer edges to center and break apart with fork.

3. Arrange cream cheese slices spoke-fashion on top; sprinkle with paprika. Cover with waxed paper and microwave on medium (50%) until almost set in center, 6 to 9 minutes. Let stand covered 5 minutes. Sprinkle with Buttered Bread Crumbs.

Buttered Bread Crumbs
Place ⅓ cup fine dry bread crumbs and 1 tablespoon margarine or butter in small bowl. Microwave on high (100%), stirring every 30 seconds, until browned and crisp, 2 to 3 minutes.

Tuna Salad Casseroles

4 servings

1½ cups thinly sliced celery
1 package (10 ounces) frozen green peas, defrosted
1 can (6½ ounces) tuna, drained
1 cup crushed potato chips
¾ cup mayonnaise or salad dressing
⅓ cup slivered almonds, toasted (page 12)
2 tablespoons lemon juice
2 teaspoons finely chopped onion
¼ teaspoon salt
½ cup crushed potato chips
¼ cup shredded Cheddar cheese

Mix all ingredients except ½ cup crushed potato chips and cheese. Pile lightly into 4 individual baking dishes or 10-ounce custard cups. Arrange dishes in circle on 12-inch plate. Sprinkle with ½ cup crushed potato chips and the cheese. Microwave uncovered on medium-high (70%) 4 minutes; rearrange baking dishes. Microwave until hot and bubbly, 3 to 5 minutes longer. Let stand 3 minutes.

Tuna Salad Casseroles

Creamy Tuna Casserole

6 to 8 servings

4 to 5 cups hot cooked noodles
2 cans (6½ ounces each) tuna, drained
1½ cups dairy sour cream
⅔ cup milk
1 can (4 ounces) mushroom stems and pieces, drained
1 can (2 ounces) sliced pimiento, drained
1 teaspoon salt
¼ teaspoon pepper

¼ cup dry bread crumbs
¼ cup grated Parmesan cheese
2 tablespoons margarine or butter, melted (page 11)
Snipped parsley

1. Mix noodles, tuna, sour cream, milk, mushrooms, pimiento, salt and pepper in 2-quart casserole. Cover casserole tightly and microwave on medium (50%) 10 minutes; stir.

2. Mix bread crumbs, cheese and margarine; sprinkle evenly over tuna mixture. Microwave uncovered on medium (50%) until hot and bubbly, 4 to 7 minutes. Sprinkle with parsley.

Seafood Puff

6 servings

2½ cups soft bread crumbs (4 to 5 slices)
1 cup shredded Cheddar cheese (about 4 ounces)
1 can (6½ ounces) tuna, drained
½ cup milk
3 eggs, separated
Grated peel of 1 medium lemon (if desired)
1 tablespoon lemon juice
1 teaspoon instant minced onion
½ teaspoon salt
¼ teaspoon dry mustard
¼ teaspoon cream of tartar

2 tablespoons margarine or butter, melted (page 11)
½ teaspoon poppy seed

1. Mix 2 cups of the bread crumbs, the cheese, tuna, milk, egg yolks, lemon peel, lemon juice, onion, salt and mustard. Beat egg whites and cream of tartar until stiff but not dry; fold into tuna mixture. Pour into 1½-quart casserole. Elevate casserole on inverted 9-inch pie plate in microwave. Cover loosely and microwave on medium (50%) 4 minutes; rotate casserole ½ turn. Microwave until center is almost set, 4 to 7 minutes longer. Let stand, covered, 5 minutes. (Center will become set while standing.)

2. Toss remaining bread, the margarine and poppy seed; sprinkle evenly over casserole. Set conventional oven control to broil and/or 550°. Broil with top 3 to 4 inches from heat until golden brown, 2 to 3 minutes.

Creamy Tuna and Peas in Popovers

Creamy Tuna and Peas in Popovers

4 *servings*

1	*can (10¾ ounces) condensed cream of chicken soup*
1	*package (10 ounces) frozen green peas*
1	*can (6½ ounces) tuna, drained*
¼	*cup milk*
5	*to 8 drops red pepper sauce*
4	*popovers, split*
¼	*cup shredded Cheddar cheese*

Mix soup, peas, tuna, milk and pepper sauce in 1½-quart casserole. Cover tightly and microwave on high (100%) 4 minutes; stir. Cover and microwave until hot and bubbly, 5 to 7 minutes longer. Spoon over popovers; sprinkle about 1 tablespoon cheese on each serving.

Reheating Popovers

Popovers need conventional dry heat to puff up, hold their shape and bake to brown crusty perfection. You can bake them ahead of time, then wrap, label and freeze no longer than 2 months. About 5 minutes before serving, remove 6 popovers from the freezer. Place them in a napkin-lined basket, cover with another napkin or paper towel and microwave on medium (50%) until warm, 3 to 4 minutes. The popovers will hold their shapes well, become tender, warm and slightly less crusty than when freshly baked. To microwave fewer than 6, decrease the reheating time. Do not overcook, as popovers can become tough.

Tuna with Chinese Vegetables

4 *servings*

1   *can (16 ounces) Chinese vege-*
     tables, rinsed and drained
1   *can (10¾ ounces) condensed*
     cream of mushroom soup
1   *can (6½ ounces) tuna, drained*
1   *cup ¼-inch diagonal slices celery*
     (about 2 medium stalks)
1   *tablespoon soy sauce*
¼ *teaspoon pepper*

1   *can (3 ounces) chow mein noodles*

1. Mix all ingredients except noodles in 1½-quart casserole. Cover tightly and microwave on high (100%) 7 minutes; stir.

2. Sprinkle chow mein noodles evenly over tuna mixture. Microwave uncovered on high (100%) until hot and bubbly, 5 to 8 minutes.

Tuna Buns

6 *sandwiches*

1   *can (6½ ounces) tuna, drained*
¾ *cup chopped celery (about*
     1 large stalk)
¼ *cup mayonnaise or salad dressing*
1   *medium dill pickle, finely chopped*
1   *tablespoon instant minced onion*
⅛ *teaspoon pepper*
6   *hamburger buns, split and*
     buttered
6   *slices process American cheese*

Mix all ingredients except buns and cheese. Fill buns with tuna mixture; add cheese slices. Arrange buns in circle on paper towel-lined 12-inch plate. Microwave uncovered on high (100%) 1 minute; rotate plate ½ turn. Microwave until cheese is melted and filling is hot, 1 to 2 minutes longer.

Tuna Buns

Salmon-Cheese Puff

4 servings

3   *eggs*
1   *cup milk*
¼   *cup dry white wine*
2   *tablespoons snipped parsley*
½   *teaspoon dry mustard*
½   *teaspoon salt*

3   *cups soft bread cubes*
    (about 6 slices)
1   *cup shredded process sharp*
    American cheese (about
    4 ounces)
1   *can (7¾ ounces) salmon, drained*

1. Beat eggs with hand beater in 1½-quart casserole; beat in milk, wine, parsley, mustard and salt. Microwave uncovered on medium-high (70%) 2 minutes; stir. Microwave until hot, 1 to 2 minutes longer.

2. Beat in remaining ingredients. Pour into 5- or 6-cup ring mold. Elevate ring mold on inverted pie plate in microwave. Cover with waxed paper and microwave on medium (50%) 5 minutes; rotate ring mold ¼ turn. Microwave until center is almost set, 4 to 7 minutes longer. Let stand 5 minutes. (Center will become set while standing.) Invert onto serving plate. Serve with lemon wedges if desired.

Shortcut Seafood and Chicken

6 servings

1   *can (16 ounces) tomatoes, broken*
    up with fork
2   *cups uncooked instant rice*
1   *package (10 ounces) frozen*
    green peas
1   *can (6½ ounces) minced clams*
1   *can (5 ounces) boned chicken*
1   *can (4½ ounces) broken shrimp,*
    rinsed and drained
2   *tablespoons instant minced onion*
1   *teaspoon paprika*
1   *teaspoon instant chicken bouillon*
¼   *teaspoon red pepper*
¼   *teaspoon turmeric*

Stir tomatoes (with liquid), rice, peas, clams (with liquid), and remaining ingredients in 3-quart casserole. Cover tightly and microwave on high (100%) 5 minutes; stir. Cover and microwave until liquid is absorbed, 6 to 9 minutes longer.

Microwaving Fish and Seafood

Delicate fish fillets are superb, cooked in a microwave. Arrange them with thickest pieces to the outside of the dish, cover tightly to steam them and microwave briefly — just until they flake easily with a fork. Be careful not to overcook since this causes toughness. If fish are to be coated (such as Breaded Lemon Fish Fillets, page 102), cook on a rack, allowing air circulation to retain crispness.

Canned tuna, salmon and shrimp can be evenly mixed into casseroles, sandwich fillings and hot salads and need only enough microwaving to cook the ingredients they are combined with.

Gingered Shrimp with Rice

6 servings

1   *pound large fresh shrimp*,
       cleaned (about 2 cups)*
1   *package (10 ounces) frozen
       green peas*
1   *large onion, sliced*
1   *cup ¼-inch diagonal slices celery
       (about 2 medium stalks)*
1   *can (8 ounces) water chestnuts,
       sliced*
2   *tablespoons soy sauce*
1   *tablespoon dry white wine or
       sherry*
1   *teaspoon crushed gingerroot or
       ½ teaspoon ground ginger*
¼   *teaspoon salt*

1   *tablespoon cornstarch*
½   *teaspoon instant chicken bouillon*
⅓   *cup cold water*
4   *cups hot cooked rice*

1. Mix shrimp, peas, onion, celery, water chestnuts, soy sauce, wine, gingerroot and salt in 2-quart casserole. Cover tightly and microwave on high (100%), stirring every 3 minutes, until shrimp are pink and vegetables are crisp-tender, 9 to 11 minutes.

2. Mix cornstarch, bouillon and water. Stir into shrimp mixture. Cover tightly and microwave on high (100%) 2 minutes; stir. Cover and microwave until thickened, 2 to 4 minutes longer. Serve shrimp over hot rice.

* One package (12 ounces) cleaned large frozen shrimp, defrosted, can be substituted for the fresh.

Oysters with Buttered Crumbs

4 or 5 servings

1   *pint shucked oysters, cut into
       halves*
⅓   *cup half-and-half*
1   *cup crushed soda crackers
       (about 20 squares)*
¼   *teaspoon salt*
⅛   *teaspoon pepper
       Dash of ground nutmeg*
⅓   *cup margarine or butter, melted
       (page 11)*

Arrange oysters in round baking dish, 8 × 1½ inches; pour half-and-half over oysters. Mix crackers, salt, pepper, nutmeg and margarine; sprinkle over oysters. Microwave uncovered on high (100%) 4 minutes; rotate baking dish ½ turn. Microwave until oysters are hot, 3 to 6 minutes longer.

Microwave Tips to Remember

1. Use the power setting first given in the recipe for every step in the recipe unless a change is indicated.
2. If your microwave has a rating of 400 to 500 watts the microwaving times will usually be longer.
3. Check your own microwave power settings with the chart on page 9. To find out what your power settings mean, you may have to refer to your microwave use and care booklet or write to the manufacturer of your microwave.

VEGETABLES

Artichokes -- French (Globe)

For 4 servings: Use 4 (1 per serving)

TO PREPARE
Remove any discolored leaves and the small leaves at the base of artichoke; trim stem even with artichoke base. Cutting straight across, slice 1 inch off top; discard top. Snip off points of the remaining leaves with scissors. Rinse artichoke under cold water.

TO MICROWAVE
Place 1 cup water, 1 teaspoon cooking oil, 1 teaspoon lemon juice, 1 small clove garlic, cut into fourths, ½ teaspoon salt and artichokes in 3-quart casserole. Cover tightly and microwave on high (100%) 7 minutes; rotate casserole ½ turn. Microwave until leaves pull out easily and bottom is tender when pierced with a knife, 7 to 9 minutes longer. Carefully remove artichokes; place upside down to drain.

TO SERVE HOT
Place artichoke upright on plate without removing choke (the fuzzy growth covering artichoke heart). Accompany with a small bowl of Hollandaise Sauce (page 220) or melted margarine or butter.

TO SERVE COLD
Refrigerate artichoke until chilled (at least 4 hours). Cut out choke by opening artichoke like a flower to reach the interior. Pull out tender center cone of leaves; scrape off exposed choke with spoon. Replace cone of leaves if desired. Accompany with Hollandaise Sauce (page 220) or melted margarine or butter. If choke has been removed, cavity can be filled with the sauce.

TO EAT
Pluck leaves one at a time. Dip base of leaf into sauce or margarine. Turn leaf meaty side down and draw between teeth, scraping off meaty portion. Discard leaf on plate. When all outer leaves have been removed, remove cone if it hasn't been previously cut out. Cut the "heart" or bottom of the artichoke — the prize section — into bite-size pieces and dip into sauce.

Pictured on previous page: Dilled Vegetables

Artichokes -- Jerusalem

For 4 servings: Use 1½ pounds

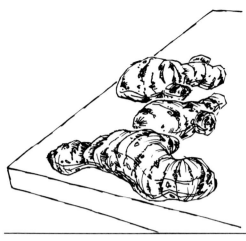

TO PREPARE
Scrub artichokes; cut into ¼-inch slices.

TO MICROWAVE
Place ¼ cup water, ¼ teaspoon salt and artichokes in 1½-quart casserole. Cover tightly and microwave on high (100%) 5 minutes; stir. Cover and microwave until crisp-tender, 4 to 6 minutes longer; stir. Let stand 5 minutes; drain.

TO SERVE
Add margarine or butter.....drizzle with lemon juice ....combine with scrambled eggs.....with soups as a garnish.....with dips as a snack.

Asparagus

For 4 servings: Use 1½ pounds

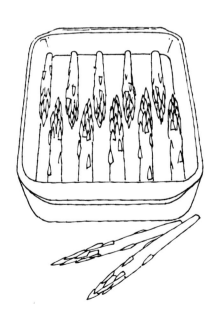

TO PREPARE
Break off tough ends as far down as stalks snap easily. Wash asparagus. Remove scales if sandy or tough. (If necessary, remove sand particles with vegetable brush.) Cut stalks into 1½-inch pieces or leave whole.

TO MICROWAVE
For cuts, place asparagus cuts in 1½-quart casserole; add ¼ cup water. For spears, arrange asparagus spears lengthwise (tips in center) in baking dish, 10 × 6 × 1½ inches; add ¼ cup water. Cover tightly and microwave on high (100%) 3 minutes; stir cuts or rotate baking dish containing spears ½ turn. Cover and microwave until crisp-tender, 2 to 3 minutes longer. Let stand 1 minute; drain.

TO SERVE
Add margarine or butter, salt and pepper.....dash of lemon juice or mace.....top with buttered crumbs..... season with allspice, dill weed, marjoram or savory.

Asparagus with Cheese Sauce

6 *servings*

3 *tablespoons water*
2 *packages (10 ounces each) frozen
     asparagus spears**

1 *can (11 ounces) condensed
     Cheddar cheese soup*
½ *teaspoon dry mustard*
½ *teaspoon Worcestershire sauce*

½ *cup Cereal Topping (right)*

1. Place water and asparagus in 1½-quart casserole. Cover tightly and microwave on high (100%) 4 minutes; stir. Cover and microwave until almost tender, 3 to 5 minutes longer; drain.

2. Mix soup, mustard and Worcestershire sauce in 2-cup measure. Microwave uncovered until hot, stirring every minute, 2 to 3 minutes.

3. Pour cheese mixture over asparagus. Microwave uncovered on high (100%) until hot and bubbly around the edges, about 2 minutes. Sprinkle with Cereal Topping.

* 1½ pounds fresh asparagus can be substituted for the frozen asparagus.

Cereal Topping
Mix ½ cup crushed corn puff cereal, 2 tablespoons margarine or butter and ¼ teaspoon marjoram in 2-cup measure. Microwave on high (100%) stirring every minute until toasted, 2 to 3 minutes.

Asparagus with Croutons

4 *servings*

½ *cup seasoned croutons*
1 *tablespoon margarine or butter*

2 *packages (10 ounces each) frozen
     cut asparagus**
1 *tablespoon margarine or butter*
1 *hard-cooked egg, chopped*

1. Place croutons and 1 tablespoon margarine in 1½-quart casserole. Microwave uncovered on high (100%) stirring every 30 seconds, until crisp, about 1½ minutes; remove croutons.

2. Place asparagus and 1 tablespoon margarine in same casserole. Cover tightly and microwave on high (100%) 3 minutes; stir. Cover and microwave until tender, 6 to 9 minutes longer. Let stand 5 minutes. Sprinkle with croutons and egg.

* 2 cans (15 ounces each) cut asparagus, drained, can be substituted for the frozen asparagus. Cover tightly and microwave on high (100%) 3 minutes; stir. Cover and microwave until hot, 2 to 4 minutes longer.

Asparagus with Water Chestnuts

Asparagus with Water Chestnuts

5 or 6 servings

⅓ cup margarine or butter
¾ teaspoon salt
⅛ teaspoon pepper
7 cups 1-inch diagonal pieces fresh
   asparagus (2 pounds spears)

1 can (8 ounces) water chestnuts,
   drained and sliced

1. Place margarine, salt, pepper and asparagus in 2-quart casserole. Cover tightly and microwave on high (100%) 7 minutes.

2. Stir in water chestnuts. Microwave uncovered on high (100%) until asparagus is crisp-tender, 5 to 7 minutes longer.

Note: If asparagus stands covered before serving, it will be very tender instead of crisp-tender.

Beans -- Green and Wax

For 4 servings: Use 1 pound

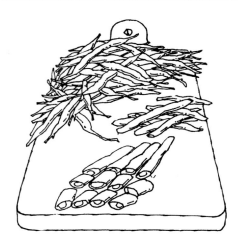

TO PREPARE
Wash beans and remove ends. Cut into 1-inch pieces.

TO MICROWAVE
Place ½ cup water, ¼ teaspoon salt and beans in 1½-quart casserole. Cover tightly and microwave on high (100%) 5 minutes; stir. Cover and microwave until tender, 4 to 7 minutes longer. Let stand 5 minutes; drain.

TO SERVE
Add margarine or butter.....drizzle with ham or bacon drippings.....top with crumbled crisply cooked bacon or buttered bread crumbs.....season with basil, dill, marjoram, nutmeg, savory or thyme.

Green Beans and Bacon

3 or 4 servings

2	*tablespoons margarine or butter*
2	*teaspoons soy sauce*
1	*teaspoon instant minced onion*
⅛	*teaspoon instant minced garlic*
1	*can (16 ounces) green beans, drained*
2	*tablespoons imitation bacon*

Place margarine, soy sauce, onion, garlic and beans in 1-quart casserole. Cover tightly and microwave on high (100%) 3 to 4 minutes; stir. Sprinkle with imitation bacon.

Cashew Green Beans

4 or 5 servings

1	*can (10¾ ounces) condensed cream of shrimp soup*
1	*teaspoon soy sauce*
1	*package (9 ounces) frozen cut green beans*
1	*can (4 ounces) mushroom stems and pieces, drained*
1	*can (16 ounces) bean sprouts, drained*
½	*cup coarsely chopped cashews or peanuts*

Mix soup and soy sauce. Layer half each of the beans, mushrooms, bean sprouts and soup mixture in 1½-quart casserole; repeat. Cover tightly and microwave on high (100%) 5 minutes; rotate casserole ½ turn. Microwave until hot and bubbly, 5 to 8 minutes longer. Sprinkle with chopped cashews. Cover and let stand 5 minutes.

Beans with Olives

4 *servings*

½ cup water
½ teaspoon seasoned salt
3 cups 1-inch pieces fresh green or
    wax beans (about 1 pound)
2 tablespoons sliced celery
1 tablespoon lemon juice
¼ cup sliced pimiento-stuffed olives

Place water, salt, beans and celery in 2-quart casserole. Cover tightly and microwave on high (100%) 5 minutes; stir. Cover and microwave until beans are tender, 5 to 7 minutes longer; drain. Cover and let stand 5 minutes. Stir in lemon juice and olives.

Green Beans with Almonds

3 *or* 4 *servings*

¼ cup slivered almonds
1 tablespoon margarine or butter

¼ teaspoon salt
1 package (9 ounces) frozen
    green beans

1. Place almonds and margarine in 1-quart casserole. Microwave uncovered on high (100%), stirring every minute, until golden, 2 to 3 minutes. Remove almonds from casserole.

2. Place salt and beans in same casserole. Cover tightly and microwave on high (100%) 3 minutes; stir. Cover and microwave until tender, 3 to 5 minutes longer. Stir in almonds.

Green Beans with Almonds

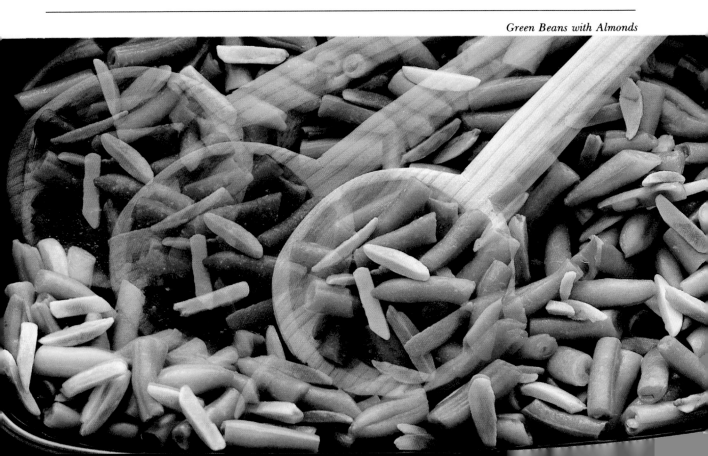

Green Beans with Bamboo Shoots

5 or 6 servings

2   *packages (9 ounces each) frozen
      French-style green beans*
2   *cans (8½ ounces each) bamboo
      shoots, drained*
1   *can (10½ ounces) condensed
      golden mushroom soup*
1   *teaspoon salt*
1   *teaspoon soy sauce*
1   *can (3 ounces) chow mein noodles
      (about 2 cups)*

Rinse beans under running cold water to separate
and remove ice crystals; drain. Mix beans, bamboo
shoots, soup, salt and soy sauce in 2-quart casserole.
Cover tightly and microwave on high (100%), stirring every 5 minutes, until beans are tender, 13 to 16
minutes. Let stand 5 minutes. Sprinkle with noodles.

Onion-Topped Green Beans

3 or 4 servings

1 *pound fresh green beans**
¼ *cup water*
½ *teaspoon salt*

1 *can (10¾ ounces) condensed cream of mushroom soup*

1 *can (3 ounces) French fried onions*

1. Cut beans into fourths lengthwise, then crosswise into 1½-inch pieces. Place beans, water and salt in 1½-quart casserole. Cover tightly and microwave on high (100%) 5 minutes; stir. Cover and microwave until crisp-tender, 4 to 6 minutes longer.

2. Stir in mushroom soup. Cover tightly and microwave on high (100%) until hot and bubbly, 2 to 3 minutes; stir.

3. Sprinkle beans with French fried onions. Microwave uncovered until onions are hot, 2 to 3 minutes.

* 2 packages (9 ounces each) frozen French-style green beans can be substituted for the fresh green beans. Drain before stirring in soup.

Italian Green Beans with Mushrooms

3 or 4 servings

1 *can (4 ounces) mushroom stems and pieces, drained (reserve 1 tablespoon liquid)*
1 *tablespoon margarine or butter*
½ *teaspoon salt*
1 *package (9 ounces) frozen Italian green beans*

1. Place reserved mushroom liquid, margarine, salt and beans in 1-quart casserole. Cover tightly and microwave on high (100%) 4 minutes.

2. Stir in mushrooms. Cover and microwave until beans are tender, 3 to 4 minutes longer.

Italian Green Beans with Mushrooms

Beans -- Green Lima

For 4 servings: Use 3 pounds (unshelled)

TO PREPARE
Wash and shell lima beans just before cooking. To shell beans, remove thin outer edge of pod with sharp knife or scissors. Beans will slip out.

TO MICROWAVE
Place ¼ cup water and lima beans in 1½-quart casserole. Cover tightly and microwave on high (100%) 7 minutes; stir. Cover and microwave until tender, 7 to 9 minutes longer. Let stand 5 minutes; drain.

TO SERVE
Add margarine or butter, salt and pepper.....season with snipped parsley, savory or sage.

Hickory Limas

2 or 3 servings

2 *tablespoons water*
¼ *teaspoon salt*
1 *package (10 ounces) frozen lima beans*

¼ *cup pasteurized process cheese spread with hickory smoke flavor**
1 *tablespoon milk*

1. Place water, salt and beans in 1-quart casserole. Cover tightly and microwave on high (100%) 4 minutes; stir. Cover and microwave until tender, 3 to 5 minutes longer.

2. Stir in cheese spread and milk. Cover tightly and microwave on high (100%) until cheese spread is melted and smooth, 1 to 2 minutes; stir.

* ¼ cup pasteurized process cheese spread with bacon or garlic can be substituted for the cheese with hickory smoke flavor.

Dilled Limas with Water Chestnuts

4 or 5 servings

3 *tablespoons water*
½ *teaspoon salt*
1 *package (10 ounces) frozen lima beans*
1 *can (8 ounces) water chestnuts*, sliced*
¼ *teaspoon dried dill weed*

Mix all ingredients in 1-quart casserole. Cover tightly and microwave on high (100%) 4 minutes; stir. Cover and microwave until tender, 4 to 6 minutes longer. Let stand 5 minutes.

* 1 package (10 ounces) frozen green peas can be substituted for the water chestnuts; use 1½-quart casserole and microwave as directed above.

Limas with Mushrooms

3 or 4 servings

2 *tablespoons margarine or butter*
½ *teaspoon salt*
1 *package (10 ounces) frozen baby lima beans*
1 *can (4 ounces) mushroom stems and pieces, drained*

Place margarine, salt, beans and mushrooms in 1-quart casserole. Cover tightly and microwave on high (100%) 4 minutes; stir. Cover and microwave until tender, 2 to 3 minutes longer. Let stand 5 minutes.

Glazed Beets

2 or 3 servings

2 *tablespoons margarine or butter, melted (page 11)*
1 *tablespoon sugar*
2 *teaspoons all-purpose flour*
¼ *teaspoon salt*
¼ *teaspoon dried dill weed*
⅛ *teaspoon pepper*
2 *tablespoons vinegar*

1 *can (16 ounces) shoestring beets, drained*

1. Mix margarine, sugar, flour, salt, dill weed, pepper and vinegar in 1-quart casserole.

2. Stir in beets. Cover tightly and microwave on high (100%) 2 minutes; stir. Cover and microwave until hot, 2 to 3 minutes longer.

Beets with Garden Herbs

2 or 3 servings

1 *can (16 ounces) whole or sliced beets, drained*
2 *tablespoons margarine or butter*
¼ *teaspoon salt*
¼ *teaspoon dried savory leaves*
¼ *teaspoon dried basil leaves*

Mix beets, margarine, salt, savory and basil in 1-quart casserole. Cover tightly and microwave on high (100%) 2 minutes; stir. Cover and microwave until hot, 2 to 3 minutes longer.

Microwaving Vegetables

Most fresh vegetables are ideal for microwaving, since they retain their fresh color and flavor and can be cooked to crisp tenderness in a short time. (An exception is fresh beets, which tend to fade in color, so we recommend microwaving canned beets just enough to reheat them.) Because fresh vegetables contain moisture, they require little added liquid. For even seasoning, salt is added to the liquid instead of the vegetables. To microwave most fresh vegetables, cover tightly and stir or rearrange (or rotate dish) after ½ of the cooking.

Broccoli

For 6 servings: Use 1½ pounds

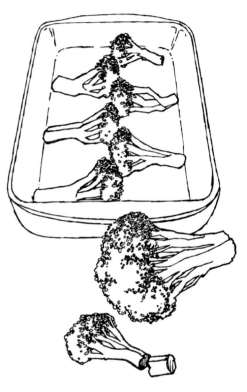

TO PREPARE
Trim off large leaves. Remove tough ends of lower stems; wash broccoli.

TO MICROWAVE
For spears, cut broccoli lengthwise into thin stalks. If stems are thicker than 1 inch, make lengthwise gashes in each stem. Place ¼ cup water and ½ teaspoon salt in baking dish, 12 × 7½ × 2 inches, or 10-inch pie plate. Arrange broccoli stalks in baking dish (tips in center). Or arrange in circle in 10-inch pie plate with tips in center of plate. Cover tightly and microwave on high (100%) 4 minutes; rotate baking dish or pie plate ½ turn. Microwave until tender, 3 to 5 minutes longer; drain.

For cuts, cut broccoli into 1-inch pieces. Place ¼ cup water and ½ teaspoon salt and broccoli in 1½-quart casserole. Cover tightly and microwave on high (100%) 4 minutes; stir. Cover and microwave until almost tender, 3 to 5 minutes longer. Let stand 5 minutes; drain.

TO SERVE
Add margarine or butter.....drizzle with lemon juice .....season with lemon pepper, nutmeg or oregano..... sprinkle with grated cheese.

Dilled Broccoli

5 or 6 servings

¼ *cup water*
½ *teaspoon salt*
1 *pound fresh broccoli*

1 *tablespoon margarine or butter*
½ *teaspoon dried dill weed*
¼ *teaspoon salt*
  Dash of pepper
2 *tablespoons half-and-half*

1. Place water and ½ teaspoon salt in baking dish, 12 × 7½ × 2 inches. Arrange broccoli stalks in baking dish (tips in center). Cover tightly and microwave on high (100%) 5 minutes; rotate baking dish ½ turn. Microwave until tender, 5 to 7 minutes longer. Let stand 5 minutes; drain.

2. Place margarine, dill weed, ¼ teaspoon salt and pepper in 1-cup measure. Microwave uncovered on high (100%) until bubbly, about 1 minute; stir in half-and-half. Pour over broccoli.

Broccoli with Bean Curd

4 *servings*

½ *pound bean curd or tofu
      (vegetable protein from
      soybeans)*
1 *package (10 ounces) frozen
      broccoli spears, defrosted*
2 *green onions (with tops)*

1 *tablespoon vegetable oil*

2 *teaspoons cornstarch*
2 *tablespoons oyster sauce*
1 *can (2 ounces) mushroom stems
      and pieces, drained (reserve
      ¼ cup liquid)*

1. Cut bean curd into ¾-inch cubes; drain thoroughly. Cut broccoli spears diagonally into 1-inch slices. Cut green onions into 2-inch pieces.

2. Place 1 tablespoon oil in 1½-quart casserole. Microwave uncovered on high (100%) until hot, 1 to 2 minutes; add bean curd. Microwave 2 minutes; stir carefully. Microwave until hot, about 1 minute longer. Remove bean curd.

3. Stir cornstarch and oyster sauce into reserved mushroom liquid in 1½-quart casserole. Microwave uncovered on high (100%) 1 minute; stir.

4. Stir in bean curd, broccoli, onions and mushrooms. Cover tightly and microwave on high (100%) until sauce is slightly thickened and vegetables are crisp-tender, 2 to 4 minutes.

Broccoli with Cheese Sauce

3 *or* 4 *servings*

1 *package (10 ounces) frozen
      chopped broccoli*

½ *can (11 ounces) condensed
      Cheddar cheese soup (⅔ cup)*
½ *cup canned French fried onions*

1. Place broccoli in 1-quart casserole. Cover tightly and microwave on high (100%) 5 minutes; stir. Cover and microwave until broccoli is tender, 2 to 3 minutes longer; drain.

2. Stir in cheese soup. Cover and microwave on high (100%) until hot, 1 to 2 minutes. Sprinkle with French fried onions.

Brussels Sprouts

For 4 servings: Use 1 pound

TO PREPARE
Remove any discolored leaves. Cut off stem ends; wash sprouts.

TO MICROWAVE
Place ¼ cup water and Brussels sprouts in 1½-quart casserole. Cover tightly and microwave on high (100%) 5 minutes; stir. Cover and microwave until tender when pierced with fork, 4 to 6 minutes longer. Let stand 5 minutes; drain.

TO SERVE
Add margarine or butter, salt and pepper.....season with garlic salt, basil, caraway seed, cumin, dill, marjoram, sage or savory.

Lemony Sprouts and Carrots (pictured on page 25)   5 *or* 6 *servings*

1   *tablespoon water*
½   *teaspoon salt*
½   *teaspoon dried basil leaves*
1   *package (10 ounces) frozen*
      Brussels sprouts

1   *can (16 ounces) small whole*
      carrots, drained

2   *tablespoons margarine or butter,*
      melted (page 11)
1   *tablespoon lemon juice*

1. Place water, salt, basil and Brussels sprouts in 1½-quart casserole. Cover tightly and microwave on high (100%) 4 minutes.

2. Stir in carrots. Cover and microwave until Brussels sprouts are tender, 5 to 7 minutes longer.

3. Mix margarine and lemon juice; drizzle over vegetables.

Brussels Sprouts with Onion

3 or 4 servings

2   *tablespoons margarine or butter*
½   *teaspoon instant beef bouillon*
1   *package (10 ounces) frozen baby*
      Brussels sprouts

1   *small onion, sliced and separated*
      into rings

1. Place margarine, bouillon and Brussels sprouts in 1-quart casserole. Cover tightly and microwave on high (100%) 3 minutes.

2. Stir in onion. Cover and microwave until tender, 3 to 5 minutes longer.

Cabbage -- Chinese or Celery

For 4 or 6 servings:
Use about 1 pound (1 medium head)

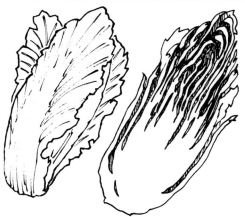

TO PREPARE
Remove root ends. Wash cabbage; shred.

TO MICROWAVE
Place ¼ cup water, ¼ teaspoon salt and cabbage in 1½-quart casserole. Cover tightly and microwave on high (100%) 2 minutes; stir. Cover and microwave until crisp-tender, 2 to 4 minutes longer. Let stand 1 minute; drain.

TO SERVE
Add margarine.....top with grated cheese or buttered crumbs.....add Hollandaise Sauce (page 220).

Cabbage -- Green Savoy and Red

For 4 servings:
Use ¾ to 1 pound (1 small head)

TO PREPARE
Remove outside leaves; wash cabbage. Shred cabbage and discard core. Or cut cabbage into 4 wedges and trim core to within ¼ inch of leaves.

TO MICROWAVE
For shredded, place ¼ cup water, ½ teaspoon salt and cabbage in 2-quart casserole. Cover tightly and microwave on high (100%) 4 minutes; stir. Cover and microwave until crisp-tender, 4 to 5 minutes longer. Let stand 3 minutes; drain.

For wedges, place ½ cup water and ½ teaspoon salt in 2-quart casserole. Arrange wedges spoke-fashion with core at outside edge of casserole. Cover tightly and microwave on high (100%) 5 minutes; rotate casserole ½ turn. Microwave until crisp-tender, 5 to 8 minutes longer. Let stand 5 minutes; drain.

TO SERVE
Add margarine or butter.....season with caraway seed, oregano, mace or dill weed.

Microwaving Cabbage

Shredded cabbage is delicious microwaved. The shredding exposes more surface area and requires minimal cooking for crisp-tender texture. Wedges, too, can be microwaved to perfection and crowned with easily microwaved sauces (pages 130 and 131).

Cabbage with Cheese and Bacon

Cabbage with Cheese and Bacon

6 *or* 7 *servings*

¼ cup water
½ teaspoon salt
6 large cabbage wedges
     (about 2 pounds)

1 can (11 ounces) condensed
     Cheddar cheese soup
½ teaspoon dry mustard
½ teaspoon celery seed
6 slices bacon, crisply cooked and
     crumbled (page 11)

1. Place water and salt in 2-quart casserole; arrange cabbage wedges spoke-fashion with core at outside edge. Cover tightly and microwave on high (100%) 6 minutes; rotate casserole ½ turn. Microwave until crisp-tender, 5 to 7 minutes longer. Drain liquid, reserving 2 tablespoons.

2. Mix reserved liquid, soup, mustard and celery seed. Pour over cabbage wedges. Cover tightly and microwave on high (100%) until hot, 3 to 5 minutes. Sprinkle with bacon.

Creamy Caraway Cabbage

3 *or* 4 *servings*

¼ cup water
¼ teaspoon salt
1 clove garlic, finely chopped
4 cups finely shredded cabbage
     (about 1 pound)

1 package (3 ounces) cream
     cheese, softened
2 tablespoons milk
½ teaspoon caraway seed
     Dash of pepper

1. Place water, salt, garlic and cabbage in 1½-quart casserole. Cover tightly and microwave on high (100%) 4 minutes; stir. Cover and microwave until tender, 2 to 4 minutes longer; drain.

2. Mix cream cheese and milk; stir in caraway seed and pepper. Stir cheese mixture into hot cabbage.

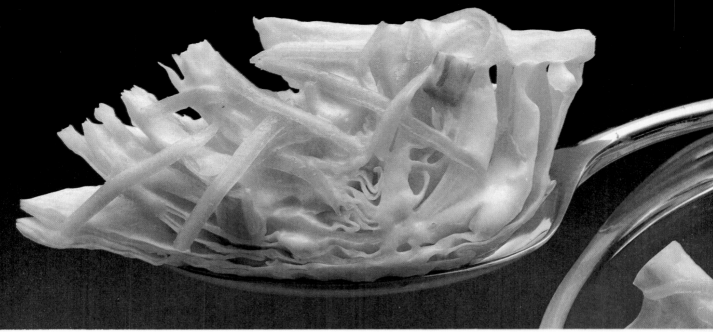

Pepper-Cheese Cabbage

Pepper-Cheese Cabbage

4 *servings*

¼ cup water
¼ teaspoon salt
6 medium cabbage wedges
     (about 1 pound)

¼ cup chopped red or green pepper
2 tablespoons margarine or butter
1 tablespoon all-purpose flour
¼ teaspoon garlic salt
     Dash of pepper
½ cup milk
¼ cup shredded Cheddar cheese

1. Place water and salt in 1½-quart casserole; arrange cabbage wedges spoke-fashion with core at outside edge. Cover tightly and microwave on high (100%) 5 minutes; rotate casserole ½ turn. Microwave until crisp-tender, 3 to 5 minutes longer; drain.

2. Place red pepper and margarine in 2-cup measure. Microwave uncovered on high (100%) until pepper is crisp-tender, about 1 minute. Blend in flour, garlic salt and pepper; stir in milk. Microwave uncovered, stirring every minute, until sauce is thickened, 2 to 3 minutes. Pour sauce over hot cabbage wedges; sprinkle with cheese.

Cabbage with Carrots

3 or 4 *servings*

4 cups finely shredded cabbage
     (about 1 pound)
1 cup coarsely shredded carrots
     (about 2 medium)
2 tablespoons water
2 tablespoons finely chopped onion
1 teaspoon salt
½ teaspoon celery seed
¼ teaspoon pepper
½ cup dairy sour cream

Mix all ingredients except sour cream in 1½-quart casserole. Cover tightly and microwave on high (100%) 3 minutes; stir. Cover and microwave until cabbage is crisp-tender, 3 to 5 minutes longer. Stir in sour cream.

Sweet-Sour Red Cabbage

4 servings

2   *tablespoons water*
2   *tablespoons vinegar or*
      lemon juice
½   *teaspoon salt*
5   *cups finely shredded red cabbage*
      (about 1¼ pounds)

4   *slices bacon, diced*

¼   *cup packed brown sugar*
2   *tablespoons all-purpose flour*
½   *cup water*
¼   *cup vinegar*
1   *teaspoon salt*
⅛   *teaspoon pepper*
1   *small onion, sliced*

    Sour cream

1. Mix 2 tablespoons water, 2 tablespoons vinegar, ½ teaspoon salt and the cabbage in 2-quart casserole. Cover tightly and microwave on high (100%) 4 minutes; stir. Cover and microwave until tender, 4 to 6 minutes longer; drain.

2. Place bacon in 1-quart casserole. Cover with paper towel and microwave on high (100%) until crisp, 3½ to 4½ minutes; drain on paper towels. Drain fat from casserole; return 1 tablespoon fat to casserole.

3. Stir brown sugar and flour into fat in casserole. Add ½ cup water, ¼ cup vinegar, 1 teaspoon salt, the pepper and onion. Microwave uncovered on high (100%), stirring every minute, until mixture thickens, 2 to 3 minutes.

4. Sprinkle bacon on sauce mixture; stir into hot cabbage. Top each serving with sour cream.

Carrots

For 4 servings: Use 1 pound

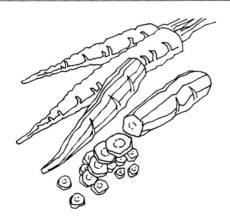

TO PREPARE
Scrape carrots and remove ends. Cut carrots crosswise into ¼-inch slices.

TO MICROWAVE
Place ¼ cup water, ¼ teaspoon salt and carrots in 1-quart casserole. Cover tightly and microwave on high (100%) 4 minutes; stir. Cover and microwave until tender, 4 to 6 minutes longer; drain.

TO SERVE
Add margarine or butter.....sprinkle with snipped parsley, mint, chives or cut green onion.....season with basil, chervil, ginger, rosemary, savory or thyme.

Microwaving Carrots

You'll find nutritious, inexpensive carrots combined with other vegetables and main dishes throughout this book. Choose fresh young carrots, cut them into uniform pieces or shred them, and enjoy the crisp-tender results. They require longer cooking than some vegetables, so they are usually added earlier in the microwaving time schedule.

Shredded Carrots and Bacon

3 *or* 4 *servings*

2	*slices bacon, cut into ½-inch pieces*
2½	*cups coarsely shredded carrots (about 4 medium)*
¼	*teaspoon salt*
	Dash of pepper
2	*tablespoons snipped parsley*

1. Place bacon in 1-quart casserole. Cover with paper towel and microwave on high (100%) until crisp, about 2 minutes. Remove bacon.

2. Stir carrots, salt and pepper into bacon fat. Cover tightly and microwave on high (100%) until tender, 4 to 6 minutes; stir. Sprinkle with bacon and parsley.

Parsley Carrots

3 *or* 4 *servings*

2	*tablespoons water*
2	*tablespoons finely chopped onion*
1	*teaspoon instant chicken bouillon*
¼	*teaspoon salt*
1	*clove garlic, finely chopped*
2½	*cups ¼-inch slices carrots (about 5 medium)*
2	*tablespoons snipped parsley*

Mix all ingredients except carrots and parsley in 1-quart casserole. Stir in carrots. Cover tightly and microwave on high (100%) 4 minutes; stir. Cover and microwave until carrots are tender, 4 to 6 minutes longer. Toss with parsley.

Parsley Carrots

Herbed Carrots and Zucchini   Carrot-Cauliflower Medley

Herbed Carrots and Zucchini

4 *servings*

  2   *tablespoons water*
 ½   *teaspoon salt*
1½   *cups ¼-inch slices carrots*
         (about 3 medium)
  3   *small onions, cut into fourths*
 ¼   *teaspoon dried dill weed**
 ⅛   *teaspoon rosemary leaves*

  2   *small zucchini, cut crosswise,*
         then lengthwise into fourths
         (about ½ pound)

1. Place water, salt, carrots, onions, dill weed and rosemary in 1½-quart casserole. Cover tightly and microwave on high (100%) 4 minutes.

2. Stir in zucchini. Cover tightly and microwave on high (100%) until vegetables are tender, 3 to 5 minutes longer.

* ¾ teaspoon fresh dill weed can be substituted for the dried dill weed.

Carrot-Cauliflower Medley

4 *servings*

  2   *tablespoons margarine or butter*
 ½   *teaspoon salt*
 ⅛   *teaspoon ground nutmeg*
1½   *cups ¼-inch slices carrots*
         (about 3 medium)
1½   *cups small flowerets cauliflower*
         (about ½ pound)
       Snipped parsley
       Grated Parmesan cheese

Place margarine, salt, nutmeg, carrots and cauliflower in 1-quart casserole. Cover tightly and microwave on high (100%) 4 minutes; stir. Cover and microwave until vegetables are crisp-tender, 2 to 4 minutes longer. Let stand 5 minutes. Sprinkle with parsley and cheese.

Dilled Vegetables (pictured on page 114)

5 or 6 servings

¼ *cup water*
½ *teaspoon salt*
2 *cups ½-inch diagonal slices carrots (about 5 medium)*
1 *small onion, sliced and separated into rings*
1 *teaspoon snipped fresh dill weed**

1 *package (10 ounces) frozen green peas*
1 *medium red or green pepper, cut into ¼-inch strips*

1. Place water, salt, carrots, onion rings and dill weed in 2-quart casserole. Cover tightly and microwave on high (100%) 5 minutes.

2. Stir in peas and pepper. Cover tightly and microwave on high (100%) until vegetables are tender, 7 to 9 minutes.

* ½ teaspoon dried dill weed can be substituted for the fresh dill weed.

Cauliflower

For 4 servings: Use about 1 pound (1 medium head)

TO PREPARE
Remove outer leaves and stalk. Cut off any discoloration; wash cauliflower. Leave whole and cut out cone-shaped center from core or separate into flowerets.

TO MICROWAVE
Place ¼ cup water and cauliflower in 1½-quart casserole. Cover tightly and microwave on high (100%) 4 minutes. Rotate casserole ¼ turn for whole cauliflower; stir flowerets. Cover and microwave until tender, 3 to 4 minutes longer; drain.

TO SERVE
Add margarine or butter, salt and pepper.....top with buttered crumbs.....season with basil, curry powder, nutmeg, celery seed or poppy seed.....top with grated Parmesan cheese or shredded cheese.

Cauliflower and Peas

4 servings

1 *package (10 ounces) frozen green peas**
1 *package (10 ounces) frozen cauliflower in cheese sauce*

Place peas in 1½-quart casserole. Pour cauliflower and cheese sauce over peas. Cover tightly and microwave on high (100%) 5 minutes; stir. Cover and microwave until vegetables are almost tender, 5 to 7 minutes longer.

* 1 package (10 ounces) frozen lima beans or Brussels sprouts can be substituted for the peas.

Celery (Pascal, Green; Golden, Bleached) *For 4 servings: Use 1 medium bunch*

TO PREPARE
Remove leaves and trim off root ends. Remove any coarse strings; wash celery. Cut stalks into 1-inch pieces (about 4 cups).

TO MICROWAVE
Place 2 tablespoons water, ¼ teaspoon salt and celery in 1½-quart casserole. Cover tightly and microwave on high (100%) 4 minutes; stir. Cover and microwave until tender, 3 to 5 minutes longer. Let stand 3 minutes; drain.

TO SERVE
Add margarine or butter.....season with mustard or instant bouillon or marjoram.

Celery with Mushrooms (pictured on page 1) *3 or 4 servings*

3 cups ¼-inch diagonal slices
    celery (6 medium stalks)
1½ cups ¼-inch slices mushrooms
    (about 4 ounces)
1½ teaspoons instant chicken
    bouillon
¼ teaspoon celery salt
2 tablespoons sliced pimiento

Mix all ingredients except pimiento in 1½-quart casserole. Cover tightly and microwave on high (100%) 3 minutes; stir. Cover and microwave until celery is crisp-tender, 2 to 4 minutes longer. Stir in pimiento.

Celery Root (Celeriac) *For 4 servings: Use 1½ pounds*

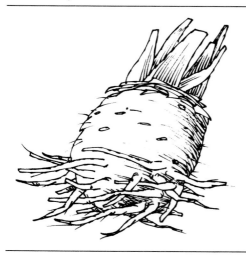

TO PREPARE
Cut off any leaves or root fibers and pare thinly. Cut into ½-inch pieces.

TO MICROWAVE
Place ¼ cup water, ¼ teaspoon salt and celery root in 1½-quart casserole. Cover tightly and microwave on high (100%) 5 minutes; stir. Cover and microwave until crisp-tender, 4 to 6 minutes longer. Let stand 1 minute; drain.

TO SERVE
Toss with ¼ cup Italian dressing, cover and refrigerate 2 hours; serve as a salad.

Corn on the Cob

Corn on the Cob

For 4 servings: Use 4 to 8 ears

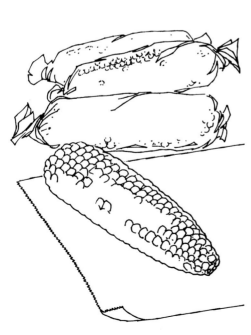

TO PREPARE
Refrigerate unhusked corn until ready to use. (Corn is best when eaten as soon after picking as possible.) Husk 4 ears corn and remove silk just before cooking.

TO MICROWAVE
Wrap each ear of corn in waxed paper; twist ends. Arrange 2 inches apart in microwave. Microwave on high (100%) 5 minutes; turn corn over and rearrange ears. Microwave until tender, 4 to 6 minutes longer. Let stand 3 minutes.

Note: Corn can be microwaved in the husk, if desired. After microwaving, grasp silk and gently pull off before removing husks.

TO SERVE
Add margarine or butter, salt and pepper.....season with chili powder, basil, celery seed or nutmeg.....cut off kernels and stir in chopped green pepper, chilies or celery.

Crunchy Corn

3 or 4 *servings*

1   *can (12 ounces) whole kernel
     corn, drained*
¼ *cup chopped celery*
¼ *teaspoon celery salt*
    Dash of pepper
1   *tablespoon margarine or butter*

Mix all ingredients in 1-quart casserole. Cover tightly and microwave on high (100%) until hot, 3 to 4 minutes; stir.

Note: Recipe can be doubled. Use 1½-quart casserole and microwave 6 to 8 minutes.

Cheesy Cucumber and Corn

4 *servings*

1   *medium cucumber, cut length-
     wise into fourths, then cross-
     wise into ½-inch pieces*
1   *can (17 ounces) whole kernel
     corn, drained*
¼ *teaspoon salt*
⅛ *teaspoon pepper*
½ *cup shredded Cheddar cheese
     (about 2 ounces)*

Mix cucumber, corn, salt and pepper in 1-quart casserole. Cover tightly and microwave on high (100%) 2 minutes; stir. Cover and microwave until vegetables are hot, 1 to 3 minutes longer. Sprinkle with shredded cheese. Cover and let stand 1 minute.

Cheesy Cucumber and Corn

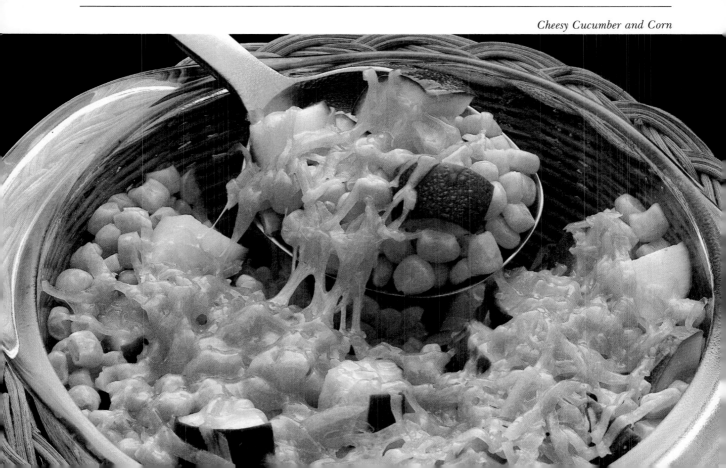

Cheese-Scalloped Corn

4 *servings*

½ *cup chopped green pepper*
  (1 small)
¼ *cup chopped onion*
2 *tablespoons margarine or butter*

2 *tablespoons all-purpose flour*
¾ *teaspoon salt*
½ *teaspoon paprika*
¼ *teaspoon dry mustard*
  Dash of pepper
¾ *cup milk*

1 *can (16 ounces) whole kernel*
  corn*, drained
½ *cup shredded Cheddar cheese*
  (about 2 ounces)
1 *egg, beaten*

⅓ *cup cracker crumbs*
1 *tablespoon margarine or butter,*
  melted (page 11)

1. Place green pepper, onion and 2 tablespoons margarine in 1½-quart casserole. Microwave uncovered on high (100%) until onion is tender, 2 to 3 minutes.

2. Stir in flour, salt, paprika, mustard and pepper. Gradually stir in milk. Microwave uncovered on high (100%), stirring every minute until mixture is thickened, 2 to 3 minutes.

3. Stir in corn, cheese and egg. Cover tightly and microwave on medium-high (70%) 5 minutes.

4. Mix crumbs and 1 tablespoon margarine; sprinkle over corn. Microwave uncovered until center is almost set, 4 to 6 minutes longer. Let stand 5 minutes.

* 1 package (10 ounces) frozen whole kernel corn, cooked and drained, can be substituted for the canned whole kernel corn.

Garlic Corn with Chilies

2 *or 3 servings*

1 *can (12 ounces) vacuum-pack*
  whole kernel corn, drained
2 *tablespoons chopped green chilies*
1 *tablespoon margarine or butter*
1 *tablespoon chopped pimiento*
1 *clove garlic, crushed*
¼ *teaspoon salt*
¼ *teaspoon basil leaves*
⅛ *teaspoon pepper*

Mix all ingredients in 1-quart casserole. Cover tightly and microwave on high (100%) until hot, 4 to 5 minutes; stir.

Tender Buttery Corn

2 *or 3 servings*

2 *cups fresh corn kernels**
  (about 4 ears)
2 *tablespoons margarine or butter*
¼ *teaspoon salt*
  Dash of pepper
  Dash of ground nutmeg

Mix corn, margarine, salt, pepper and nutmeg in 1-quart casserole. Cover tightly and microwave on high (100%) 3 minutes; stir. Cover and microwave until tender, 3 to 4 minutes longer. Let stand 5 minutes.

* 1 package (10 ounces) frozen whole kernel corn can be substituted for the fresh corn.

Eggplant

For 4 servings: Use 1½ pounds (1 medium)

TO PREPARE
Just before cooking, wash eggplant and, if desired, pare. Cut into ½-inch cubes or ¼-inch slices.

TO MICROWAVE
For cubes, place 2 tablespoons water, ½ teaspoon salt and eggplant in 1½-quart casserole. Cover tightly and microwave on high (100%) until tender, stirring every 2 minutes, 6 to 8 minutes; drain.

For slices, place 2 tablespoons water and ½ teaspoon salt in 9-inch pie plate. Overlap eggplant slices in a circle around edge of pie plate. Cover tightly and microwave on high (100%) 3 minutes; rotate pie plate ½ turn. Microwave until tender, 3 to 5 minutes longer; drain.

TO SERVE
Add margarine or butter.....sprinkle with grated Parmesan cheese or shredded mozzarella cheese .....season with garlic salt, allspice, chili powder or oregano.

Chili Eggplant with Tomatoes

4 servings

6   *slices bacon, cut into 1-inch pieces*

¼   *cup chopped onion*
¼   *cup chopped green chilies*
1   *clove garlic, finely chopped*
½   *teaspoon salt*

2   *cups ½-inch pieces eggplant (about ½ pound)*
2   *medium tomatoes, cut into eighths*
1   *small zucchini, cut into ½-inch slices*

1. Place bacon in 1½-quart casserole. Cover with paper towel and microwave on high (100%) 3 minutes; stir. Cover and microwave until crisp, 2 to 3 minutes longer; drain on paper towel. Drain fat from casserole; return 1 tablespoon fat to casserole.

2. Stir onion, chilies, garlic and salt into fat in casserole. Cover tightly and microwave on high (100%) until onion is tender, 1 to 2 minutes.

3. Mix in eggplant, tomatoes, zucchini and bacon. Cover tightly and microwave on high (100%) 3 minutes; stir. Cover and microwave until eggplant is almost tender, 3 to 5 minutes longer; stir. Cover and let stand 5 minutes.

Standing Time for Vegetables

Standing time is built into some vegetable recipes for even heating, uniform texture and development of flavor. However, many vegetables do not require a standing time and should be served immediately. If it is necessary to let these vegetables stand before serving, shorten the microwave time slightly to avoid overcooking.

Vegetable-Stuffed Eggplant

Vegetable-Stuffed Eggplant

4 servings

1 *medium eggplant*
     (about 1½ pounds)

2 *tablespoons all-purpose flour*
¼ *cup margarine or butter*
2 *tablespoons chopped green pepper*
2 *tablespoons finely chopped onion*
1 *clove garlic, chopped*
½ *teaspoon salt*
⅛ *teaspoon pepper*
2 *tablespoons half-and-half*
½ *cup coarsely chopped peanuts*
1 *jar (2 ounces) chopped pimientos,*
     drained
1 *tablespoon grated Parmesan*
     cheese

1. Cut a lengthwise slice from side of eggplant. Remove and cube enough eggplant to measure 3 cups.

2. Mix eggplant, flour, margarine, green pepper, onion, garlic, salt and pepper in 1½-quart casserole. Cover tightly and microwave on high (100%) 2 minutes; stir. Cover and microwave until mixture is thickened and eggplant is hot, 1 to 2 minutes longer. Stir in half-and-half, peanuts and pimiento. Fill eggplant shell with mixture; sprinkle with cheese.

3. Place eggplant shell on serving plate. Microwave uncovered on high (100%) until eggplant is tender, 4 to 6 minutes. Let stand 5 minutes.

Greens (Spinach, Beet Tops, Chicory Escarole, Mustard Greens)

For 4 servings: Use 1 pound

CHICORY

MUSTARD GREENS

BEET TOPS

TO PREPARE
Remove root ends and imperfect leaves. Wash greens several times, lifting out of the water each time; drain.

TO MICROWAVE
Place greens with just the water that clings to the leaves in 3-quart casserole or bowl. Cover tightly and microwave on high (100%) 3 minutes; stir. Cover and microwave until tender, 3 to 5 minutes longer. Let stand 3 minutes; drain.

TO SERVE
Season with dill, marjoram, mint, nutmeg, rosemary or onion.....drizzle with lemon juice or vinegar..... sprinkle with crumbled bacon or grated cheese.

Spinach and Broccoli

3 or 4 servings

2 tablespoons water
1 teaspoon salt
1 package (10 ounces) frozen chopped spinach
1 package (10 ounces) frozen chopped broccoli
1 tablespoon margarine or butter
1 tablespoon lemon juice

Place water, salt, spinach and broccoli in 1½-quart casserole. Cover tightly and microwave on high (100%) 8 minutes; break up and stir. Cover and microwave until tender, 4 to 6 minutes longer; drain. Stir in margarine and lemon juice.

Spinach with Peanuts

4 servings

1 package (10 ounces) frozen leaf spinach

1 egg
2 teaspoons all-purpose flour
¼ teaspoon salt
¼ teaspoon lemon juice
Dash of pepper
1 tablespoon finely chopped onion
¼ cup chopped peanuts

1. Place spinach in 1-quart casserole. Cover tightly and microwave on high (100%) 4 minutes; stir. Cover and microwave until tender, 2 to 3 minutes longer; drain.

2. Beat egg, flour, salt, lemon juice and pepper until smooth. Stir egg mixture and onion into spinach. Cover tightly and microwave on medium-high (70%) 3 minutes; stir. Microwave until hot, 2 to 3 minutes longer. Sprinkle with peanuts. Let stand 5 minutes.

Spinach with Bacon

2 or 3 servings

1 *package (10 ounces) frozen chopped spinach*
1 *small onion, thinly sliced*
½ *teaspoon salt*
   Dash of pepper
3 *slices bacon, crisply cooked and crumbled (page 11)*

Place spinach, onion, salt and pepper in 1-quart casserole. Cover tightly and microwave on high (100%) 4 minutes; break up and stir. Cover and microwave until spinach is tender, 2 to 4 minutes longer. Sprinkle with bacon.

Kohlrabi

For 3 or 4 servings: Use 1½ pounds (6 to 8 medium)

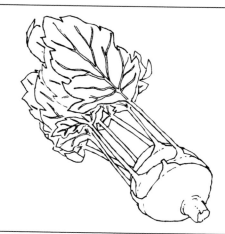

TO PREPARE
Trim off root ends and vinelike stems. Wash and pare kohlrabi. Cut into ¼-inch slices.

TO MICROWAVE
Place ¼ cup water, ¼ teaspoon salt and kohlrabi in 1-quart casserole. Cover tightly and microwave on high (100%) 3 minutes; stir. Cover and microwave until tender, 3 to 5 minutes longer. Let stand 1 minute; drain.

TO SERVE
Season with dill or thyme.....stir in snipped chives .....add a dash of Worcestershire sauce.

Leeks

For 4 servings: Use 2 pounds (about 6 medium)

TO PREPARE
Cut roots from leeks; remove woody green tops to within 2 inches of white part (save greens for soup or stew). Peel outside layer of bulbs. Cut large leeks lengthwise into fourths for pieces of similar size. Wash in cold water, spreading leaves to clean.

TO MICROWAVE
Place ¼ cup water, ½ teaspoon salt and leeks in 1½-quart casserole. Cover tightly and microwave on high (100%) 3 minutes; rotate casserole ½ turn. Microwave until tender, 3 to 5 minutes longer. Let stand 1 minute; drain.

TO SERVE
Drizzle with French dressing .....sprinkle with grated cheese.....serve with roasts.

Mushrooms

For 4 servings: Use 1 pound

TO PREPARE
Rinse mushrooms and trim off stem ends. Slice mushrooms parallel to stem in ¼-inch slices.

TO MICROWAVE
Place mushrooms in 1½-quart casserole. Cover tightly and microwave on high (100%) 2 minutes; stir. Cover and microwave until tender, 1 to 3 minutes longer. Let stand 1 minute; drain. Stir in 1 tablespoon margarine or butter.

TO SERVE
Season with salt, marjoram, oregano, rosemary, savory or tarragon.....combine with hot cooked peas, green beans or lima beans.

Garlic Mushrooms

2 servings

2 tablespoons margarine or butter
1½ teaspoons cornstarch
¼ teaspoon salt
  Dash of oregano
3 cups ¼-inch slices mushrooms
  (about 8 ounces)
1 small clove garlic,
  finely chopped
  Snipped parsley

Place margarine, cornstarch, salt, oregano, mushrooms and garlic in 1-quart casserole. Cover tightly and microwave on high (100%) 1 minute; stir. Cover and microwave until hot, 1 minute longer. Sprinkle with parsley.

Okra

For 4 servings: Use 1 pound

TO PREPARE
Remove tips; wash okra and cut into ½-inch slices.

TO MICROWAVE
Place ¼ cup water, ¼ teaspoon salt and okra in 1½-quart casserole. Cover tightly and microwave on high (100%) 3 minutes; stir. Cover and microwave until tender, 2 to 3 minutes longer. Let stand 1 minute.

TO SERVE
Add dash of vinegar or lemon juice.....combine with tomatoes.....use in soups or casseroles.

Okra-Corn-Tomato Medley

Okra-Corn-Tomato Medley

6 servings

4	*slices bacon, cut into ½-inch pieces*
2	*cups ½-inch slices okra* (about ¾ pound)*
2	*medium tomatoes, peeled and cut into eighths*
1	*cup fresh corn kernels (about 2 ears)*
½	*cup chopped onion*
¼	*teaspoon salt*
4	*to 6 drops hot pepper sauce*

1. Place bacon in 2-quart casserole. Cover with paper towel and microwave on high (100%) until crisp, about 4 minutes.

2. Stir in okra, tomatoes, corn, onion, salt and pepper sauce. Cover tightly and microwave on high (100%) 5 minutes; stir. Cover and microwave until corn is tender, 5 to 7 minutes longer.

* 1 package (10 ounces) frozen cut okra, defrosted, can be substituted for the fresh okra.

Onions (Small White, Yellow or Red)

For 4 servings:
Use 1½ pounds (8 to 10)

TO PREPARE
Peel onions under running cold water (to prevent eyes from watering).

TO MICROWAVE
Place ¼ cup water, ¼ teaspoon salt and onions in 2-quart casserole. Cover tightly and microwave on high (100%) 3 minutes; stir. Cover and microwave until tender, 3 to 5 minutes longer. Let stand 3 minutes; drain.

TO SERVE
Add margarine or butter.....season with basil, ginger, oregano or thyme.....sprinkle with grated cheese.

Onions and Peas with Nutmeg

4 servings

1 *package (10 ounces) frozen green peas*
1 *package (10 ounces) frozen small onions in cheese sauce*

¼ *teaspoon ground nutmeg*
⅛ *teaspoon salt*

1. Place peas in 1½-quart casserole. Pour onions and cheese sauce over peas. Cover tightly and microwave on high (100%) 5 minutes.

2. Stir in nutmeg and salt. Cover tightly and microwave on high (100%) until vegetables are tender, 6 to 8 minutes longer; stir.

Onions and Peas with Nutmeg

Hollandaise Onions

2 or 3 servings

Prepare Hollandaise Sauce (below). Place 1 jar (16 ounces) small whole onions*, drained, in 1-quart casserole. Cover tightly and microwave on high (100%) until hot, 3 to 4 minutes. Stir and drain again. Pour Hollandaise Sauce over onions.

* 2 cups cooked whole onions (page 146) can be substituted for the jar of onions.

Hollandaise Sauce

⅓ cup margarine or butter

2 tablespoons lemon juice
1 tablespoon water
2 egg yolks

1. Place margarine in 2-cup measure. Microwave uncovered on high (100%) until melted, 45 to 60 seconds.

2. Add lemon juice and water. Beat in egg yolks gradually with fork. Microwave uncovered on medium (50%) 45 seconds; stir. Microwave until thickened, stirring every 15 seconds, 15 to 30 seconds longer. (Do not overcook or sauce will curdle.)

Parsnips

For 4 servings: Use 1½ pounds (6 to 8)

TO PREPARE
Scrape or pare. Cut into ¼-inch slices.

TO MICROWAVE
Place ¼ cup water, ¼ teaspoon salt and parsnips in 1-quart casserole. Cover tightly and microwave on high (100%) 4 minutes; stir. Cover and microwave until tender, 4 to 6 minutes longer. Let stand 1 minute.

TO SERVE
Add margarine or butter.....sprinkle with snipped parsley.....season with allspice.

Pineapple Parsnips

4 or 5 servings

6 medium parsnips, cut crosswise, then lengthwise into ¼-inch strips (1½ pounds)
1 can (8¼ ounces) crushed pineapple, drained
1 teaspoon sugar
½ teaspoon salt
⅛ teaspoon pepper
2 tablespoons margarine or butter

Place parsnips, pineapple, sugar, salt and pepper in 2-quart casserole. Dot with margarine. Cover tightly and microwave on high (100%) 4 minutes; stir. Cover and microwave until parsnips are tender, 4 to 6 minutes longer. Let stand 5 minutes.

Chinese Pea Pods

For 3 servings: Use 1 pound

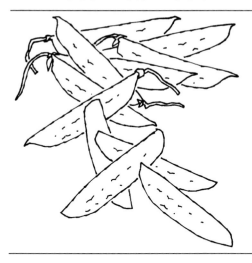

TO PREPARE
Wash pea pods; remove tips and strings.

TO MICROWAVE
Place ¼ cup water, ¼ teaspoon salt and pea pods in 1½-quart casserole. Cover tightly and microwave on high (100%) 3 minutes; stir. Cover and microwave until crisp-tender, 3 to 5 minutes longer. Let stand 3 minutes; drain.

TO SERVE
Drizzle with small amount of soy sauce.....refrigerate until chilled and add to tossed salads.....combine with sliced water chestnuts.

Green Peas

For 4 servings: Use 3 pounds (unshelled)

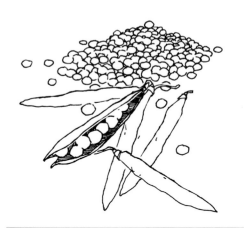

TO PREPARE
Wash and shell peas just before cooking.

TO MICROWAVE
Place ¼ cup water and ½ teaspoon salt and peas in 1½-quart casserole. Cover tightly and microwave on high (100%) 4 minutes; stir. Cover and microwave until tender, 4 to 6 minutes longer. Let stand 3 minutes; drain.

TO SERVE
Add margarine.....season with allspice, basil, chervil, marjoram, mint, rosemary, savory, thyme or tarragon.....combine with carrots, onion or mushrooms.

Curried Peas and Celery

3 or 4 servings

2   *tablespoons margarine or butter*
½   *teaspoon salt*
½   *teaspoon curry powder*
1   *cup thin slices celery*
       (about 2 medium stalks)
1   *package (10 ounces) frozen*
       green peas

Place all ingredients in 1-quart casserole. Cover tightly and microwave on high (100%) 3 minutes; stir. Cover and microwave until peas are tender, 3 to 5 minutes longer.

Dilled Peas and Cauliflower

3 servings

1 *tablespoon water*
¼ *teaspoon salt*
1 *tablespoon margarine or butter*
1 *package (10 ounces) frozen
       cauliflower*
¼ *teaspoon dill weed*

1 *package (10 ounces) frozen
       green peas*
2 *tablespoons grated Parmesan
       cheese*

1. Place water, salt, margarine, cauliflower and dill weed in 1½-quart casserole. Cover tightly and microwave on high (100%) 4 minutes.

2. Stir in peas. Cover and microwave until vegetables are tender, 5 to 7 minutes. Sprinkle with cheese.

Peas with Mushrooms and Tomatoes

4 servings

1 *can (16½ ounces) green peas,
       drained*
1 *can (2 ounces) mushroom stems
       and pieces, drained*
¼ *teaspoon salt*
⅛ *teaspoon pepper*
1 *tablespoon margarine or butter*

1 *tomato, cut into 1-inch wedges*

1. Mix peas, mushrooms, salt, pepper and margarine in 1-quart casserole. Cover tightly and microwave on high (100%) 3 minutes; stir.

2. Arrange tomato wedges in circle on top of vegetables. (See photograph.) Cover and microwave until tomatoes are hot, 2 to 4 minutes longer.

Peas with Mushrooms and Tomatoes

Peppers -- Green Bell

For 4 servings:
Use 2 green peppers if sliced, 4 if stuffed

TO PREPARE
Wash 2 green peppers; remove stems, seeds and membranes. Leave whole or cut into thin slices.

TO MICROWAVE
Place peppers in 1½-quart casserole. Cover tightly and microwave on high (100%) 2 minutes; stir. Cover and microwave until crisp-tender, 2 to 3 minutes longer. Let stand 1 minute.

TO SERVE
Add margarine or butter, salt and pepper.....combine with tomatoes or cooked mushrooms.

Rice-Stuffed Peppers

4 servings

4	*medium green peppers*
2	*cups chopped tomato*
⅔	*cup uncooked instant rice*
½	*cup chopped onion*
¼	*cup raisins*
¼	*cup snipped parsley*
2	*tablespoons sunflower kernels*
2	*tablespoons margarine or butter*
¾	*teaspoon salt*
½	*teaspoon curry powder*
¼	*teaspoon pepper*
½	*cup water*

1. Cut thin slice from stem end of each pepper. Remove seeds and membranes; rinse. Arrange peppers in circle in 9- or 10-inch pie plate.

2. Mix remaining ingredients except water. Fill each pepper with ⅔ cup mixture. Spoon 2 tablespoons water into each pepper.

3. Cover loosely and microwave 6 minutes on high (100%); rotate pie plate ½ turn. Microwave until peppers are crisp-tender, 4 to 5 minutes longer.

Peppers and Corn in Tomato Sauce

4 servings

1	*medium green pepper, cut into ½-inch strips*
1	*cup ¼-inch diagonal slices celery*
¼	*cup finely chopped onion*
1	*can (7 ounces) whole kernel corn, drained*
½	*teaspoon dried basil leaves*
½	*teaspoon salt*
1	*can (8 ounces) tomato sauce*
	Garlic Croutons (right)

Mix all ingredients except Garlic Croutons in 1½-quart casserole. Cover tightly and microwave on high (100%) 5 minutes; stir. Cover and microwave until green peppers are tender, 5 to 7 minutes longer. Sprinkle with Garlic Croutons.

Garlic Croutons
Mix 2 tablespoons margarine or butter, ¼ teaspoon garlic powder and 1 cup toasted bread cubes. Microwave uncovered on high (100%) until crisp and dry, stirring every minute, 1 to 2 minutes.

Potatoes -- Small New

For 4 or 5 servings: Use 1½ pounds (10 to 14)

TO PREPARE
Wash potatoes of similar size lightly and leave whole. Pierce potatoes to allow steam to escape, or pare narrow strip around centers.

TO MICROWAVE
Place ¼ cup water, ½ teaspoon salt and potatoes in 2-quart casserole, arranging larger potatoes at outside edge of casserole, small potatoes in center. Cover tightly and microwave on high (100%) 5 minutes; stir. Cover and microwave until tender, 5 to 7 minutes longer. Let stand 3 minutes; drain.

TO SERVE
Drizzle with lemon juice.....sprinkle with snipped parsley, chives or green onion.....sprinkle with paprika.

New Potatoes with Onions

4 or 5 servings

¼   *cup water*
½   *teaspoon salt*
10   *to 14 small new potatoes*
       (about 1½ pounds)

2   *tablespoons margarine or butter*
½   *teaspoon grated lemon peel*
1   *tablespoon lemon juice*
½   *teaspoon salt*
⅛   *teaspoon pepper*
     Dash of dried dill weed
1   *green onion, chopped*

1. Prepare potatoes as directed above. Place water, salt and potatoes in 2-quart casserole. Cover tightly and microwave on high (100%) 5 minutes; stir. Cover and microwave until tender, 4 to 6 minutes longer; drain.

2. Mix remaining ingredients except onion in 1-cup measure. Microwave uncovered on high (100%) until bubbly, about 1 minute; stir in onion. Pour mixture over potatoes.

Microwaving Vegetables with Skins or Shells

Round or oval vegetables (and fruits) with skins or shells need to be partially pared or pricked in several places to allow steam to escape and prevent bursting while microwaving. Cooking such foods as potatoes also illustrates an important microwave principle — cooking time increases as the number of potatoes increases. Choose vegetables of similar size for best results.

Potatoes -- White

For 4 servings: Use 1½ pounds (4 medium)

TO PREPARE
For whole potatoes, scrub oval potatoes (rather than long shapes) of similar size. Pierce potatoes to allow steam to escape. Or cut into 1-inch pieces.

TO MICROWAVE
For whole potatoes, arrange potatoes about 2 inches apart in circle in microwave. (If potatoes are long, old or dry, wrap each in waxed paper before placing in microwave. For crisper potato skins, sprinkle each dampened potato with salt.) Microwave potatoes uncovered on high (100%) until tender, 11 to 13 minutes. Let stand 5 minutes. (Potatoes hold their heat well; if microwaving a second vegetable, cook potatoes first).

For cut-up potatoes, place ½ cup water, ½ teaspoon salt and potatoes in 2-quart casserole. Cover tightly and microwave on high (100%) 6 minutes; stir. Cover and microwave until tender, 5 to 7 minutes longer.

TO SERVE
Add margarine or butter, salt and pepper.....season with bay leaf, caraway seed, dill, mint, poppy seed or sage.....top whole potatoes with seasoned sour cream or yogurt.

Potatoes -- Sweet

For 4 servings: Use 1½ pounds (about 4 medium)

TO PREPARE
Wash sweet potatoes of similar size but do not pare. Pierce potatoes to allow steam to escape.

TO MICROWAVE
Arrange potatoes about 2 inches apart in circle on paper towel in microwave. Microwave uncovered on high (100%) until tender when pierced with fork, 8 to 10 minutes. Let stand 5 minutes.

TO SERVE
Add margarine or butter, salt and pepper.....season with cinnamon, cloves or ginger.

Pineapple-Nut Sweet Potatoes

Pineapple-Nut Sweet Potatoes

4 *servings*

1   *can (18 ounces) vacuum-pack*
     sweet potatoes, drained
¾   *teaspoon salt*
1   *can (8¼ ounces) crushed*
     pineapple, drained
¼   *cup coarsely chopped nuts*
1   *tablespoon packed brown sugar*
1   *cup miniature marshmallows*
     or 10 or 11 large marsh-
     mallows, cut-up
     Ground nutmeg

1. Layer sweet potatoes, salt, pineapple, nuts, brown sugar and ½ cup of the marshmallows in 1½-quart casserole. Cover tightly and microwave on high (100%) until hot, 5 to 7 minutes.

2. Sprinkle with remaining marshmallows. Microwave uncovered until marshmallows are puffed, about 1 minute longer. Sprinkle with nutmeg.

Orange Sweet Potatoes

4 *or 5 servings*

1   *can (18 ounces) vacuum-pack*
     sweet potatoes, drained
¼   *teaspoon salt*
⅓   *cup orange marmalade*

Place potatoes in 1-quart casserole. Sprinkle with salt; spoon marmalade on potatoes. Cover loosely and microwave on high (100%) 4 minutes; stir and spoon marmalade on potatoes. Cover and microwave until hot, 1 to 2 minutes longer; stir.

Squash -- Summer (Pattypan, Straightneck and Crookneck, Zucchini)

For 4 servings: Use 1½ pounds

TO PREPARE
Wash squash; remove stem and blossom ends but do not pare. Cut into ½-inch slices or cubes.

TO MICROWAVE
Place ¼ cup water, ¼ teaspoon salt and squash in 1½-quart casserole. Cover tightly and microwave on high (100%) 4 minutes; stir. Cover and microwave until almost tender, 3 to 4 minutes longer (pattypan 5 to 7 minutes); stir. Cover squash and let stand 1 minute; drain.

TO SERVE
Add margarine or butter, garlic salt and pepper.....season with basil, marjoram, oregano or rosemary.....sprinkle with grated Parmesan or shredded mozzarella cheese.

Crookneck Squash and Green Pepper

3 or 4 servings

4 *cups ½-inch slices crookneck squash (about 1¼ pounds)*
2 *tablespoons margarine or butter*
⅓ *cup chopped green pepper*
2 *green onions (with tops), sliced*
½ *teaspoon salt*
¼ *teaspoon ground turmeric*

Mix all ingredients in 1½-quart casserole. Cover tightly and microwave on high (100%) 3 minutes; stir. Cover and microwave until squash is crisp-tender, 3 to 5 minutes longer.

Squash with Mushrooms

3 or 4 servings

1 *tablespoon margarine or butter*
1 *teaspoon salt*
1½ *cups ¼-inch slices yellow crookneck squash (½ pound)*
1 *medium onion, sliced*
¼ *teaspoon ground ginger*
⅛ *teaspoon ground turmeric*

1 *cup whole small mushrooms (about 4 ounces)*
2 *teaspoons lemon juice*

1. Place margarine, salt, squash, onion, ginger and turmeric in 1½-quart casserole. Cover tightly and microwave on high (100%) 2 minutes; stir. Cover and microwave until vegetables are almost tender, 2 to 3 minutes longer.

2. Stir in mushrooms and lemon juice. Cover tightly and microwave on high (100%) until mushrooms are hot, 2 to 3 minutes.

Zucchini Italian-Style

4 servings

6   *small zucchini (about 1½*
      pounds)
⅛   *teaspoon salt*
2   *tablespoons bottled Italian salad*
      dressing
⅛   *teaspoon Italian herb seasoning*
      Grated Parmesan cheese

Cut unpared zucchini in half crosswise, then lengthwise into fourths. Place salt and zucchini slices in 1½-quart casserole; sprinkle with salad dressing and herb seasoning. Cover tightly and microwave on high (100%) 3 minutes; stir. Cover and microwave until tender, 2 to 3 minutes longer. Sprinkle with Parmesan cheese and paprika, if desired.

Squash -- Summer (Spaghetti)

For 6 servings:
Use about 2½ pounds (1 medium)

TO PREPARE
Pierce squash to allow steam to escape.

TO MICROWAVE
Place squash on paper towel in microwave. Microwave on high (100%) 8 minutes; turn squash over. Microwave until tender, 8 to 11 minutes longer; let stand 10 minutes. Cut in half crosswise; scoop out seeds. Unwind spaghetti-like flesh with fork and serve like pasta.

TO SERVE
Add margarine, salt and pepper.....sprinkle with grated Parmesan cheese.....season with allspice, basil, cinnamon, ginger or sage.....top with spaghetti sauce.

Squash -- Winter (Acorn)   *For 4 servings: Use about 2 pounds (2 medium)*

TO PREPARE
Pierce squash of similar size to allow steam to escape.

TO MICROWAVE
Place squash 2 inches apart in microwave. Microwave on high (100%) 6 minutes. Carefully cut into halves; remove seeds. Arrange squash halves cut-sides down in baking dish, 12 × 7½ × 2 inches. Cover tightly and microwave on high (100%) until tender, 6 to 9 minutes longer. Let stand 3 minues.

TO SERVE
Remove from rind and mash with cream or orange juice, nutmeg, brown sugar.....sprinkle with crumbled cooked bacon or grated orange peel.

Pecan Squash

4 servings

2 *acorn squash (about 1 pound each)*

⅔ *cup graham cracker crumbs or soda cracker crumbs*
⅓ *cup coarsely chopped pecans*
⅓ *cup margarine or butter, softened (page 11)*
3 *tablespoons packed brown sugar*
⅛ *teaspoon salt*
¼ *teaspoon ground nutmeg*

Whole cranberry sauce

1. Pierce each whole squash in several places to allow steam to escape; place 2 inches apart in microwave. Microwave on high (100%) 6 minutes. Cut squash crosswise in halves; remove seeds and arrange cut-sides down on serving plate. Cover tightly and microwave until tender, 7 to 9 minutes longer. Remove stem; cut thin slice from pointed end to prevent tipping.

2. Mix remaining ingredients except cranberry sauce. Arrange squash halves cut-sides up on serving plate. Spoon ¼ of the crumb mixture into each squash half. Microwave uncovered on high (100%) until filling is hot, 3 to 5 minutes.

3. Top each squash half with cranberry sauce.

Pecan Squash

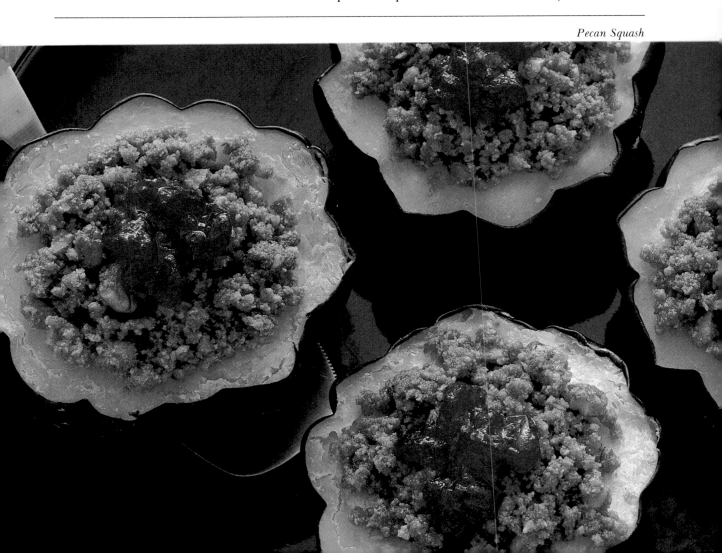

Tomatoes

For 4 servings: Use 2 pounds (about 6 medium)

TO PREPARE
Wash tomatoes; cut into 8 wedges or ½-inch slices. Peel tomatoes before cutting if desired. To remove skin easily, dip tomato into boiling water 30 seconds, then into cold water. Or scrape surface of tomato with blade of knife to loosen; peel.

TO MICROWAVE
Place tomatoes in 2-quart casserole. Cover tightly and microwave on high (100%) 4 minutes for wedges, 3 minutes for slices; gently stir. Cover and microwave until hot, wedges 3 to 4 minutes, slices 2 to 3 minutes. Let stand 1 minute.

TO SERVE
Add margarine or butter, salt and pepper.....season with allspice, basil, bay leaf, chives, fennel, marjoram, oregano, sage or tarragon.

Stewed Tomatoes with Limas

4 servings

1   can (8 ounces) stewed tomatoes
⅓   cup chopped celery
        (1 large stalk)
½   teaspoon dried thyme leaves
¼   teaspoon mustard seed
¼   teaspoon salt
⅛   teaspoon pepper

1   package (10 ounces) frozen
        lima beans

1. Mix tomatoes (with liquid), celery, thyme, mustard seed, salt and pepper in 1½-quart casserole. Cover tightly and microwave on high (100%) 3 minutes.

2. Stir in lima beans. Cover tightly and microwave on high (100%) until beans are tender, 4 to 6 minutes.

Tomatoes with Cabbage

4 or 5 servings

1   teaspoon instant beef bouillon
¼   teaspoon dried basil leaves
1   can (16 ounces) tomato wedges,
        drained (reserve ⅓ cup
        liquid)
3   cups finely shredded cabbage
        (about ¾ pound)

Mix bouillon, basil, reserved tomato liquid and cabbage in 2-quart casserole. Cover tightly and microwave on high (100%) 4 minutes; stir in tomatoes. Cover and microwave until cabbage is crisp-tender and tomatoes are hot, 3 to 5 minutes longer.

Savory Tomatoes

4 *servings*

4   *medium tomatoes*
      (about 1⅓ pounds)
   Salt and pepper

⅓   *cup coarsely crushed crumbs*
      (cereal, crackers, croutons,
      onion rings)
¼   *teaspoon crushed basil, oregano*
      or savory leaves
⅓   *cup shredded Cheddar cheese*

1. Remove stem ends from tomatoes; cut tomatoes in half. Arrange cut-sides up in circle on 10-inch pie plate or dinner plate. Season with salt and pepper.

2. Mix crumbs and herbs; mound on tomatoes. Microwave uncovered on high (100%) 2 minutes; rotate pie plate ½ turn. Sprinkle tomatoes with cheese. Microwave until tomatoes are hot and cheese is melted, about 2 minutes longer. Garnish with parsley if desired.

Stuffed Tomatoes (pictured on page 1)

6 *servings*

6   *firm medium tomatoes*
      (about 2 pounds)
1   *cup crumbled herb-seasoned*
      stuffing mix
¼   *cup shredded process American*
      cheese
¼   *teaspoon salt*
⅛   *teaspoon pepper*

1. Remove stem ends from tomatoes. Scoop out pulp, leaving ½-inch walls. Chop pulp; mix with stuffing mix, cheese, salt and pepper.

2. Fill tomatoes with stuffing; arrange in circle in 9-inch pie plate. Cover loosely and microwave on high (100%) 3 minutes; rotate pie plate ½ turn. Microwave until tomatoes are hot, 3 to 4 minutes longer. Garnish with parsley if desired.

Five-Vegetable Combo

Five-Vegetable Combo

5 *or* 6 *servings*

2　*tablespoons margarine or butter*
½　*teaspoon salt*
1　*can (16 ounces) whole tomatoes,
　　drained and cut into halves*
1　*package (9 ounces) frozen green
　　beans, broken apart*
1　*cup ¼-inch diagonal slices celery
　　(about 2 medium stalks)*
1　*cup ¼-inch diagonal slices
　　carrots (about 2 medium)*

½　*green pepper, cut into strips*

1. Mix margarine, salt, tomatoes, beans, celery and carrots in 2-quart casserole. Cover tightly and microwave on high (100%) 6 minutes.

2. Stir in green pepper. Cover tightly and microwave on high (100%) until peppers are tender, 7 to 9 minutes.

Turnips -- Yellow (Rutabagas)

For 4 servings:
Use 1½ pounds (1 large or 2 small)

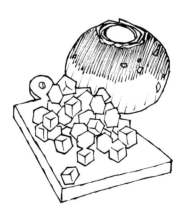

TO PREPARE
Wash and pare thinly. Cut into ½-inch pieces.

TO MICROWAVE
Place ½ cup water, ½ teaspoon salt and rutabagas in 2-quart casserole. Cover tightly and microwave on high (100%) stirring every 5 minutes until tender, 14 to 17 minutes. Let stand 1 minute; drain.

TO SERVE
Add margarine or butter.....season with dill, poppy seed, thyme.....mash and stir in snipped onion or chives and season with dash of Worcestershire sauce.

Gingered Rutabagas

4 or 5 servings

¼ cup water
1 teaspoon salt
4 cups ½-inch pieces rutabagas
      (about 1½ pounds)
1 tablespoon sugar
¼ teaspoon ground ginger

Place all ingredients in 1½-quart casserole. Cover tightly and microwave on high (100%) 8 minutes; stir. Cover and microwave until tender, 8 to 10 minutes longer. Let stand 5 minutes.

Turnips -- White

For 4 servings: Use 1½ pounds (6 medium)

TO PREPARE
If necessary, cut off tops. Wash and pare thinly; cut into ½-inch pieces.

TO MICROWAVE
Place ¼ cup water, ½ teaspoon salt and turnips in 2-quart casserole. Cover tightly and microwave on high (100%) stirring every 4 minutes, until tender, 12 to 14 minutes. Let stand 1 minute; drain.

TO SERVE
Season with dill, poppy seed or thyme.....stir in snipped onion or chives and a dash of Worcestershire sauce .....mash and add a small amount of cream and a sprinkling of nutmeg.

Turnips with Cheese Sauce

4 servings

½ cup water
1 teaspoon salt
⅛ teaspoon pepper
4 medium turnips (about 1 pound)
1 small onion, sliced
1 cup ¼-inch slices celery

2 tablespoons cornstarch
⅓ cup cold water
5 or 6 drops red pepper sauce

½ cup shredded Cheddar cheese
      (about 2 ounces)
   Paprika

1. Cut turnips into 2 × 1½-inch strips. Place ½ cup water, salt, pepper, turnips, onion and celery in 2-quart casserole. Cover tightly and microwave on high (100%) 6 minutes; stir. Cover and microwave until tender, 6 to 8 minutes longer. Drain vegetables, reserving ¼ cup liquid.

2. Mix cornstarch and ⅓ cup cold water in 2-cup measure. Stir in reserved liquid and red pepper sauce. Microwave uncovered on high (100%) to boiling, stirring every minute, 2 to 3 minutes.

3. Stir in cheese just until melted. Pour sauce on hot vegetables; sprinkle with paprika.

BREADS
&GRAINS

Baking Powder Biscuits (pictured on pages 146 and 239) *1 dozen biscuits*

⅓ *cup shortening*
1¾ *cups all-purpose or whole wheat flour (not stone-ground)*
2½ *teaspoons baking powder*
¾ *teaspoon salt*
  About ¾ cup milk

  Paprika Topping (below)

1. Cut shortening into flour, baking powder and salt with pastry blender until mixture resembles fine crumbs. Stir in just enough milk so dough leaves side of bowl and rounds up into a ball. (Too much milk makes dough sticky, not enough makes biscuits dry.)

2. Turn dough onto lightly floured surface. Knead lightly 10 times. Roll ½ inch thick. Cut with floured 2-inch biscuit cutter. Arrange 6 biscuits with sides almost touching in circle on 10-inch plate lined with 2 paper towels; brush tops of biscuits with Paprika Topping. Microwave uncovered on high (100%) 1 minute; rotate plate ½ turn. Microwave until no longer doughy, 1 to 2 minutes longer. Let stand 1 minute; remove to rack. Repeat with remaining biscuits.

Note: After microwaving, biscuits can be broiled if desired. Omit Paprika Topping. Set conventional oven control to broil and/or 550°. Arrange microwaved biscuits on cookie sheet; brush tops with melted margarine or butter. Broil with tops about 2 inches from heat until golden brown, 2 to 4 minutes.

Paprika Topping
Mix 1 tablespoon melted margarine or butter (page 11) and ⅛ teaspoon paprika.

Cornmeal Biscuits: Substitute ½ cup yellow cornmeal for ½ cup of the flour. Brush tops with melted margarine; sprinkle with 1½ teaspoons cornmeal.

Rye Biscuits: Substitute ¾ cup rye flour for ¾ cup of the all-purpose flour. Brush tops of biscuits with Paprika Topping.

Wheat Germ Biscuits: Substitute ¼ cup wheat germ for ¼ cup of the flour. Brush tops with melted margarine; sprinkle with 1 teaspoon wheat germ.

Microwaving Biscuits

Since baking powder biscuits come out of the microwave as snowy-white as they went in, they need help to get that golden, just-baked look. You can brush them with Paprika Topping (above) before microwaving. The topping works well with chicken too. Another way to give biscuits golden tops is to brush with margarine after microwaving and broil, above.

Pictured on previous page: Chili-Cheese Savory Hot Bread Slices, Cornmeal Bread, Butterscotch-Pecan Puffs, Pilaf with Tomatoes and Peppers

Biscuit Ring

1 biscuit ring

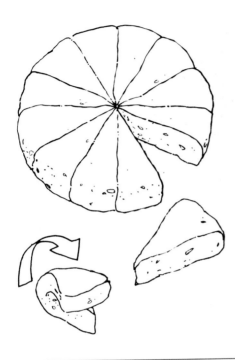

1. Place ⅓ cup margarine or butter in small bowl. Microwave uncovered on high (100%) until melted, 45 to 60 seconds.

2. Prepare Baking Powder Biscuits dough (opposite). Turn dough onto lightly floured surface. Knead lightly 10 times. Roll into 8-inch round. Cut dough into 12 wedges; fold each wedge in half crosswise. Dip wedges into margarine, coating all sides. Roll in Cinnamon-Sugar Coating or Herb-Cheese Coating (below). Arrange wedges, point sides down, in 8-cup ring dish. Elevate ring dish on inverted dinner plate in microwave. Microwave uncovered on medium (50%) 4 minutes; rotate ring dish ½ turn. Microwave until no longer doughy, 3 to 6 minutes longer.

Cinnamon-Sugar Coating: Mix ½ cup granulated or brown sugar and ¾ teaspoon cinnamon.

Herb-Cheese Coating: Mix ½ cup grated Parmesan cheese, ¾ teaspoon Italian herb seasoning and ½ teaspoon paprika.

Herb-Cheese Biscuit Ring

Shortcakes

½ dozen shortcakes

⅓ cup shortening
2 cups all-purpose flour
2 tablespoons sugar
3 teaspoons baking powder
1 teaspoon salt
¾ cup milk

1 tablespoon margarine or butter,
       melted (page 11)
⅛ teaspoon cinnamon

1. Cut shortening into flour, sugar, baking powder and salt until mixture resembles fine crumbs. Stir in milk just until blended. Gently smooth dough into a ball on lightly floured cloth-covered board. Knead 20 to 25 times. Roll to ½-inch thickness; cut with floured 3-inch cutter.

2. Arrange shortcakes in circle with sides almost touching on 12-inch plate lined with 2 paper towels. Mix margarine and cinnamon; brush over tops of shortcakes. Microwave uncovered on high (100%) 1 minute; rotate plate ½ turn. Microwave until short-cakes are no longer doughy, 2 to 4 minutes longer. Let stand 3 minutes.

Butterscotch-Pecan Puffs (pictured on page 163)

½ dozen puffs

¼ cup margarine or butter
¼ cup packed brown sugar
18 pecan halves
      Ground cinnamon

1 cup buttermilk baking mix
⅓ cup cold water
2 to 3 teaspoons grated orange peel

1. Arrange 6 six-ounce custard cups in circle on 12-inch plate. Place 2 teaspoons margarine in each cup. Microwave uncovered on high (100%) until margarine is melted, about 1 minute. Place 2 teaspoons brown sugar and 3 pecan halves in each cup; sprinkle with cinnamon. Microwave uncovered on high (100%) until hot and bubbly, 1 to 2 minutes.

2. Mix baking mix, water and orange peel until soft dough forms; beat vigorously 20 strokes. Spoon evenly onto mixture in cups. Microwave uncovered on high (100%) 1 minute; rotate plate ½ turn. Microwave until tops spring back when touched lightly, 1 to 2 minutes longer. Immediately invert cups on serving plate; leave cups over puffs a few minutes.

Microwaving Muffins

To add color as well as flavor to muffins and cupcakes, which do not brown in the microwave, ingredients (such as cornmeal, molasses, chocolate, cranberries and apricots, to name a few) are mixed in, toppings (marmalade, cinnmon-sugar) are added before microwaving, or the muffin tops are dipped in a coating. Muffins can be made into individual upside-down cakes too — such as Butterscotch Pecan Puffs. Custard cups hold slightly more batter than muffin rings. Follow specific recipe for which kind to use. You can improvise your own reusable muffin ring — cut paper hot-drink cups down to 2 inches high. Place a paper liner in each cup and arrange them in a circle on a plate for easy rotating.

Cinnamon Puffs

Cinnamon Puffs

7 puffs

1	*cup buttermilk baking mix*
¼	*cup milk*
1	*egg*
2	*tablespoons sugar*
1	*tablespoon margarine or butter,*
	softened (page 11)
⅛	*teaspoon ground nutmeg*
¼	*cup sugar*
½	*teaspoon ground cinnamon*
3	*tablespoons margarine or butter,*
	melted (page 11)

1. Place paper liners in 7 six-ounce custard cups. Arrange cups in circle on 12-inch plate.

2. Mix baking mix, milk, egg, sugar, margarine and nutmeg. Stir until smooth, about 15 seconds. Fill muffin cups ½ full. Microwave uncovered on high (100%) 1 minute; rotate plate ¼ turn. Microwave until tops spring back when touched lightly, 1 to 2 minutes longer. Remove puffs.

3. Mix ¼ cup sugar and the cinnamon. Dip tops of puffs into melted margarine, then into cinnamon-sugar mixture.

Muffins

1½ dozen muffins

1   *egg*
¾   *cup milk*
½   *cup vegetable oil*
2   *cups all-purpose or whole wheat*
      flour (not stone-ground)
⅓   *cup sugar*
3   *teaspoons baking powder*
1   *teaspoon salt*
      Cinnamon-Sugar (below)

1. Place paper liners in 6 muffin cups, 2½ × 1½ inches, or 6-ounce custard cups. Arrange cups in circle on 12-inch plate.

2. Beat egg; stir in milk and vegetable oil. Stir in remaining ingredients except Cinnamon-Sugar all at once just until flour is moistened (batter will be lumpy). Fill muffin cups about ½ full. Sprinkle with Cinnamon-Sugar. Microwave uncovered on high (100%) 1 minute; rotate plate ½ turn. Microwave until wooden pick inserted in center comes out clean, 30 to 60 seconds longer. (Parts of muffins will appear moist but will continue to cook while standing.) Let stand 1 minute; remove to rack. Repeat with remaining batter and additional cupcake liners.

Cinnamon-Sugar
Mix 1 tablespoon granulated sugar and ⅛ teaspoon ground cinnamon.

Apple-Nut Muffins: Stir in 1 cup finely chopped, pared apple with the milk and ½ teaspoon ground cinnamon with the flour. Substitute packed brown sugar for the granulated sugar. Sprinkle tops with mixture of ¼ cup packed brown sugar, ¼ cup finely chopped nuts and ½ teaspoon ground cinnamon before microwaving. Increase first microwave time by 30 seconds.

Cranberry-Orange Muffins: Stir in 1 cup (about 4 ounces) cranberry halves and 1 tablespoon grated orange peel with the milk. Sprinkle tops with Cinnamon-Sugar before microwaving.

Date-Nut Muffins: Stir in ¾ cup chopped dates and ½ cup finely chopped nuts with the milk. Increase sugar to ⅔ cup. Sprinkle tops with Cinnamon-Sugar and ¼ cup finely chopped nuts before microwaving.

Prune-Apricot Muffins: Stir in ½ cup cut-up dried prunes and ½ cup cut-up dried apricots with the milk. Stir in ⅛ teaspoon ground cloves with the flour.

Honey-Orange Muffins

1½ dozen muffins

1 egg
¾ cup milk
½ cup vegetable oil
2 tablespoons grated orange peel
2 cups all-purpose or whole wheat
    flour (not stone-ground)
⅓ cup honey
3 teaspoons baking powder
1 teaspoon salt
    Orange marmalade

1. Place paper liners in 6 muffin cups, 2½ × 1½ inches, or 6-ounce custard cups. Arrange cups in circle on 12-inch plate.

2. Beat egg; stir in milk, vegetable oil and orange peel. Stir in remaining ingredients except orange marmalade all at once just until flour is moistened (batter will be lumpy). Fill muffin cups about ½ full. Spoon 1 teaspoon orange marmalade onto each muffin. Sprinkle with Cinnamon-Sugar (opposite) if desired. Microwave uncovered on high (100%) 1 minute; rotate plate ½ turn and rearrange custard cups. Microwave until wooden pick inserted in center comes out clean, 1½ to 2½ minutes longer. (Parts of muffins will appear moist but will continue to cook while standing.) Let stand 1 minute; remove to rack. Repeat with remaining batter and cupcake liners.

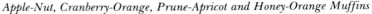

Apple-Nut, Cranberry-Orange, Prune-Apricot and Honey-Orange Muffins

Corn Muffins

1 dozen muffins

3	*tablespoons margarine or butter, softened (page 11)*
2	*tablespoons sugar*
2	*eggs*
1¼	*cups buttermilk baking mix*
⅔	*cup yellow cornmeal*
½	*teaspoon salt*
¾	*cup milk*

1. Place paper liners in 6 muffin cups, 2½ × 1¼ inches or 6-ounce custard cups. Arrange cups in circle on 12-inch plate.

2. Mix margarine and sugar. Beat in eggs, 1 at a time; mix in remaining ingredients. Beat vigorously 1 minute (batter will be slightly lumpy). Fill muffin cups ½ full. Microwave uncovered on high (100%) 1 minute; rotate plate ½ turn. Microwave until tops spring back when touched lightly and are almost dry, 1½ to 2 minutes longer. Let stand 1 minute; remove to rack. Repeat with remaining batter and additional cupcake liners.

Molasses-Bran Muffins

1½ dozen muffins

¾	*cup milk*
1	*cup whole bran cereal*
1	*egg*
½	*cup vegetable oil*
½	*cup raisins*
⅓	*cup molasses*
1⅔	*cups all-purpose flour*
2	*teaspoons baking powder*
½	*teaspoon baking soda*
½	*teaspoon ground cinnamon*

1. Prepare muffin cups as directed in step 1, Muffins (page 168).

2. Pour milk on whole bran cereal; let stand 1 minute. Beat egg; stir in cereal mixture, vegetable oil, raisins and molasses. Stir in remaining ingredients all at once until flour is moistened (batter will be lumpy). Fill muffin cups ½ full. Microwave as directed in step 2, Muffins (page 168).

Microwaving Quick Breads and Cakes

Using the doneness tests given in these recipes is especially important to avoid overcooking. Since microwave cooking patterns vary so much, check at minimum time, use the doneness test in the recipe, then add more cooking if necessary.

Standing time is indicated in many recipes to finish cooking the bottom, center or top without drying out the side. Some recipes call for placing the hot food directly on a heatproof surface instead of on a rack. This traps the heat and continues the cooking.

Ring-shaped or round dishes are ideal for microwaving breads and cakes; oblong or square shapes generally tend to cook faster at the ends or corners and may need a lower power setting. The volume for ring dishes is given in cups. To measure the volume of a container, fill it to the top with water, keeping track of the amount needed to fill it.

To improvise a ring-shaped dish, place a drinking glass about 2 inches across or a 6-ounce custard cup right side up in the center of a casserole or round baking dish. Make sure the dish is the same volume as the dish called for in the recipe, by measuring the volume, then subtracting the volume of the glass.

Pumpkin Bread

Pumpkin Bread

1 *bread ring*

¼   cup graham cracker crumbs

1⅓   cups all-purpose flour
1⅓   cups sugar
   1   cup pumpkin (½ of 16-ounce
         can)
   ⅓   cup water
   ⅓   cup shortening
   2   eggs
   1   teaspoon baking soda
   ¾   teaspoon salt
   ½   teaspoon ground cinnamon
   ½   teaspoon ground cloves
   ¼   teaspoon baking powder
   ⅓   cup coarsely chopped nuts
   ⅓   cup raisins

1. Generously grease 9-cup ring dish; coat with graham cracker crumbs.

2. Mix remaining ingredients except nuts and raisins; beat until smooth. Stir in nuts and raisins. Pour into ring dish. Elevate ring dish on inverted dinner plate in microwave. Cover with waxed paper and microwave on medium-high (70%) 6 minutes; rotate ring dish ½ turn. Microwave until top of bread is dry and springs back when touched lightly, 6 to 8 minutes longer.

3. Let cool 10 minutes on heatproof surface (do not use rack). Invert on dish and let cool completely before slicing. To store, wrap and refrigerate no longer than 10 days.

Zucchini Bread: Substitute 1½ cups shredded zucchini (about 1 medium) for the pumpkin. Add 1 teaspoon vanilla; decrease cloves to ¼ teaspoon.

Brown Bread (pictured at left)

2 loaves

1 cup buttermilk
½ cup all-purpose or rye flour
½ cup whole wheat flour
    (not stone-ground)
½ cup cornmeal
⅓ cup molasses
1 teaspoon baking soda
½ teaspoon salt
1 cup raisins

Beat all ingredients except raisins in 3½-quart bowl on low speed, scraping bowl constantly, 30 seconds. Beat on medium speed, scraping bowl constantly, 30 seconds longer. Stir in raisins. Pour ½ of batter (about 1 cup) into greased 2-cup measure. Cover tightly and microwave on medium (50%) 3 minutes; rotate measure ½ turn. Microwave until no longer doughy, 2 to 4 minutes longer. Let stand 5 minutes; unmold. Repeat with remaining batter. Serve with margarine or softened cream cheese if desired.

Note: Brown Bread is best served warm.

Molasses Bread Ring: Pour batter into greased 5- or 6-cup ring dish. Elevate ring dish on inverted dinner plate in microwave. Cover tightly and microwave on medium (50%) 5 minutes; rotate ring dish ½ turn. Microwave until no longer doughy, 5 to 7 minutes longer. Let cool 10 minutes on heatproof surface (do not use rack). Unmold.

Orange-Date Nut Bread (pictured at left)

1 bread ring

⅓ cup finely chopped nuts

1¼ cups all-purpose flour
½ cup milk
½ cup chopped nuts
½ cup chopped dates
⅓ cup vegetable oil
¼ cup sugar
¼ cup honey
1 egg
2 teaspoons grated orange peel
1¾ teaspoons baking powder
½ teaspoon salt

1. Generously grease 5- or 6-cup ring dish; coat with ⅓ cup finely chopped nuts.

2. Mix remaining ingredients; beat 30 seconds. Pour into ring dish. Microwave uncovered on medium-high (70%), rotating ring dish ¼ turn every 3 minutes, until wooden pick inserted near center comes out clean, 8 to 10 minutes. Let cool 5 minutes on heatproof surface (do not use rack). Remove from dish and let cool completely before slicing. To store, wrap and refrigerate no longer than 10 days.

Whole Wheat Apricot Nut Bread: Substitute whole wheat flour (not stone ground) for the all-purpose flour. Substitute ½ cup finely cut-up dried apricots for the dates.

Orange-Date Nut Bread   Brown Bread

Orange-Cinnamon Coffee Ring

1 coffee cake ring

1½   cups all-purpose flour
1½   cups packed brown sugar
 ⅓   cup firm margarine or butter

 1   cup dairy sour cream
 1   egg
 1   tablespoon grated orange peel
 ¾   teaspoon baking soda
 ½   teaspoon ground cinnamon
 ⅓   cup chopped nuts

1. Mix flour, brown sugar and margarine until crumbly. Generously grease 8-cup ring dish; coat with ¼ cup crumbly mixture. Reserve ¾ cup remaining mixture for topping.

2. Stir sour cream, egg, orange peel, baking soda and cinnamon into remaining crumbly mixture just until moistened. Spread evenly in ring mold. Sprinkle with reserved crumbly mixture and the nuts. Microwave uncovered on high (100%) 3 minutes; rotate ring dish ½ turn. Microwave until wooden pick inserted near center comes out clean, 3 to 5 minutes longer. Let cool 10 minutes on heatproof surface (do not use rack). Invert on plate; cover with serving plate and invert again.

Streusel Coffee Cake

1 bundt coffee cake

    Streusel (below)

 ¼   cup graham cracker crumbs

 2   cups all-purpose flour
 1   cup sugar
 3   teaspoons baking powder
 1   teaspoon salt
 ⅓   cup margarine or butter, softened
      (page 11)
 1   cup milk
 1   egg

    Lemon Glaze (page 175)

1. Prepare Streusel.

2. Generously grease 12-cup bundt dish; coat with graham cracker crumbs.

3. Beat remaining ingredients except glaze in 3½-quart bowl on low speed 30 seconds. Beat on medium speed, scraping bowl occasionally, 2 minutes. Spread half of the batter in prepared dish; sprinkle with 1½ cups of the Streusel. Top with remaining batter and Streusel. Microwave uncovered on high (100%), rotating dish ¼ turn every 4 minutes, until top springs back when touched lightly, 12 to 14 minutes. Let cool 10 minutes on heatproof surface (do not use rack). Invert on serving plate.

4. Prepare Lemon Glaze. Drizzle over coffee cake.

Streusel
 ⅔   cup chopped nuts
 ½   cup packed brown sugar
 ⅓   cup all-purpose flour
 ¼   cup firm margarine or butter
 ¾   teaspoon ground cinnamon

Mix all ingredients until crumbly.

Blueberry Coffee Cake

1 bundt coffee cake

¼ *cup graham cracker crumbs*

  *Streusel Coffee Cake batter
    (page 174)*
2 *cups fresh or frozen (defrosted
    and drained) blueberries*

  Lemon Glaze (below)

1. Generously grease 12-cup bundt cake dish; coat with graham cracker crumbs.

2. Prepare Streusel Coffee Cake batter as directed. Spread ½ of the batter in prepared dish. Sprinkle ½ of blueberries over batter. Spread with remaining batter and sprinkle remaining blueberries on top. Microwave uncovered on high (100%), rotating cake dish ¼ turn every 4 minutes, until top springs back when touched lightly, 12 to 14 minutes. Let cool on heatproof surface 10 minutes (do not use rack).

3. Invert coffee cake onto serving plate. Drizzle with Lemon Glaze.

Lemon Glaze
Mix 1 cup powdered sugar, ¼ teaspoon grated lemon peel and 1 tablespoon lemon juice until smooth. Add a few drops additional lemon juice, if necessary, until glaze is of desired consistency.

Blueberry Coffee Cake

Walnut Coffee Ring

1 coffee cake ring

½ *cup chopped walnuts*
¼ *cup granulated sugar*
½ *teaspoon ground cinnamon*

3 *tablespoons margarine or butter*

¼ *cup packed brown sugar*
2 *tablespoons corn syrup*

2 *cups buttermilk baking mix*
½ *cup cold water*
1 *tablespoon grated orange peel
    (if desired)*
¼ *cup margarine or butter, melted
    (page 11)*

1. Mix ¼ cup of the walnuts, the granulated sugar and cinnamon; reserve.

2. Place 3 tablespoons margarine in 8-cup ring dish. Microwave uncovered on high (100%) until melted, 30 to 45 seconds.

3. Stir in brown sugar, corn syrup and the remaining nuts; spread evenly. Microwave uncovered on high (100%) until hot and bubbly, 2 to 3 minutes.

4. Stir baking mix, water and orange peel to a soft dough. Drop ½ of the dough onto brown sugar mixture and drizzle with 2 tablespoons of the melted margarine. Sprinkle with reserved walnut mixture; drizzle with remaining margarine. Top with remaining dough. Elevate ring dish on inverted pie plate in microwave. Microwave uncovered on medium-high (70%) 3 minutes; rotate ring dish ½ turn. Microwave until no longer doughy, 2 to 4 minutes longer. Invert on serving plate; leave dish over cake a few minutes.

Reheating Breads

Biscuits, muffins, coffee cakes and some brown breads are best served warm. To reheat, place the amount you need on a paper towel or napkin (do not cover) and follow the directions below. Medium (50%) power is recommended, to avoid overheating. Always check at minimum time, because breads are porous and cook quickly. Overcooking toughens breads and causes fillings, frostings and fruits in breads to get too hot, since fillings heat even more quickly than breads. Breads should be warm, not hot and steamy.

Microwave Reheat Directions

Medium (50%) Power

Servings	Room Temperature	Frozen
1	15 to 30 seconds	45 seconds to 1¼ minutes
2	25 to 40 seconds	60 seconds to 1½ minutes
3	35 to 60 seconds	1¼ to 1½ minutes
4	45 seconds to 1¼ minutes	1½ to 3 minutes

This timing applies to muffins and biscuits 2 to 3 inches in diameter, coffee cake pieces about 2½ inches square and 2-inch wedges from bundt or ring shapes. Increase or decrease microwave times according to the size of the breads you are reheating.

Glazed Sour Cream Coffee Cake

Glazed Sour Cream Coffee Cake

One 8-inch round cake

½ cup sugar
¼ cup margarine or butter, softened
    (page 11)
1 egg
½ teaspoon vanilla
1 cup all-purpose or whole wheat
    flour (not stone-ground)
½ teaspoon baking powder
½ teaspoon baking soda
¼ teaspoon salt
¾ cup dairy sour cream

Filling (below)

Light Brown Glaze (below)

Light Brown Glaze
2 *tablespoons margarine or butter*
1 *cup powdered sugar*
½ *teaspoon vanilla*
2 *to 3 teaspoons milk*

1. Place sugar, margarine, egg and vanilla in 1½-quart bowl. Beat on medium speed, scraping bowl occasionally, 2 minutes. Beat in flour, baking powder, baking soda and salt alternately with sour cream on low speed.

2. Prepare Filling.

3. Spread ½ of the batter in round baking dish, 8 × 1½ inches, and sprinkle with ½ of the filling; repeat. Microwave uncovered on high (100%) until top springs back when touched lightly, 5 to 7 minutes. Let cool 10 minutes on heatproof surface (do not use rack). Drizzle with Light Brown Glaze.

Filling
Mix 3 tablespoons brown sugar, 3 tablespoons chopped nuts and ½ teaspoon ground cinnamon.

Place margarine in 2-cup measure. Microwave uncovered on high (100%) until melted and brown, 2 to 3 minutes. Stir in powdered sugar and vanilla. Mix in milk, 1 teaspoon at a time, until glaze is of desired consistency.

White Bread

2 loaves

2 *packages active dry yeast*
¾ *cup warm water (105 to 115°)*
2 *cups lukewarm milk (scalded then cooled)*
3 *tablespoons sugar*
3 *tablespoons shortening*
1 *tablespoon salt*
7 *to 8 cups all-purpose flour*

1. Dissolve yeast in warm water in 4-quart bowl. Stir in milk, sugar, shortening, salt and 4 cups of the flour. Beat until smooth. Mix in enough remaining flour to make dough easy to handle.

2. Turn dough onto lightly floured surface; knead until smooth and elastic, about 10 minutes. Place dough in greased bowl; turn greased side up. Cover with waxed paper and microwave on low (10%) 5 minutes; rotate bowl ½ turn. Microwave 5 minutes longer. Let stand covered until indentation remains when touched, 10 to 15 minutes.

3. Punch down dough; divide into halves. Roll each half into rectangle, 18 × 9 inches. Fold 9-inch sides crosswise into thirds, overlapping ends. Roll up tightly, beginning at narrow end. Pinch edge of dough into roll to seal well; press in ends of roll. Press each end with side of hand to seal; fold ends under.

4. Place loaves seam sides down in 2 greased loaf dishes, 9 × 5 × 3 or 8½ × 4½ × 2½ inches. Brush lightly with margarine if desired. Cover each loaf with waxed paper and microwave on low (10%) 5 minutes; rotate each loaf ½ turn. Microwave 5 minutes longer. Let stand, covered, until indentation remains when lightly touched, 5 to 8 minutes.

5. Heat conventional oven to 425°. Place loaves on low rack so that tops of loaf dishes are in center of oven. Dishes should not touch each other or sides of oven. Bake until loaves are deep golden brown and sound hollow when tapped, 20 to 30 minutes. Immediately remove from dishes. Brush tops of loaves with margarine; cool on racks.

Cornmeal Bread: Substitute 1 cup yellow cornmeal for 1 cup of the second addition of flour. Mix ¼ cup yellow cornmeal and 1 teaspoon paprika. Coat greased loaf dishes with ½ of mixture. After brushing loaves with margarine, sprinkle with remaining cornmeal.

Cracked Wheat Bread: Substitute brown sugar for the granulated sugar. Substitute 2⅔ cups cracked wheat for 2⅔ cups of the second addition of flour.

White Bread, continued

To proof the White Bread dough, place it in a greased bowl and cover with a sheet of waxed paper.

Microwave on low (10%) 5 minutes; rotate bowl ½ turn, microwave 5 minutes longer. Let stand 10 minutes.

Test for rising after 10 minutes. Press fingertips ½ inch into dough. An indentation should remain.

To proof the White Bread loaves, cover them with waxed paper; microwave on low (10%) 5 minutes.

Rotate each loaf ½ turn; microwave 5 minutes. Let stand 5 minutes longer. Test with fingertips.

Bake bread in conventional preheated 425° oven until loaves sound hollow when tapped, 20 to 30 minutes.

CAUTION!

Unless your microwave has a low (10% of full power) setting, DO NOT PROOF these bread loaves in the microwave! With higher than 10% power, parts of the dough will start to cook and form a crust before the rest of the dough has had a chance to rise. For microwave users who have a setting as low as 10%, microwave proofing saves over an hour's time.

For crusty, appetizing loaves after proofing, we recommend baking White Bread and its variations in a conventional oven. Don't forget that you can use your microwave to scald the milk. Pour it into a 2-cup measure and heat it on high (100%) to just below the boiling point, 2 to 4 minutes. (Tiny bubbles will form around edge.) Watch carefully.

An example of a yeast dough that can be proofed and cooked in the microwave is the rich, moist Apple-Raisin Coffee Cake, page 180. This is an upside-down cake, so the top is colorful and it is a ring shape (ideal for microwaving), but it too needs a low (10%) setting for proofing.

Apple-Raisin Coffee Cake

1 cake ring

Apple Topping (below)

1   *package active dry yeast*
¾   *cup warm water (105 to 115°)*
¼   *cup sugar*
¼   *cup shortening*
1   *egg*
1   *teaspoon salt*
1¼ *cups all-purpose flour*
1   *cup whole wheat flour
      (not stone-ground)*
½   *cup raisins*
½   *cup chopped nuts*

1. Prepare Apple Topping.

2. Dissolve yeast in warm water in 3½-quart bowl. Add sugar, shortening, egg, salt and all-purpose flour. Beat 2 minutes on medium speed, scraping bowl frequently. Stir in whole wheat flour, raisins and nuts; continue stirring until smooth. Drop batter by tablespoonfuls onto Apple Topping in ring dish; spread evenly. Cover with waxed paper and micro-wave on low (10%) 6 minutes. Let stand, covered, until indentation remains when lightly touched with floured finger, about 30 minutes.

3. Microwave uncovered on high (100%) 4 minutes; rotate ring dish ½ turn. Microwave until no longer doughy and top springs back when touched lightly, 4 to 6 minutes longer. Let cool 10 minutes on heat-proof surface (do not use rack). Invert dish on serving plate; leave dish over cake a few minutes.

Apple Topping

⅓   *cup margarine or butter*
½   *cup packed brown sugar*
2   *tablespoons light corn syrup*
1   *teaspoon ground cinnamon*
2   *cups ¼-inch apple slices
      (1 to 2 medium)*

Place margarine in small bowl. Microwave uncovered on high (100%) until melted, 45 to 60 seconds. Stir in sugar, syrup and cinnamon; pour into 8-cup ring dish. Overlap apple slices on butter-sugar mixture.

Drop yeast batter onto apple topping in ring-shaped dish. Spread evenly.

Proof in microwave 6 minutes. Let stand covered until an indentation from fingers remains.

After cooking, let cool 10 minutes. Invert on plate; lift dish off and serve.

Savory Hot Bread Slices

12 one-inch slices

1. Spread top sides of 12 one-inch slices French bread (½ of 1-pound loaf) or 6 individual French rolls, split, with one of the Seasoned Spreads (below).

2. Reassemble bread slices; place in paper napkin-lined basket or on dinner plate. Cover with paper towel and microwave on medium (50%) 1 minute; rotate basket ½ turn. Microwave until bread slices are warm, 1 to 1½ minutes longer.

Seasoned Spreads
Place ¼ cup margarine or butter in small bowl. Microwave uncovered on medium-low (30%) until softened, 15 to 30 seconds. Mix with one of the following.

Chili-Cheese: ½ cup shredded sharp Cheddar cheese (about 2 ounces), 1 tablespoon chopped green chilies and ½ teaspoon Worcestershire sauce.

Herb-Cheese: 2 teaspoons grated Parmesan cheese, ½ teaspoon snipped parsley, ⅛ teaspoon dried oregano leaves, and dash of garlic salt.

Onion: ¼ teaspoon instant minced onion or 1 teaspoon snipped chives.

Crusty Blue Cheese Slices

12 one-inch slices

½ loaf (½ pound) French bread
3 tablespoons margarine or butter
2 tablespoons crumbled blue cheese
1 tablespoon grated Parmesan
 cheese

1. Cut loaf diagonally into 1-inch slices. Place margarine and blue cheese in small bowl. Microwave uncovered on medium-low (30%) until softened, 15 to 30 seconds. Stir in Parmesan cheese; spread mixture on one side of each slice of bread.

2. Reassemble loaf; place in paper napkin-lined basket or on dinner plate. Cover with paper towel and microwave on medium (50%) 1 minute; rotate basket ½ turn. Microwave until bread slices are warm, 30 to 60 seconds longer.

Cheesy French Bread (pictured at right)

12 one-inch slices

½ loaf (½ pound) French bread
½ cup shredded sharp Cheddar
    cheese (about 2 ounces)
¼ cup mayonnaise or salad dressing
2 teaspoons snipped parsley
1 teaspoon prepared mustard
¼ teaspoon hickory-smoked salt

Cut loaf diagonally into 1-inch slices. Mix remaining ingredients; spread mixture on one side of each slice of bread. Reassemble loaf; place in paper napkin-lined basket or on dinner plate. Cover with paper towel and microwave on medium (50%) 1 minute; rotate basket ½ turn. Microwave until warm and cheese starts to melt, 1 to 1½ minutes longer.

Curried Raisin Bread (pictured at right)

4 servings

3 tablespoons crunchy peanut butter
2 tablespoons mayonnaise or
    salad dressing
¼ to ½ teaspoon curry powder
8 slices raisin bread (½ of
    1-pound loaf)

Mix peanut butter, mayonnaise and curry powder; spread mixture on one side of each slice of bread. Reassemble loaf with spread sides together; place in paper napkin-lined basket or on dinner plate. Cover with paper towel and microwave on medium (50%) 1 minute; rotate basket ½ turn. Microwave until warm, 30 to 60 seconds longer. To serve, cut each sandwich into 3 lengthwise strips.

Cream Cheese-Filled Rolls (pictured at right)

6 rolls

1. Mix ½ teaspoon dill weed and 1 package (3 ounces) cream cheese, softened (page 13). Spread cheese mixture in breaks of 6 butterfly rolls or Parker House rolls. Place rolls in paper napkin-lined basket or in circle on dinner plate. Cover with paper towel and microwave on medium (50%) until rolls are warm, 1 to 2 minutes.

Reheating Baked Breads

French breads retain their crustiness and tenderness and rolls their freshness when reheated — with or without special fillings — for a brief time in the microwave. Covering reassembled French loaves and butterfly rolls loosely helps to heat them quickly without making them too soft on top.

To save last minute fuss, slice and assemble the "fix-ups" early, then microwave them in the paper napkin-lined basket you will serve them in. (Check to be sure there are no metal parts on the basket.) Rotate once for even heating and presto — fragrant breads, savory fillings, seasonings blended — warm from your microwave! (For reheating other breads, pancakes and popovers, see pages 176, 275 and 109.)

Top to Bottom: Cheesy French Bread, Curried Raisin Bread, Cream Cheese-Filled Rolls

Cracked Wheat (Bulgur) with Green Peas

Cracked Wheat (Bulgur) with Green Peas   6 *servings*

2¼   *cups hot water*
1   *cup uncooked cracked wheat
        (bulgur)*
½   *cup chopped onion
        (about 1 medium)*
1   *clove garlic, finely chopped*
2   *tablespoons margarine or butter*
2   *teaspoons instant beef or
        chicken bouillon*
½   *teaspoon dill weed*
½   *teaspoon salt*

1   *package (10 ounces) frozen
        green peas*

1. Mix all ingredients except frozen peas in 2-quart casserole. Cover tightly; microwave on high (100%) 12 minutes.

2. Stir in peas. Cover tightly and microwave on high (100%) until bulgur is tender and water is absorbed, 7 to 11 minutes longer.

Hot Cooked Rice

2⅔ to 3 cups

Mix 2 cups uncooked instant rice, 1½ cups hot water and ½ teaspoon salt in 2-quart casserole. Cover tightly and microwave on high (100%) until rice is tender and water is absorbed, 6 to 8 minutes; stir.

Chicken-Flavored Rice

4 to 6 servings

1 *can (10½ ounces) condensed*
  chicken broth (about
  1¼ cups)
2 *cups uncooked instant rice*
¼ *cup chopped onion*
  (about 1 medium)
¼ *cup dry white wine*
  Dash of ground turmeric
1 *to 2 tablespoons margarine*
  or butter
  Grated Parmesan cheese
  (if desired)

Mix all ingredients except margarine and cheese in 2-quart casserole. Cover tightly and microwave on high (100%) 5 minutes; stir. Cover and microwave until rice is tender and water is absorbed, 5 to 7 minutes longer. Stir in margarine. Cover and let stand 5 minutes. Sprinkle with cheese.

Pilaf with Tomatoes and Peppers (pictured on page 162)

4 servings

1 *cup hot water*
1 *cup coarsely chopped tomato,*
  (about 1 medium)
¾ *cup uncooked instant rice*
¼ *cup chopped green pepper*
1 *tablespoon margarine or butter*
1 *teaspoon instant minced onion*
½ *teaspoon instant beef bouillon*
½ *teaspoon salt*

Mix all ingredients in 1½-quart casserole. Cover tightly and microwave on high (100%) 8 minutes; stir. Cover and microwave until rice is tender and water is absorbed, 7 to 9 minutes longer.

Microwaving Pasta or Rice

Cooking pasta or regular rice alone in the microwave takes about as much time as range-top cooking, although these foods are sometimes microwaved with other ingredients in casseroles.

Instant rice is a natural for microwaving, and pasta and rice, when conventionally cooked, do reheat beautifully. To reheat conventionally cooked pasta in your microwave, see page 244.

Parsley-Mushroom Rice

6 servings

1½ cups uncooked instant rice
1½ cups hot water
¼ cup margarine or butter
¼ cup finely chopped onion
1 small clove garlic, finely
      chopped
2 teaspoons instant chicken
      bouillon
¼ teaspoon dried basil leaves

1 can (4 ounces) mushroom stems
      and pieces, drained
2 tablespoons snipped parsley
   Grated Parmesan cheese
      (if desired)

1. Mix all ingredients except mushrooms, parsley and cheese in 1½-quart casserole. Cover tightly and microwave on high (100%) 7 minutes.

2. Stir in mushrooms. Cover tightly and microwave on high (100%) until rice is tender and water is absorbed, 4 to 6 minutes longer. Stir in parsley and sprinkle with cheese.

Parsley-Mushroom Rice

Curried Rice with Almonds

4 to 6 servings

¼ cup chopped onion
  (about 1 small)
2 tablespoons margarine or butter

¾ cup uncooked regular rice
1½ teaspoons instant chicken
  bouillon
¼ teaspoon ground allspice
¼ teaspoon ground turmeric
⅛ to ¼ teaspoon curry powder
  Dash of pepper
2⅔ cups hot water
¼ cup slivered almonds, toasted
  (page 12)

1. Place onion and margarine in 3-quart casserole. Cover tightly and microwave on high (100%) until onion is crisp-tender, 2 to 3 minutes.

2. Stir in rice, bouillon, allspice, turmeric, curry powder and pepper. Mix in water. Cover tightly and microwave on high (100%) 7 minutes; stir. Cover and microwave until liquid is almost absorbed, 8 to 10 minutes longer; stir. Cover and let stand 10 minutes (rice will absorb liquid while standing). Stir in almonds.

Skillet Cornmeal Mush

4 servings

2½ cups hot water
¾ cup cornmeal
¾ teaspoon salt

2 tablespoons margarine or butter
  All-purpose flour
  Quick Maple-Flavor Syrup
  (below)

1. Mix water, cornmeal and salt in 2-quart casserole. Microwave uncovered on high (100%) 3 minutes; stir. Microwave until mixture thickens and boils, 3 to 5 minutes longer. Spread in greased loaf dish, 9 × 5 × 3 or 8½ × 4½ × 2½ inches. Cover and refrigerate until firm, about 12 hours.

2. To serve, invert pan to unmold; cut loaf into ½-inch slices. Heat margarine on conventional range in 10-inch skillet until melted. Coat slices with flour; cook in margarine over low heat until light brown on both sides. Serve hot with syrup.

Quick Maple-Flavor Syrup
1 cup light corn syrup
1 tablespoon margarine or butter
¼ teaspoon maple flavoring
⅛ teaspoon vanilla

Place corn syrup and margarine in 2-cup measure. Microwave uncovered on high (100%) until margarine is melted, 1 to 2 minutes. Stir in maple flavoring and vanilla.

Complementary Cooking

Some foods are best when both microwaving and conventional cooking are used. Skillet Cornmeal Mush after microwaving needs surface cooking for a crusty coating. Pancakes need conventional cooking, but can be reheated in the microwave. Two-crust pies, after microwaving until the filling bubbles, need a conventional oven for that last beautiful browning and drying, but pie shells made with margarine can be microwaved to a beautiful, flaky finish.

Cherry Nut Cake

Cherry Nut Cake

One 8-inch round cake

1⅔	*cups all-purpose flour*
1	*cup packed brown sugar*
¼	*cup cocoa*
1	*teaspoon baking soda*
½	*teaspoon salt*
⅓	*cup chopped almonds*
1	*jar (6 ounces) maraschino cherries, drained and chopped (reserve syrup)*
⅓	*cup vegetable oil*
1	*teaspoon vinegar*
¼	*teaspoon vanilla*

Fluffy Pink Frosting (below)

1. Mix flour, brown sugar, cocoa, baking soda, salt and almonds with fork. Add enough water to reserved cherry syrup to measure 1 cup. Stir syrup-water mixture and the remaining ingredients except Fluffy Pink Frosting into flour mixture. Pour into round baking dish, 8 × 1½ inches. Elevate baking dish on inverted 9-inch pie plate in microwave. Microwave uncovered on medium (50%), rotating baking dish ¼ turn every 5 minutes, until top springs back when touched lightly, 15 to 17 minutes. (Center top may appear moist but will continue to cook while standing). Let cool on heatproof surface (do not use rack).

2. Frost with Fluffy Pink Frosting or sprinkle with powdered sugar.

Fluffy Pink Frosting

¼	*cup sugar*
2	*tablespoons light corn syrup*
1	*tablespoon water*
1	*egg white*
½	*teaspoon vanilla*
4	*drops red food color*

1. Mix sugar, corn syrup and water in 2-cup measure. Microwave uncovered on high (100%) until mixture boils, about 1 minute.

2. Beat egg white in 1½-quart bowl until soft peaks form. Pour hot syrup very slowly in thin stream into egg white, beating constantly on medium speed. Add vanilla and food color; beat on high speed until stiff peaks form.

Pictured on previous page: Glazed Oranges with Kiwis, Jeweled Fruitcake, Trifle, Chocolate Toffee Bars, Whole Wheat Apple Pie

Carrot-Pineapple Cupcakes

About 1½ dozen cupcakes

1⅓ cups all-purpose flour
1 cup sugar
1 teaspoon ground cinnamon
¾ teaspoon baking soda
½ teaspoon salt
¼ teaspoon ground nutmeg
1 cup grated carrot
(about 1 medium)
½ cup vegetable oil
½ cup drained, crushed pineapple
2 eggs
¼ cup chopped nuts
Browned Butter Frosting (right)

1. Place paper liners in 6 muffin cups, 2½ × 1¼ inches, or 6-ounce custard cups. Arrange cups in circle on 12-inch plate.

2. Mix flour, sugar, cinnamon, baking soda, salt and nutmeg. Stir in remaining ingredients except Browned Butter Frosting, just until dry ingredients are moistened. Fill muffin cups half full. Microwave uncovered on high (100%) 2 minutes; rotate plate ½ turn. Microwave until wooden pick inserted in center comes out clean, about 1 minute longer. (Parts of cupcakes will appear moist but will continue to cook while standing.) Let stand 1 minute; remove to rack. Repeat 2 times with remaining batter and additional cupcake liners. Frost with Browned Butter Frosting. Refrigerate any leftover cupcakes.

Browned Butter Frosting
Place ¼ cup margarine or butter in 4-cup measure. Microwave uncovered on high (100%) until melted and brown, 3 to 4 minutes. Stir in 2 cups powdered sugar. Mix in 1 teaspoon vanilla and 2 to 3 tablespoons milk until of spreading consistency.

Note: These little cakes can be used unfrosted as muffins.

Carrot-Pineapple Cupcakes

Blueberry Cake with Lemon Custard

Blueberry Cake with Lemon Custard
One 8-inch round cake

Lemon Custard (below)

1 *package (13.5 ounces) wild*
    blueberry muffin mix
2 *tablespoons sugar*
1 *tablespoon grated lemon peel*
¾ *teaspoon ground nutmeg*
1 *tablespoon graham cracker*
    crumbs

1. Prepare Lemon Custard.

2. Prepare muffin mix as directed on package except—stir in sugar, lemon peel and nutmeg with the muffin mix. Pour batter into round baking dish, 8 × 1½ inches. Sprinkle graham cracker crumbs over batter.

3. Microwave uncovered on high (100%) 2 minutes; rotate baking dish ½ turn. Microwave until top springs back when touched lightly, 2 to 3 minutes longer. Let cool 10 minutes on heatproof surface (do not use rack). Serve with Lemon Custard. Refrigerate any leftover custard.

Lemon Custard
¾ *cup milk*
1 *egg, slightly beaten*
2 *tablespoons sugar*
2 *teaspoons grated lemon peel*

Mix all ingredients in 2-cup measure. Microwave uncovered on medium-high (70%), briskly stirring with fork every minute, until thick, 3½ to 4½ minutes. Stir, cover and refrigerate until cooled, about 1 hour.

Quick Date Cake

One 8-inch square cake

1   *package (14 ounces) date bar mix*
½   *cup hot water*
2   *eggs*
1   *teaspoon baking powder*
½   *cup chopped walnuts*
½   *cup raisins (if desired)*
      Lemon-Scotch Topping (below)

Mix date filling and hot water. Stir in crumbly mix, eggs, baking powder, walnuts and raisins. Spread in greased baking dish, 8 × 8 × 2 inches. Microwave uncovered on high (100%), rotating dish ¼ turn every 2 minutes, until top springs back when touched lightly, 6 to 8 minutes. Let cool 5 minutes on heatproof surface (do not use rack). Spread warm cake with Lemon-Scotch Topping.

Lemon-Scotch Topping

⅔   *cup packed brown sugar*
½   *cup finely chopped walnuts*
2   *tablespoons lemon juice*
2   *tablespoons margarine or butter*

Mix all ingredients in 4-cup measure. Microwave uncovered on high (100%) until hot and bubbly, 1 to 2 minutes.

Jeweled Fruitcake (pictured on page 188)

1 bundt or 8 individual cakes

8   *ounces dried apricots*
        (about 2 cups)
8   *ounces pitted dates*
        (about 1½ cups)
9   *ounces Brazil nuts*
        (about 1½ cups)
1   *cup red and green maraschino*
        cherries
5   *ounces red and green candied*
        pineapple, cut up
        (about 1 cup)
¾   *cup all-purpose flour*
¾   *cup packed brown sugar*
½   *teaspoon ground nutmeg*
½   *teaspoon baking powder*
½   *teaspoon salt*
3   *eggs*
¼   *teaspoon vanilla*
¼   *cup graham cracker crumbs*

      Jelly Glaze (right, if desired)

1. Mix all ingredients except graham cracker crumbs and Jelly Glaze. Grease 8-cup bundt cake dish; coat with graham cracker crumbs. Pour batter evenly into cake dish.

2. Microwave uncovered on medium (50%), rotating cake dish ¼ turn every 5 minutes, until cake begins to pull away from sides of dish, 22 to 30 minutes. Let stand 15 minutes on heatproof surface (do not use rack). Remove from dish; let cool completely. Drizzle cake with ¼ cup brandy if desired. Wrap in double thickness of plastic wrap or in aluminum foil and store in refrigerator no longer than 4 weeks. To serve, pour Jelly Glaze over cake and cut into thin slices.

Jelly Glaze
Place ¼ cup currant jelly in 1-cup measure. Microwave uncovered on high (100%) until hot, about 1 minute; stir. Pour over fruitcake before serving.

Mini Fruitcakes: Grease eight 6-ounce custard cups; coat with ⅓ cup graham cracker crumbs. Pour ¾ cup batter into each cup; press firmly. Place 4 cups at a time on 10-inch dinner plate. Microwave uncovered on medium (50%), rotating plate ¼ turn every 5 minutes, until wooden pick inserted in center comes out clean, 15 to 17 minutes.

Glazed Pound Cake

1 *bundt cake*

⅓	to ½ *cup graham cracker crumbs*
2¾	*cups sugar*
1¼	*cups margarine or butter, softened (page* 11)
5	*eggs*
1	*teaspoon vanilla*
3	*cups all-purpose flour*
1	*teaspoon baking powder*
¼	*teaspoon salt*
1	*cup evaporated milk*

Orange Glaze (below)

1. Generously grease 16-cup plastic bundt cake dish; coat with graham cracker crumbs. Beat sugar, margarine, eggs and vanilla in 3½-quart bowl on low speed, scraping bowl constantly, 30 seconds. Beat on high speed, scraping bowl occasionally, 5 minutes. Beat in flour, baking powder and salt alternately with milk on low speed. Pour into dish.

2. Microwave uncovered on medium (50%), rotating dish ¼ turn every 5 minutes, 15 minutes. Rotate dish ¼ turn again.

3. Microwave uncovered on high (100%) 3 minutes; rotate dish ¼ turn. Microwave until cake top springs back when lightly touched, 3 to 6 minutes. (Parts of cake may appear moist but will continue to cook while standing.) Let cool 10 minutes on heatproof surface (do not use rack). Remove from pan.

4. Prepare Orange Glaze.

5. Make many holes of varying depths in inverted cake with 5-inch skewer. Pour glaze into holes; let stand until syrup is absorbed, about 30 minutes. To serve, sprinkle with powdered sugar and garnish with orange slices if desired.

Orange Glaze

¾	*cup sugar*
¾	*cup sweet white wine*
¾	*cup orange juice*
1	*teaspoon grated orange peel*

Mix sugar, wine, orange juice and orange peel in 4-cup measure. Microwave uncovered on high (100%), 2 minutes; stir. Microwave until bubbly, 2 to 3 minutes longer.

Meringue-Topped Pound Cake

8 servings

Chocolate-Almond Pudding
  (below)

3   egg whites
¼   teaspoon cream of tartar
6   tablespoons powdered sugar
½   teaspoon vanilla
¼   cup slivered almonds

8   slices pound cake

1. Prepare Chocolate-Almond Pudding; refrigerate.

2. Beat egg whites and cream of tartar in 1½-quart bowl until foamy. Beat in powdered sugar, 1 tablespoon at a time; continue beating until stiff peaks form. Beat in vanilla; fold in almonds.

3. Drop 8 mounds egg white mixture (about ⅓ cup each) in circle on 12-inch plate. Microwave uncovered on high (100%) until set, 1 to 2 minutes. Let stand 1 minute; remove from plate.

4. Top each slice pound cake with meringue and about 2 tablespoons pudding.

Chocolate-Almond Pudding

3   tablespoons sugar
1   tablespoon cornstarch
    Dash of salt
1   cup milk
1   ounce unsweetened chocolate,
    cut up

1   egg yolk, slightly beaten
1   tablespoon margarine or butter,
    softened (page 11)
1   tablespoon almond-flavored
    liqueur
1   teaspoon vanilla

1. Mix sugar, cornstarch and salt in 4-cup measure. Gradually stir in milk; add chocolate. Microwave uncovered on high (100%) 2 minutes; stir with fork. Microwave to boiling, 1 to 2 minutes longer.

2. Stir at least half of the hot mixture gradually into egg yolk. Blend into hot mixture in measure. Microwave uncovered on medium (50%) to boiling, 1 to 2 minutes. Stir in margarine, liqueur and vanilla. Cover surface of pudding with plastic wrap to prevent skin from forming. Refrigerate until cooled, about 1 hour.

Meringue-Topped Pound Cake

Lemon-Coconut Pudding Cake

6 servings

2   *eggs, separated*
¼   *teaspoon cream of tartar*
1   *teaspoon grated lemon peel*
¼   *cup lemon juice*
1   *cup milk*
1   *cup sugar*
¼   *cup all-purpose flour*
¼   *teaspoon salt*
¼   *cup toasted coconut (page 12)*

Whipped topping
Maraschino cherries

1. Beat egg whites and cream of tartar in 1½-quart bowl until stiff peaks form; set aside. Beat egg yolks slightly. Beat in lemon peel, lemon juice and milk. Add sugar, flour and salt; beat until smooth. Fold into beaten egg whites. Pour into 1-quart casserole; sprinkle with coconut.

2. Pour 1 cup very hot water in 1½-quart casserole in microwave. Carefully set casserole of pudding mixture in 1½-quart casserole. Microwave uncovered on medium-high (70%) until wooden pick inserted in center comes out clean, 10 to 12 minutes. Serve with whipped topping and a cherry.

Peanut-Fudge Pudding Cake

9 servings

1   *cup all-purpose flour*
¾   *cup sugar*
2   *tablespoons cocoa*
2   *teaspoons baking powder*
¼   *teaspoon salt*
½   *cup milk*
½   *cup chunky peanut butter*
2   *tablespoons vegetable oil*
1   *teaspoon vanilla*

1   *cup packed brown sugar*
¼   *cup cocoa*
1¾ *cups hot water*
    Ice cream

1. Mix flour, sugar, 2 tablespoons cocoa, baking powder and salt in a 2-quart casserole. Stir in milk, peanut butter, oil and vanilla until smooth.

2. Sprinkle with brown sugar and ¼ cup cocoa. Pour hot water over batter. Microwave uncovered on medium (50%) 9 minutes; rotate casserole ¼ turn. Microwave on high (100%) until top is almost dry, 5 to 7 minutes longer. While warm, spoon into dessert dishes and top with ice cream. Spoon sauce over ice cream.

Butterscotch Sundae Cake: Omit peanut butter. Add 1 package (6 ounces) butterscotch chips (1 cup). Decrease brown sugar to ½ cup and the ¼ cup cocoa to 2 tablespoons.

Chocolate Sundae Cake: Substitute 1 cup chopped nuts for the peanut butter.

Marshmallow-Fudge Sundae Cake: Omit peanut butter. Add ½ cup chopped nuts and ½ cup miniature marshmallows. Decrease brown sugar to ½ cup.

Raisin-Fudge Sundae Cake: Omit peanut butter. Add 1 cup raisins. Decrease brown sugar to ½ cup.

Apricot Upside-Down Gingerbread

9 servings

¼ cup margarine or butter
½ cup packed brown sugar
9 maraschino cherry halves
1 can (17 ounces) apricot halves, drained

1 package (14.5 ounces) gingerbread mix
Whipped topping

1. Place margarine in baking dish, 8 × 8 × 2 inches. Microwave uncovered on high (100%) until melted, 45 to 60 seconds. Sprinkle brown sugar on margarine. Arrange cherries and apricots on sugar mixture.

2. Prepare gingerbread mix as directed except — decrease water to ¾ cup. Pour batter over fruit. Elevate on 9-inch pie plate in microwave. Microwave uncovered on high (100%) 5 minutes; rotate baking dish ¼ turn. Microwave until gingerbread begins to pull away from sides of dish, 5 to 7 minutes longer. Let stand 5 minutes. Invert dish onto plate; leave dish over cake 5 minutes. Serve with topping.

Apple Upside-Down Gingerbread: Substitute 2 cups thinly-sliced apples (about 2 medium) for the apricots. Overlap in 3 rows in dish.

Lemon Upside-Down Gingerbread: Substitute 1 lemon for apricots. Cut lemon into 9 very thin slices (about ⅛ inch thick); cut each slice into fourths.

Apricot Upside-Down Gingerbread

Trifle (pictured on page 189)

8 *servings*

2 *cups milk*
1 *package (3⅛ ounces) vanilla
    pudding and pie filling*

12 *ladyfingers**
3 *tablespoons rum*
2 *cups sliced fresh strawberries*

1 *cup chilled whipping cream*
¼ *cup packed brown sugar*
½ *teaspoon vanilla*
2 *tablespoons slivered almonds,
    toasted (page 12)*

1. Stir milk into pudding mix in 4-cup measure. Microwave uncovered on high (100%) 3 minutes; stir with fork. Microwave to boiling, stirring every minute, 2 to 3 minutes longer. Cover surface of pudding with plastic wrap to prevent skin from forming. Refrigerate until cooled, about 2 hours.

2. Split ladyfingers lengthwise; arrange in 2-quart serving bowl, using as many as needed to line bowl. Sprinkle rum over ladyfingers. Layer pudding, strawberries and remaining ladyfingers in bowl.

3. Beat whipping cream, brown sugar and vanilla in chilled bowl until stiff. Spread over trifle; sprinkle with almonds. Refrigerate at least 1 hour. To serve, spoon into dessert dishes.

* 8 slices Glazed Pound Cake (page 194), about ½ inch thick, can be substituted for the ladyfingers. Omit Orange Glaze from pound cake; if desired, sprinkle remaining cake with powdered sugar or serve with fresh fruit.

Cherry Nut Cobbler

6 *servings*

1 *can (21 ounces) cherry pie filling*
¼ *teaspoon almond extract*

1 *cup buttermilk baking mix*
1 *tablespoon sugar*
¼ *cup milk*
1 *tablespoon margarine or butter,
    softened (page 11)*
2 *tablespoons almonds,
    toasted (page 12)*

1. Mix pie filling and almond extract in 1½-quart casserole. Microwave uncovered on medium-high (70%) 4 minutes; stir.

2. Mix baking mix, sugar, milk and margarine with fork until soft dough forms; beat vigorously 20 strokes. Stir in almonds. Drop 6 spoonfuls dough in circle on hot cherry mixture. Microwave uncovered on medium-high (70%) until top of dough is almost dry, 4 to 7 minutes. Let cool 10 minutes before serving. Serve with light cream if desired.

Blueberry Cobbler: Substitute 1 can (21 ounces) blueberry pie filling and ½ teaspoon grated orange peel for the cherry pie filling and almond extract.

Peach Cobbler: Substitute 1 can (21 ounces) peach pie filling and ¼ teaspoon ground mace for the cherry pie filling and almond extract.

Two-Fruit Shortcakes

Two-Fruit Shortcakes

4 *servings*

2   *tablespoons packed brown sugar*
1   *tablespoon cornstarch*
½   *cup orange juice*
¼   *cup water*

   Shortcakes (page 166)
2   *cups fresh raspberries,*
     strawberries or blueberries
2   *large firm bananas, sliced*
½   *cup whipped topping*

1. Mix brown sugar and cornstarch in 4-cup measure; stir in orange juice and water. Microwave uncovered on high (100%) stirring every minute, to boiling, about 2 minutes. Cover and refrigerate until cooled, about 1 hour.

2. Prepare and microwave shortcakes. Split shortcakes crosswise while hot. Fold raspberries and bananas into orange sauce. Fill and top shortcakes with fruit. Add spoonful of whipped topping to each shortcake.

Rhubarb with Strawberries

6 *servings*

4   *cups 1-inch pieces rhubarb*
     (about 1 pound)
¾   *to 1 cup sugar*
¼   *cup water*
1   *cup halved, fresh strawberries*

Mix rhubarb, sugar and water in 2-quart casserole. Cover tightly and microwave on high (100%) 5 minutes; stir. Cover and microwave until rhubarb is tender and slightly transparent, 3 to 5 minutes longer. Stir in strawberries.

Fruit with Currant Sauce

4 *servings*

⅓   *cup currant jelly*

2   *plums, cut into halves*
2   *peaches or pears, cut into halves*

1. Place jelly in 1-cup measure. Microwave uncovered on high (100%) until melted, about 1 minute; stir until smooth.

2. Arrange fruits cut sides down in 1½-quart casserole. Pour jelly over fruits. Cover tightly and microwave on high (100%) until fruits are almost tender when pierced with fork, 3 to 4 minutes. Let stand 3 minutes. Serve warm or chilled.

Flaming Fruit

8 *to* 10 *servings*

8   *to 10 scoops vanilla ice cream*
      (about ½ cup each)

1   *jar (10 ounces) currant jelly*

1   *cup pitted dark sweet cherries,*
      drained (reserve 2
      tablespoons syrup)
1   *can (11 ounces) mandarin*
      oranges, drained
¼   *cup rum*
1   *teaspoon grated orange peel*

¼   *cup brandy*

1. Scoop ice cream onto cookie sheet, freeze until ice cream is hard, about 2 hours.

2. Place jelly in 1-quart casserole. Microwave uncovered on high (100%), stirring every minute, until melted, 2 to 3 minutes.

3. Stir in cherries, reserved syrup, oranges, rum and orange peel. Microwave uncovered on high (100%) until hot, 1 to 2 minutes.

4. Pour brandy into 1-cup measure. Microwave uncovered on high (100%) 15 seconds. Fill metal ladle or serving spoon with brandy; pour remaining brandy over cherries and oranges. Ignite brandy in ladle and pour over fruit. Serve hot over ice cream.

Flaming Fruit

Berry Crumble

4 *to* 6 *servings*

3 *cups raspberries or blueberries*
    or 1 package (12 or 16
    ounces) frozen raspberries
    or blueberries
2 *tablespoons lemon juice*
⅔ *cup packed brown sugar*
½ *cup all-purpose or whole*
    wheat flour
⅔ *cup quick-cooking oats*
⅓ *cup margarine or butter, softened*
    (page 11)
¾ *teaspoon ground cinnamon*
¼ *teaspoon salt*
    Cream or ice cream

Spread raspberries in baking dish, 8 × 8 × 2 inches. Sprinkle with lemon juice. Mix brown sugar, flour, oats, margarine, cinnamon and salt; sprinkle on top. Microwave uncovered on high (100%), until raspberries are hot and bubbly, 7 to 10 minutes. Let stand 10 minutes. Serve warm with cream.

Banana Sundaes

4 *servings*

4 *scoops vanilla ice cream*
    (about ½ cup each)

⅓ *cup packed brown sugar*
¼ *cup margarine or butter*
½ *teaspoon ground cinnamon*
¼ *cup coffee-flavored liqueur*

4 *firm medium bananas*
4 *maraschino cherries (if desired)*

1. Scoop ice cream onto cookie sheet; freeze until ice cream is hard, about 2 hours.

2. Place brown sugar, margarine and cinnamon in 2-quart casserole. Microwave uncovered on high (100%) until hot and bubbly, 2 to 3 minutes; stir in liqueur.

3. Cut bananas into ½-inch diagonal slices; carefully stir into syrup. Microwave uncovered on high (100%) until bananas are hot, about 2 minutes. Serve hot over ice cream. Garnish each serving with a cherry.

Marmalade Pears

4 *servings*

⅓ *cup orange marmalade*
¼ *cup orange juice*
4 *pears, cut into halves**

½ *cup dairy sour cream*
1 *tablespoon orange marmalade*
   Mint leaves (if desired)

1. Mix ⅓ cup marmalade and the orange juice in baking dish, 8 × 8 × 2 inches or round baking dish, 8 × 1½ inches. Arrange pears cut sides down in sauce. Cover tightly and microwave on high (100%) until pears are almost tender when pierced with fork, 4 to 6 minutes. Let stand 3 minutes. Spoon into bowls; refrigerate.

2. Swirl sour cream and 1 tablespoon orange marmalade; spoon over pears. Garnish with mint leaves.

* 2 cans (16 ounces each) pear halves, drained, can be substituted for the fresh pear halves. Microwave until pears are hot, 3 to 4 minutes.

Glazed Oranges with Kiwis (pictured on page 188)

4 *servings*

3 *large seedless oranges*

¼ *cup sugar*
2 *teaspoons cornstarch*
½ *cup water*

1 *kiwi fruit, cut up, or*
   ½ cup raspberries or
   blueberries

1. Cut thin slivers of peel from 1 orange with vegetable parer or sharp knife, being careful not to cut into white membrane. Cover peel with boiling water; let stand 5 minutes. Drain.

2. Mix sugar and cornstarch in 2-cup measure; stir in water and orange peel. Microwave uncovered on high (100%), stirring every minute with fork, until thickened, 2 to 3 minutes. Let cool 5 minutes.

3. Pare oranges, cutting deep enough to remove all white membrane. Cut into slices. Pour syrup over slices; cover and refrigerate about 1 hour. Just before serving, fold in kiwi fruit.

Chocolate-Almond Brownies (pictured at right)   *About 2 dozen bars*

⅓ *cup shortening*
2 *ounces unsweetened chocolate*

1 *cup sugar*
¾ *cup all-purpose flour*
½ *teaspoon baking powder*
½ *teaspoon salt*
2 *eggs*
½ *cup chopped almonds*
½ *cup finely chopped almond paste*
       or semisweet chocolate chips

1. Place shortening and chocolate in baking dish, 8 × 8 × 2 inches. Microwave uncovered on medium-high (70%) until melted, 3 to 4 minutes.

2. Stir in remaining ingredients except almond paste. Mix in almond paste. Spread batter evenly. Elevate baking dish on inverted dinner plate in microwave. Microwave uncovered on medium (50%) 4 minutes; rotate baking dish ¼ turn. Microwave, rotating dish ¼ turn every 2 minutes, until wooden pick inserted about 1 inch from center comes out clean, 4 to 8 minutes longer. Let cool on heatproof surface (do not use rack). Cut into bars, about 2 × 1¼ inches.

Note: Store any leftover almond paste in refrigerator.

Chocolate Toffee Bars (pictured on page 189)   *About 2 dozen bars*

¼ *cup packed brown sugar*
3 *tablespoons margarine or butter*
½ *cup all-purpose flour*

1 *egg, beaten*
½ *cup packed brown sugar*
1 *tablespoon all-purpose flour*
½ *teaspoon baking powder*
½ *teaspoon vanilla*
¼ *teaspoon salt*
½ *cup semisweet chocolate chips*
½ *cup chopped nuts*

Chocolate Glaze (right)

1. Mix ¼ cup brown sugar and the margarine. Stir in ½ cup flour. Press firmly and evenly in baking dish, 8 × 8 × 2 inches. Elevate baking dish on inverted dinner plate in microwave. Microwave uncovered on medium (50%) 2 minutes; rotate baking dish ¼ turn. Microwave until mixture appears almost dry, 2 to 4 minutes longer. Let stand 5 minutes.

2. Mix egg, ½ cup brown sugar, 1 tablespoon flour, the baking powder, vanilla and salt. Stir in chocolate chips and nuts. Spread over cooked layer. Microwave (do not elevate) uncovered on medium (50%), rotating baking dish ¼ turn every 3 minutes, until bars begin to lose glossiness on top, 7 to 10 minutes. (Do not overcook.) Cover loosely and let stand 5 minutes.

4. Drizzle with Chocolate Glaze. Cut into bars, about 2 × 1¼ inches. Refrigerate until chocolate is firm, about 30 minutes.

Chocolate Glaze
Place 1 tablespoon cocoa, 1 tablespoon margarine or butter and 1 tablespoon water in 2-cup measure. Microwave uncovered on high (100%) until margarine is melted, 20 to 30 seconds; stir. Add ½ cup powdered sugar; mix until smooth.

Chocolate-Almond Brownies   Coconut Chews

Coconut Chews

About 2 dozen bars

⅓ cup powdered sugar
⅓ cup margarine or butter, softened
      (page 11)
¾ cup all-purpose or whole
      wheat flour

1 egg
½ cup packed brown sugar
1 tablespoon all-purpose flour
¼ teaspoon baking powder
¼ teaspoon salt
¼ teaspoon vanilla
¼ cup chopped walnuts
¼ cup flaked coconut
      Orange Frosting (right)

1. Mix powdered sugar and margarine. Stir in ¾ cup flour. Press firmly and evenly in baking dish, 8 × 8 × 2 inches. Elevate baking dish on inverted dinner plate in microwave. Microwave uncovered on medium (50%) 2 minutes; rotate baking dish ¼ turn. Microwave until mixture appears almost dry, 2 to 4 minutes longer.

2. Mix remaining ingredients except Orange Frosting. Spread over cooked layer. Microwave (do not elevate) uncovered on medium (50%) 3 minutes; rotate baking dish ¼ turn. Microwave until filling is set, 3 to 5 minutes longer; let cool on heatproof surface (do not use rack). Frost with Orange Frosting. Cut into bars, about 2 × 1¼ inches.

Orange Frosting
Place 1 tablespoon margarine or butter in 2-cup measure. Microwave uncovered until melted, about 15 seconds. Add 1 cup powdered sugar, 1 tablespoon orange juice and 1 teaspoon lemon juice; mix until smooth.

Pecan Chews: Substitute ½ cup chopped pecans for the walnuts and coconut.

Standard Pastry

9-inch One-crust Pastry
6 *tablespoons margarine*
1 *cup all-purpose or whole wheat flour (not stone-ground)*
½ *teaspoon salt*
2 *to 3 tablespoons cold water*

9-inch Two-crust Pastry
¾ *cup margarine*
2 *cups all-purpose or whole wheat flour (not stone-ground)*
1 *teaspoon salt*
4 *to 5 tablespoons cold water*

1. Cut margarine into flour and salt until particles are size of small peas. Sprinkle water in, 1 tablespoon at a time, tossing with fork until all flour is moistened and pastry almost cleans side of bowl (1 to 2 teaspoons water can be added if necessary).

2. Gather pastry into a ball; shape into flattened round on lightly floured cloth-covered board. (For Two-crust Pie, divide pastry into halves and shape into 2 rounds.) Roll pastry 2 inches larger than inverted pie plate with floured stockinet-covered rolling pin. Fold pastry into fourths; unfold and ease into plate, pressing firmly against bottom and side.

Microwaved 9-inch Pie Shell
Trim overhanging edge of pastry 1 inch from rim of plate. Fold and roll pastry under, even with plate; flute (page 208). (Hook fluted edge over edge of pie plate to prevent shrinking and help pastry retain its shape.) Prick bottom and side thoroughly with fork. Elevate pie plate on inverted dinner plate in microwave. Microwave uncovered on high (100%) until pastry looks dry and flaky, 5 to 7 minutes; let cool.

9-inch Two-crust Pie
Turn desired filling into pastry-lined pie plate. Trim overhanging edge of pastry ½ inch from rim of plate. Roll other round of pastry. Fold into fourths; cut slits so steam can escape. Place over filling and unfold. Trim overhanging edge of pastry 1 inch from rim of plate. Fold and roll top edge under lower edge, pressing on rim to seal; flute. Microwave as directed in recipes (pages 208 and 273).

Variations for Dessert Pastry

For flavor, texture and/or color in your pie crusts, stir one of the following into the flour for 9-inch One-crust Pastry: ⅛ teaspoon ground allspice, ½ cup finely shredded Cheddar cheese, 1 teaspoon ground cinnamon, ¼ cup yellow cornmeal, 1½ teaspoons grated lemon or orange peel, 2 tablespoons finely chopped nuts, 1 tablespoon toasted sesame seed or 2 tablespoons wheat germ. Double the amount for Two-crust Pastry.

Chocolate-Topped Peanut Pie

Chocolate-Topped Peanut Pie

One 9-inch pie

Cookie Pat Crust (below)

⅓   cup margarine or butter

1   cup corn syrup
⅔   cup sugar
1   tablespoon all-purpose flour
½   teaspoon salt
3   eggs
1   cup salted peanuts, coarsely
      chopped

½   cup semisweet chocolate chips

1. Prepare cookie crust.

2. Place margarine in 2½-quart bowl. Microwave uncovered on high (100%) until margarine is melted, 45 to 60 seconds.

3. Stir in corn syrup, sugar, flour, salt and eggs; beat with hand beater until smooth. Stir in peanuts. Microwave uncovered on medium (50%), stirring every 2 minutes, until hot, 5 to 7 minutes.

4. Pour mixture into crust. Elevate pie plate on inverted dinner plate in microwave. Microwave uncovered on medium (50%), rotating ¼ turn every 3 minutes, until filling is almost set, 9 to 13 minutes.

5. Sprinkle with chocolate chips. Let stand 30 minutes. Refrigerate at least 2 hours.

Cookie Pat Crust
½   cup margarine or butter
1   cup all-purpose flour
¼   cup finely chopped peanuts
¼   cup powdered sugar

Place margarine in 1½-quart bowl. Microwave uncovered on medium-low (30%) until soft, 30 to 45 seconds. Mix in remaining ingredients with hands to form soft dough. Press with floured fingers firmly and evenly against bottom and side of 9-inch pie plate. Elevate pie plate on inverted dinner plate in microwave. Microwave on high (100%) 3 minutes; rotate ½ turn. Microwave until dry and flaky, 2 to 4 minutes longer. Let cool on heatproof surface (do not use rack).

Southern Blueberry Pie

One 9-inch pie

Microwaved 9-inch Pie Shell
  (page 206)
¼ cup yellow cornmeal

3 cups fresh or frozen (defrosted
     and drained) blueberries
½ cup sugar
1 tablespoon plus 2 teaspoons
     cornstarch
¼ teaspoon salt
¼ teaspoon ground cinnamon
⅔ cup water

¼ cup grenadine syrup
2 teaspoons lemon juice

Sour Cream or Whipped Cream
  Topping (right)

1. Prepare pie shell as directed except — stir in ¼ cup cornmeal with the flour.

2. Spread blueberries in pie shell. Mix sugar, cornstarch, salt and cinnamon in 4-cup measure. Stir in water. Microwave uncovered on high (100%) stirring every minute until thickened and clear, 3 to 4 minutes.

3. Stir in grenadine syrup and lemon juice. Pour on blueberries in pie shell. Refrigerate at least 2 hours.

4. Serve with Sour Cream or Whipped Cream Topping.

Sour Cream Topping
Mix 1 cup dairy sour cream, 2 tablespoons sugar and 1 teaspoon vanilla.

Whipped Cream Topping
Beat ½ cup chilled whipping cream and 1 tablespoon packed brown sugar in chilled bowl until stiff.

Fresh Apple Pie (pictured on page 188)

One 9-inch pie

9-inch Two-crust Pastry
  (page 206)

¾ cup sugar
¼ cup all-purpose or whole wheat
     flour (not stone-ground)
½ teaspoon ground nutmeg
½ teaspoon ground cinnamon
   Dash of salt
6 or 7 cups thinly sliced pared tart
     apples (about 6 medium)
2 tablespoons margarine or butter

1. Prepare pastry.

2. Mix sugar, flour, nutmeg, cinnamon and salt. Stir in apples. Turn into pastry-lined pie plate; dot with margarine. Cover with top crust that has slits cut in it; seal and flute. Microwave uncovered on high (100%) until filling begins to bubble through slits in crust, 10 to 12 minutes.

3. Transfer pie to conventional oven (do not preheat). Bake at 450° until crust is brown and flaky, 12 to 18 minutes.

Fluting Pie Edges

Fluting the rim around one- and two-crust pies adds a festive touch. To make a *rope edge* (page 188), place your thumb on the pastry rim at an angle. Pinch pastry between your thumb and first knuckle of your index finger; repeat as your hand moves around pie. To make a *pinch edge* (right), place index finger on the inside of pastry rim, with thumb and index finger on the outside. Pinch pastry into "v" shape; pinch again to sharpen points as your hand moves around pie. Hook fluted points over rim of plate with thumb and finger.

Tart Shells

6 tart shells

1. Prepare 9-inch One-crust Pastry (page 206) except — roll into 13-inch circle about ⅛ inch thick. Cut circle into six 4½-inch rounds. Shape pastry rounds over backs of six 6-ounce custard cups, making pleats so pastry will fit closely. Prick thoroughly with fork to prevent puffing.

2. Arrange custard cups in circle on 12-inch plate. Microwave uncovered on high (100%) 3 minutes; rotate plate ½ turn. Microwave until tart shells are dry and flaky, about 2 minutes longer. Let stand 5 minutes. Loosen edge of each tart with tip of knife; carefully remove each tart shell from cup. Let cool on rack.

Note: To cut circles easily, cut around a 10-ounce custard cup; the diameter measures about 4½ inches.

Roll pastry on cloth-covered board into 13-inch circle.

Cut circle around custard cups into six 4-inch rounds.

Shape pastry rounds over backs of custard cups.

Prick pastry rounds with fork to prevent puffing.

Loosen cooked tarts with knife tip before removing.

Add filling and topping for Cheesecake Tarts (page 211).

Cheesecake Tarts (pictured at left)

6 *tarts*

Tart Shells (page 210)

1 *package (8 ounces) cream cheese*
⅓ *cup sugar*
1 *egg*
1 *teaspoon grated lemon peel*
1 *teaspoon vanilla*

Cheesecake Topping (right)

1. Prepare tart shells.

2. Place cream cheese in 1½-quart bowl. Microwave uncovered on medium (50%) until softened, 60 to 90 seconds. Add sugar, egg, lemon peel and vanilla; beat with hand beater until smooth, about 2 minutes. Microwave uncovered on medium (50%), stirring every 2 minutes, until hot and thickened, 4 to 5 minutes.

3. Spread about 3 tablespoons cheese mixture in each tart shell. Prepare Cheesecake Topping; carefully spread over tarts. Refrigerate until chilled, about 1½ hours. Serve wth sweetened strawberries if desired.

Cheesecake Topping
Mix ½ cup dairy sour cream, 1 tablespoon sugar and 1 teaspoon vanilla.

Custard

About 6 servings

2½ *cups milk*

4 *eggs*
⅓ *cup sugar*
Dash of salt
1 *teaspoon vanilla*
Nutmeg

1. Pour milk into 4-cup measure. Microwave uncovered on high (100%) 4 minutes.

2. Beat eggs, sugar, salt and vanilla in 1½-quart bowl. Gradually stir in hot milk. Pour into 6-cup ring mold. Sprinkle with nutmeg. Cover loosely and microwave on medium (50%) until edges begin to set, 5 to 8 minutes; rotate ring mold ½ turn. Microwave on medium-low (30%) until knife inserted in 3 or 4 places halfway between center and edge comes out clean, 5 to 7 minutes longer. Cover and refrigerate 3 hours. Loosen around sides with knife and unmold.

Individual Custards: Pour custard mixture into eight 6-ounce custard cups. Sprinkle with nutmeg. Arrange cups in circle on 12-inch plate. Cover with waxed paper and microwave on medium (50%) until edges begin to set, 5 to 8 minutes, rotate plate ½ turn. Microwave on medium-low (30%) until centers are almost set, 5 to 7 minutes longer. (Remove individual custards as centers become set; check remaining custards every minute.)

Mallow Mint Parfaits

6 servings

24   *large marshmallows*
½   *cup milk*
1   *teaspoon vanilla*
⅛   *teaspoon salt*
6   *drops peppermint extract*
6   *drops red or green food color*

  Chocolate Cookie Crumbs (right)

1   *cup chilled whipping cream*

1. Place marshmallows and milk in 3-quart casserole. Cover tightly and microwave on high (100%) until marshmallows are melted, 3 to 4 minutes. Stir in vanilla, salt, peppermint extract and food color. Refrigerate, stirring occasionally, until mixture mounds slightly when dropped from spoon, about 20 minutes.

2. Prepare Chocolate Cookie Crumbs.

3. Beat whipping cream in chilled bowl until stiff. Stir marshmallow mixture until smooth; fold into whipped cream. Layer creamy mixture and Chocolate Cookie Crumbs in each of 6 parfait glasses, using about 2 tablespoons crumbs for each glass, and ending with crumbs on top. Refrigerate at least 1 hour.

Chocolate Cookie Crumbs
Mix ¾ cup chocolate cookie crumbs (about 14 chocolate wafers), 2 tablespoons margarine or butter and 1 tablespoon sugar in 2-cup measure. Microwave uncovered on high (100%) until margarine is melted, about 1 minute; stir. Let cool 10 minutes.

Mallow Mint Parfaits

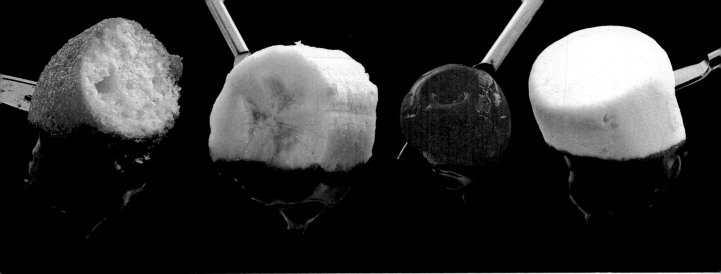

Spiced Chocolate Fondue

6 to 8 servings

1 *package (12 ounces) semisweet chocolate chips*
½ *cup light corn syrup*

¼ *cup milk*
2 *tablespoons coffee-flavored liqueur*
¼ *teaspoon ground cinnamon*
  Dippers (right)

1. Place chocolate chips and corn syrup in 4-cup measure. Microwave uncovered on medium (50%), until mixture can be stirred smooth, 1½ to 2 minutes.

2. Stir in milk, liqueur and cinnamon. Microwave uncovered on medium (50%), stirring every minute, until warm, 2 to 3 minutes. Pour into fondue pot or chafing dish to keep warm. If mixture becomes too thick, stir in small amount of milk. Serve with Dippers and fondue forks.

Dippers
Cake doughnut slices, banana slices, cherries, marshmallows, cake cubes and pretzels.

Golden Fondue

About 6 servings

1 *cup sugar*
3 *tablespoons cornstarch*
¼ *teaspoon salt*
1 *cup orange juice*
¼ *cup lemon juice*
¼ *cup hot water*

1 *tablespoon margarine or butter*
1 *teaspoon grated orange peel*
1 *teaspoon grated lemon peel*
  Dippers (right)

1. Mix sugar, cornstarch and salt in 1½-quart casserole. Slowly stir in orange juice, lemon juice and water. Microwave uncovered on high (100%), stirring every 2 minutes, until mixture thickens and boils, 6 to 7 minutes.

2. Stir in margarine, orange peel and lemon peel. Pour into dessert fondue pot to keep warm. Serve with Dippers and fondue forks.

Dippers
Cake cubes, cantaloupe balls, cream cheese squares rolled in toasted sesame seed, nut-stuffed dates, doughnut slices, cake doughnuts and day-old gingerbread squares.

APPETIZERS & SNACKS

Clear Beef Soup

Clear Beef Soup

6 *servings (about ½ cup each)*

3   *cups hot water*
1   *tablespoon instant beef bouillon*
1   *teaspoon soy sauce*

6   *mushrooms*
6   *thin lemon slices*
6   *parsley sprigs*

1. Mix water, bouillon and soy sauce in 4-cup measure. Microwave uncovered on high (100%) to boiling, 5 to 7 minutes.

2. Slice mushrooms into 6 small bowls; add lemon slices and broth. Garnish with parsley.

French Onion Soup (pictured on page 214)

4 *servings (about 1 cup each)*

2   *medium onions, sliced*
2   *tablespoons margarine or butter*

2   *cans (10½ ounces each) condensed beef broth**
2   *cups hot water*
1   *teaspoon Worcestershire sauce*

Thin slices French bread, toasted
Grated Parmesan cheese

1. Place onions and margarine in 2-quart casserole. Cover tightly and microwave on high (100%) 2 minutes; stir. Cover and microwave until tender, 2 to 3 minutes.

2. Stir in broth, water and Worcestershire sauce. Cover tightly and microwave on high (100%) to boiling, 8 to 10 minutes.

3. Divide ½ of soup among 4 bowls; add toast. Pour remaining hot soup over toast; sprinkle with cheese.

* If desired, ¼ cup finely chopped carrots, ¼ cup finely chopped celery, 2 sprigs parsley, 2 small bay leaves and ⅛ teaspoon thyme leaves can be added to the beef broth. Microwave until vegetables are tender, 10 to 12 minutes; strain.

Pictured on previous page: Fruit-Nut Nibbles, French Onion Soup, Mulled Tomato Juice, Party Cheese Log, Chocolate Caramel Apples

Cream of Almond Soup

Cream of Almond Soup

8 *servings (about ½ cup each)*

1	*tablespoon margarine or butter*
1	*tablespoon all-purpose flour*
¾	*teaspoon salt*
⅛	*teaspoon pepper*
1½	*cups chicken broth or bouillon*
½	*cup finely chopped almonds, toasted*
2	*cups half-and-half*
2	*teaspoons grated lemon peel*
	Paprika
	Snipped parsley

1. Place margarine in 1½-quart casserole. Microwave uncovered on high (100%) until melted, 15 to 30 seconds. Stir in flour, salt and pepper. Gradually stir in chicken broth and almonds. Cover tightly and microwave 2 minutes; stir. Cover and microwave to boiling, 1 to 3 minutes longer.

2. Stir in half-and-half. Cover tightly and microwave on medium-high (70%) until hot, 4 to 6 minutes; stir. Sprinkle with lemon peel, paprika and parsley.

Zucchini Soup

8 *servings (about ⅔ cup each)*

3	*cups sliced zucchini (about ¾ pound)*
3	*tablespoons chopped onion*
1	*clove garlic, crushed*
1	*can (10¾ ounces) cream of mushroom soup (⅔ cup)*
2	*cups water*
1	*teaspoon salt*
⅛	*teaspoon dried oregano leaves*
	Dash of pepper
	Sour cream

1. Place zucchini, onion and garlic in 2-quart casserole. Cover tightly and microwave on high (100%) 3 minutes; stir. Cover and microwave until vegetables are tender, 2 to 4 minutes longer.

2. Place remaining ingredients except sour cream with zucchini mixture in blender container. Cover and blend on medium-high speed until smooth, about 30 seconds.

3. Return mixture to casserole. Cover tightly and microwave on high (100%) 3 minutes; stir. Cover and microwave until hot and bubbly, 2 to 4 minutes longer. Top each serving with spoonful of sour cream.

Beet-Cabbage Soup

8 *servings (½ cup each)*

1 *tablespoon plus 1 teaspoon*
    instant beef bouillon
1½ *cups boiling water*
1 *can (16 ounces) shoestring beets*
2 *cups coarsely shredded cabbage*
    (about ½ pound)
3 *tablespoons finely chopped onion*
1 *teaspoon sugar*

1 *tablespoon vinegar*
    Plain yogurt

1. Stir beef bouillon, water, beets (with liquid), cabbage, onion and sugar in 1½-quart casserole. Cover tightly and microwave on high (100%) 5 minutes; stir. Cover and microwave until cabbage is tender, 7 to 9 minutes longer.

2. Stir in vinegar; refrigerate until chilled. Top each serving with spoonful of yogurt.

Fruit Soup

6 *servings (about ½ cup each)*

2 *tablespoons sugar*
2 *tablespoons cornstarch*
    Dash of salt
⅔ *cup medium red wine*
1 *cup hot water*

¼ *teaspoon ground nutmeg*
1 *cup cranberry juice*

3 *cups assorted fresh fruit*
    (strawberries, sliced bananas,
    seedless green grapes,
    cut-up cantaloupe)
    Sour cream or whipped topping

1. Mix sugar, cornstarch and salt in 1½-quart casserole; stir in wine and water. Cover tightly and microwave on high (100%) 2 minutes; stir. Cover and microwave until mixture is thickened and clear, 2 to 4 minutes longer.

2. Stir in nutmeg and cranberry juice. Cover and refrigerate until chilled.

3. Stir in fruit. Top each serving with spoonful of sour cream.

Note: Fruit Soup can also be served as a dessert.

Fruit Soup

Taco Salad Dip

About 3½ cups dip

½ *pound ground beef*

1 *can (15½ ounces) mashed refried beans*
1 *can (8 ounces) tomato sauce*
1 *package (1¼ ounces) taco seasoning mix*
¼ *cup finely chopped onion (about 1 small)*
¼ *cup finely chopped green pepper*
2 *to 3 drops red pepper sauce*
1 *small clove garlic, finely chopped*

Sour Cream Topping (right)
Finely shredded lettuce
Shredded Cheddar cheese
Corn chips

1. Crumble ground beef into 1½-quart casserole. Cover loosely and microwave on high (100%) until very little pink remains, 2½ to 3½ minutes; stir and drain.

2. Stir in beans, tomato sauce, seasoning mix, onion, green pepper, pepper sauce and garlic. Cover tightly and microwave on high (100%) 3 minutes; stir. Spread mixture in 9-inch pie plate. Cover and microwave until hot and bubbly, 3 to 4 minutes longer.

3. Mound Sour Cream Topping in center of beef mixture; sprinkle with shredded lettuce and cheese. Serve with corn chips.

Sour Cream Topping
Mix ½ cup dairy sour cream, 1 tablespoon grated American cheese food and ⅛ teaspoon chili powder.

Curried Tuna Dip

1½ *cups dip*

1 *package (8 ounces) cream cheese*

1 *teaspoon curry powder*
1 *can (6½ ounces) chunk tuna,*
  drained

1. Place cream cheese in 1-quart casserole. Microwave uncovered on medium (50%) until cheese is softened, 1 to 1½ minutes.

2. Stir in curry powder and tuna. Microwave uncovered on high (100%) 1 minute; stir. Microwave until hot, 1 to 2 minutes longer; stir.

Artichoke Hearts with Hollandaise Dip

3 *or 4 servings*

Place 1 package (9 ounces) frozen artichoke hearts, 1 lemon slice and 1 tablespoon water in 1-quart casserole. Cover tightly and microwave on high (100%) 3 minutes; stir. Cover and microwave until tender, 2 to 4 minutes longer; drain. Refrigerate until chilled, about 3 hours. Serve artichokes and Hollandaise Sauce (below) with wooden picks.

Hollandaise Sauce
3 *tablespoons margarine or butter*

1 *tablespoon lemon juice*
2 *teaspoons water*
1 *egg yolk*

1. Place margarine in 1-cup measure. Microwave uncovered on high (100%) until margarine is melted, 30 to 45 seconds.

2. Add lemon juice and water. Beat in egg yolk with fork. Microwave uncovered on medium (50%), stirring every 15 seconds, until thickened, 40 to 65 seconds. (Do not overcook or dip will curdle.) Cover and refrigerate until chilled but no longer than 2 days. Before serving, stir in 1 teaspoon hot water if necessary for smooth consistency. Refrigerate any leftover dip.

Red Bean and Bacon Dip

1½ cups dip

3 slices bacon, diced

1 can (8 ounces) red kidney beans,
   drained

1 cup dairy sour cream
1 tablespoon chopped green pepper
1 teaspoon instant minced onion
¼ teaspoon salt
⅛ teaspoon garlic powder
⅛ teaspoon pepper
   Tortilla chips

1. Place bacon in 1½-quart casserole. Cover with paper towel and microwave on high (100%) 2 minutes; stir. Cover and microwave until crisp, 1 to 2 minutes longer.

2. Stir in beans; mash with fork. Cover tightly and microwave on high (100%) until hot, 2 to 3 minutes.

3. Stir remaining ingredients except tortilla chips into bean mixture. Cover tightly and microwave on high (100%) until hot, about 1 minute. Serve with tortilla chips.

Bacon Crackers

About 3 dozen appetizers

½ cup mayonnaise or salad
   dressing
1 teaspoon Worcestershire sauce
¼ teaspoon salad seasoning
⅛ teaspoon paprika
1 cup shredded Cheddar cheese
   (about 4 ounces)
4 slices bacon, crisply cooked
   and crumbled (page 11)
3 tablespoons chopped salted
   peanuts
2 tablespoons chopped onion
32 to 36 round crackers

Mix mayonnaise, Worcestershire sauce, salad seasoning and paprika. Stir in cheese, bacon, peanuts and onion. Spread about ½ tablespoon mixture over each cracker. Arrange 8 or 9 crackers at a time in circle on plate. Microwave uncovered on high (100%) until hot and puffed, about 30 seconds.

Bacon Crackers

Party Cheese Log (pictured on page 214)

About 6 servings

1 *package (8 ounces) cream cheese*
¼ *cup crumbled blue cheese*
   (about 2 ounces)
1 *cup shredded sharp Cheddar*
   cheese (about 4 ounces)
¼ *cup finely chopped onion*
   (about 1 small)
1 *tablespoon Worcestershire sauce*

⅓ *cup finely snipped parsley or*
   chopped nuts

1. Place cream cheese in 1-quart bowl. Microwave uncovered on medium (50%) 1 minute; stir in blue and Cheddar cheeses, onion and Worcestershire sauce. Microwave until cheeses are softened, about 1 minute longer.

2. Beat cheese mixture on low speed until blended; beat on medium speed, scraping bowl constantly, until fluffy, about 1 minute. Refrigerate 1 hour.

3. Using waxed paper, shape cheese mixture into 6-inch log shape; roll in parsley. Cover; refrigerate until firm, about 2 hours.

Appetizer Pâté

About 1 cup spread

8 *ounces chicken livers*
½ *cup hot water*
1 *teaspoon instant chicken bouillon*
¼ *cup chopped onion*
¼ *teaspoon dried basil leaves*

3 *slices bacon, crisply cooked*
   (page 11) and crumbled
¼ *cup margarine or butter,*
   softened (page 11)
¼ *teaspoon dry mustard*
⅛ *teaspoon garlic salt*
   Dash of pepper

Snipped parsley
Sesame seed crackers

1. Prick chicken livers with fork and place in 1½-quart casserole with water, bouillon, onion and basil. Cover tightly and microwave on high (100%) 3 minutes; stir. Cover and microwave on medium (50%) until no longer pink, 8 to 10 minutes longer. Let cool about 15 minutes. Drain, reserving ¼ cup broth.

2. Chop chicken livers; mix with reserved broth and remaining ingredients except parsley and crackers. Place in blender container. Cover and blend on high speed until smooth, scraping blender container frequently, about 2 minutes. Mound in serving dish. Cover and refrigerate at least 3 hours but no longer than 2 days.

3. Sprinkle with parsley and serve with crackers.

Individual Appetizer Pâtés: Divide mixture among eight 1¾-inch paper nut cups. At serving time, peel off paper cups and invert on individual plates.

Microwaving Appetizers

Your "microwave helper" is especially good with appetizers — from starter soups to cheese spreads and fondues to hot individual nibbles that can be heated and served on the same paper plate. For casual party snack menus with timing and reheating tips, see pages 254 to 259.

Golden Mushrooms

Golden Mushrooms

About 4 dozen appetizers

1	*pound medium mushrooms*
¼	*cup chopped onion*
¼	*cup chopped celery*
	(about 1 small stalk)
3	*tablespoons margarine or butter*
1½	*cups soft bread crumbs*
¼	*teaspoon salt*
¼	*teaspoon dried marjoram*
¼	*teaspoon pepper*
⅛	*to ¼ teaspoon ground turmeric*

1. Cut stems from mushrooms; finely chop enough stems to measure ⅓ cup. Mix chopped mushroom stems, onion, celery and margarine in 1-quart casserole. Microwave uncovered on high (100%) until onion is tender, 2 to 3 minutes. Stir in bread crumbs, salt, marjoram, pepper and turmeric.

2. Fill mushroom caps with stuffing mixture; arrange mushrooms filled sides up (smallest mushrooms in center) on two 10-inch plates. Microwave one plate at a time uncovered on high (100%) 2 minutes; rotate plate ½ turn. Microwave until hot, 1 to 2 minutes longer.

Basic Meatballs

About 2 dozen meatballs

1	*pound ground beef*
½	*cup dry bread crumbs*
¼	*cup milk*
¼	*cup finely chopped onion*
	(about 1 small)
1	*egg*
1	*teaspoon Worcestershire sauce*
¾	*teaspoon salt*
⅛	*teaspoon pepper*

Mix all ingredients; shape by tablespoonfuls into 1½-inch balls. (For ease in shaping meatballs, occasionally wet hands with cold water.) Arrange meatballs in baking dish, 12 × 7½ × 2 inches. Cover loosely and microwave on high (100%) 3 minutes; rearrange meatballs. Cover and microwave until no longer pink inside, 5 to 7 minutes longer. Let stand 3 minutes; drain.

Tiny Coconut-Chutney Meatballs

About 8 dozen meatballs

Basic Meatballs (page 223)
½ *cup flaked coconut*

⅓ *cup currant or grape jelly*
⅓ *cup chopped chutney or chutney sauce*
2 *tablespoons dry red wine or orange juice*
2 *teaspoons dry mustard*

1. Prepare Basic Meatballs except — add coconut before mixing ingredients and shape mixture by teaspoonfuls into ¾-inch balls. Arrange in 2 baking dishes, 8 × 8 × 2 inches. Cover loosely and microwave one dish at a time on high (100%) 3 minutes; rearrange meatballs. Cover and microwave until no longer pink inside, 1 to 3 minutes longer.

2. Mix remaining ingredients in 2-quart casserole. Cover tightly and microwave on high (100%) 2 minutes; stir in meatballs. Cover and microwave until meatballs are hot, 2 to 4 minutes longer. Serve with wooden picks.

Chili-Cheese Meatballs

About 3 dozen meatballs

Basic Meatballs (page 223)

8 *ounces pasteurized process cheese spread loaf, cut up*

1 *small tomato, chopped*
1 *tablespoon chopped green chilies*

1. Prepare and microwave Basic Meatballs as directed, except — shape mixture by rounded teaspoonfuls into 1¼-inch balls.

2. Place cheese in 1-quart casserole. Microwave uncovered on high (100%) until melted, 1 to 2 minutes.

3. Stir in tomato and chilies. Microwave until tomato is hot, 1 to 2 minutes. Transfer meatballs to serving dish with slotted spoon. Serve with cheese mixture and wooden picks.

Chili-Cheese Meatballs

Cocktail Wiener Kabobs   Teriyaki Kabobs

Cocktail Wiener Kabobs

1 dozen kabobs

24 *cocktail wieners*
 1 *small zucchini, cut into 12 slices*
 1 *can (4 ounces) button*
      mushrooms, drained
12 *small cherry tomatoes*
12 *large pimiento-stuffed olives*
½ *medium green pepper,*
      cut into 1-inch squares
      Lemon Butter (right)

Alternate 2 wieners and the vegetables on each bamboo skewer. Place kabobs on 12-inch plate; brush with Lemon Butter. Cover with waxed paper and microwave on high (100%) until hot, 3 to 4 minutes.

Lemon Butter
Mix 2 tablespoons melted margarine or butter, 1 teaspoon lemon juice and dash of red pepper sauce.

Teriyaki Kabobs

7 or 8 kabobs

 1 *pound beef round steak,*
      1¼ inches thick
¼ *cup soy sauce*
 2 *tablespoons water*
 2 *tablespoons honey*
¼ *teaspoon garlic salt*
¼ *teaspoon ground allspice*
⅛ *teaspoon ground ginger*

 2 *bunches green onions*

1. Trim fat and bone from beef steak; cut beef into strips, 1¼ × ¼ inch. Place in glass bowl. Mix remaining ingredients except onions; pour over beef.

2. Trim green tops from onions; cut onions into 1-inch pieces. Alternate 3 pieces meat and 2 pieces onion on each bamboo skewer.

3. Arrange skewers in baking dish, 12 × 7½ × 2 inches or on 12-inch plate. Cover loosely and microwave on high (100%) 2 minutes; rotate baking dish ½ turn. Microwave until almost done, 1 to 2 minutes longer; let stand 3 minutes.

Barbecued Ham Nibbles

About 4 dozen appetizers

1. Prepare Zesty Barbecue Sauce (below).

2. Trim fat from 1 fully cooked center-cut smoked ham slice, ¾ inch thick (about 1½ pounds). Cut ham into 1-inch pieces. Secure on wooden picks and arrange in baking dish, 12 × 7½ × 2 inches. Cover tightly and microwave on high (100%) 3 minutes; rotate baking dish ½ turn. Microwave until hot, 2 to 4 minutes longer. Serve with Zesty Barbecue Sauce.

Zesty Barbecue Sauce
½   *cup catsup*
2   *tablespoons chopped onion*
2   *tablespoons packed brown sugar*
1   *teaspoon Worcestershire sauce*
¼   *teaspoon dry mustard*
1   *clove garlic, finely chopped*

Mix all ingredients in 2-cup measure. Cover loosely and microwave on high (100%) 2 minutes; stir. Cover and microwave until sauce is hot and bubbly, about 1 minute longer.

Little Barbecued Ribs

About 1 dozen appetizers

2   *pounds fresh pork spareribs,*
    cut across bones into halves
¼   *cup soy sauce*
¼   *cup chili sauce*
2   *tablespoons packed brown sugar*
2   *tablespoons dry white wine*
2   *small cloves garlic, finely chopped*

1. Cut spareribs between each rib into individual pieces. Place ribs meaty sides up in baking dish, 12 × 7½ × 2 inches. Mix remaining ingredients; spoon over ribs. Cover and refrigerate at least 2 hours.

2. Remove ½ each of ribs and marinade. Cover with waxed paper and microwave on medium (50%), rotating baking dish ½ turn every 3 minutes until done, 24 to 26 minutes. Repeat.

Glazed Pork Tenderloin Appetizers

6 small sandwiches

1   *pork tenderloin (10 to 12*
    ounces)
⅛   *teaspoon salt*
¼   *cup tomato preserves or*
    orange marmalade
1   *drop liquid smoke (if desired)*

12   *slices party rye bread (about*
    2 inches in diameter)

1. Place pork tenderloin on roasting rack in dish. Mix salt, preserves and liquid smoke; brush half of mixture on tenderloin. Cover with waxed paper and microwave on medium (50%) 6 minutes; turn tenderloin over. Brush with remaining preserves. Cover and microwave until meat thermometer registers 170°, 3 to 5 minutes longer; let stand 3 minutes.

2. Cut meat diagonally into thin slices. For each serving, place 2 slices meat between 2 slices rye bread. Serve with additional tomato preserves if desired.

Bacon Wrap-Arounds

1 dozen appetizers

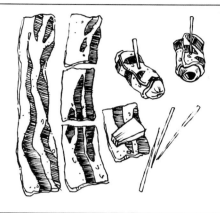

1. Cut 4 bacon slices into thirds. Wrap a bacon slice around any of the following: large pitted black olive, 2 dried apricot halves, cooked Brussels sprout half, bite-size piece of cooked artichoke heart, pineapple chunk, frankfurter chunk, bite-size piece of smoked cocktail sausage. Fasten with wooden pick.

2. Arrange Wrap-Arounds in circle on paper towel-lined plate. Cover with paper towel and microwave on high (100%) 3 minutes; rotate plate ¼ turn. Microwave until bacon is crisp, 2 to 4 minutes longer. Remove from paper towel while hot.

Chili-Shrimp with Bacon

About 2 dozen appetizers

1 *package (9 ounces) frozen deveined and peeled shrimp (about 20)*
1 *tablespoon water*

½ *cup chili sauce*
½ *clove garlic, finely chopped*

10 *slices bacon, cut into halves*

1. Arrange frozen shrimp in circle in 9-inch pie plate; add water. Cover tightly and microwave on high (100%) 2 minutes; rotate pie plate ½ turn. Microwave until almost done, 2 to 3 minutes longer; drain.

2. Mix chili sauce and garlic; pour over shrimp. Cover and refrigerate about 1 hour.

3. Layer ⅓ of bacon between towels on 10-inch plate. Repeat 2 times. Microwave on high (100%) until partially cooked, 4 to 6 minutes. Wrap each shrimp in bacon piece; secure with wooden pick.

4. Arrange 10 shrimp at a time in circle on paper towel-lined plate. Cover with paper towel and microwave on high (100%) until bacon is crisp, 3 to 4 minutes.

Pour chili-garlic sauce on cooked shrimp; refrigerate.

Microwave bacon in paper towels until partly cooked.

Microwave bacon-wrapped shrimp until bacon is crisp.

Lemon-Gingered Shrimp   Oysters Parmesan

Lemon-Gingered Shrimp

15 or 16 appetizer servings

1½ *pounds medium frozen deveined and peeled shrimp*
¼   *cup soy sauce*
¼   *cup lemon juice*
2   *tablespoons sugar*
2   *tablespoons dry white wine*
¼   *teaspoon ground ginger*

1. Arrange frozen shrimp in baking dish, 12 × 7½ × 2 inches. Mix soy sauce, lemon juice, sugar, wine and ginger. Pour over shrimp and stir. Cover tightly and microwave on high (100%) 6 minutes; stir. Cover and microwave until done, 6 to 8 minutes longer.

2. To serve hot, let stand 5 minutes. To serve cold, refrigerate about 3 hours. Remove shrimp from marinade with slotted spoon; arrange on serving plate. Garnish with green onion tops if desired.

Oysters Parmesan (pictured at left)   12 *oysters*

Rock salt
12 medium oysters in shells,
      shucked (page 13)
¼ cup dairy sour cream
½ cup grated Parmesan cheese
¼ cup cracker crumbs
¼ cup margarine or butter,
      melted (page 11)
½ teaspoon dry mustard

1. Fill two 9-inch pie plates ½-inch deep with rock salt (about 2 cups each plate). Place oyster on deep half of shell; discard other half. Spoon 1 teaspoon sour cream onto oyster in each shell. Mix Parmesan cheese, crumbs, margarine and mustard. Spoon about 2 teaspoons cheese mixture onto each oyster.

2. Arrange filled shells in circle on rock salt. Microwave one plate at a time uncovered on high (100%) 1 minute; rotate pie plate ½ turn. Microwave until oysters are hot and bubbly, 1½ to 2½ minutes longer.

Note: If desired, oysters can be microwaved without rock salt. Decrease microwave time by 1 minute.

Oysters Rumaki   2 *dozen appetizers*

12 slices bacon, cut into halves

24 large fresh or frozen (defrosted)
      shucked oysters
½ teaspoon salt
¼ teaspoon pepper

1. Layer ⅓ of bacon between paper towels on 10-inch plate. Repeat 2 times. Microwave on high (100%) until partially cooked, 4 to 6 minutes.

2. Drain oysters; dry on paper towels. Sprinkle oysters with salt and pepper. Wrap each in bacon piece; secure with wooden pick. (At this point rumakis can be covered and refrigerated about 2 hours). Arrange 12 rumakis at a time in circle on plate lined with 2 paper towels, or microwave rack in baking dish. Cover with paper towel and microwave on high (100%) 3 minutes; rotate plate ½ turn. Microwave until bacon is crisp, 3 to 4 minutes longer.

Parslied Scallops   About 4 *appetizer servings*

1 package (12 ounces) frozen
      scallops

⅓ cup bottled oil-and-vinegar
      dressing
3 tablespoons snipped parsley
1 clove garlic, finely chopped
      Paprika

1. Arrange scallops in 9-inch pie plate. Cover tightly and microwave on high (100%) 2 minutes; rotate pie plate ½ turn. Microwave until almost tender, 4 to 5 minutes longer. Let stand 1 minute; drain thoroughly.

2. Mix dressing, parsley and garlic; pour over scallops in pie plate. Refrigerate about 4 hours, stirring occasionally. Sprinkle with paprika and serve with wooden picks.

Fruit-Nut Nibbles (pictured on page 214)

About 12 cups snack

3 cups honey graham cereal
1⅓ cups salted peanuts
1 cup dried banana chips
2 tablespoons margarine or
    butter, melted (page 11)
2 tablespoons honey
½ teaspoon ground cinnamon
¼ teaspoon salt

4 cups popped corn (about ¼
    cup unpopped)
1 cup flaked coconut
1 cup raisins

1. Mix cereal, peanuts and banana chips in 3-quart casserole or bowl. Mix margarine, honey, cinnamon and salt; pour over cereal mixture, tossing until evenly coated. Microwave uncovered on high (100%) 2 minutes; stir. Microwave until toasted, 1 to 2 minutes longer. Watch carefully so mixture does not burn.

2. Stir in popcorn, coconut and raisins. Sprinkle with additional salt if desired. Let cool about 1 hour. Store in tightly covered container no longer than 1 week.

Pretzel-Cereal Snack

About 8 cups snack

½ cup margarine or butter
1 teaspoon garlic salt
1 teaspoon Worcestershire sauce
½ teaspoon celery salt

4 cups crispy corn puff cereal
2 cups pretzel sticks
2 cups salted mixed nuts

1. Place margarine, garlic salt, Worcestershire sauce and celery salt in 3-quart casserole or bowl. Microwave uncovered on high (100%) until margarine is melted, 45 to 60 seconds; stir.

2. Stir in cereal, pretzels and nuts; toss until well coated. Microwave uncovered on high (100%) stirring every 2 minutes, until toasted, 6 to 8 minutes. Let cool about 30 minutes.

Crunchy Cinnamon S'mores

About 1½ dozen squares

1 package (5.75 ounces) milk
    chocolate chips or 5 bars
    (1.2 ounces each) milk
    chocolate, broken
    into pieces
⅓ cup light corn syrup
1 tablespoon margarine or butter
½ teaspoon vanilla
¼ teaspoon ground cinnamon

4 cups honey graham cereal
1½ cups miniature marshmallows

1. Mix chocolate chips, corn syrup, margarine, vanilla and cinnamon in 3-quart casserole. Cover tightly and microwave on high (100%) to boiling, 2½ to 3 minutes; stir.

2. Fold in cereal until completely coated with chocolate; fold in marshmallows. Press mixture evenly with buttered back of spoon in greased baking pan, 9 × 9 × 2 inches. Let stand at room temperature about 1 hour. Cut into about 2-inch squares.

Cereal-Chocolate Clusters

About 3 dozen clusters

16   *large marshmallows or 2 cups*
        miniature marshmallows
 1   *package (6 ounces) semisweet*
        chocolate chips
⅓   *cup margarine or butter*

½   *teaspoon vanilla*
1½   *cups whole bran cereal*
 1   *cup flaked coconut*

1. Place marshmallows, chocolate chips and margarine in 2-quart casserole. Cover tightly and microwave on high (100%) 2 minutes; stir. Cover and microwave until mixture can be stirred smooth, 1 to 2 minutes longer.

2. Stir in vanilla, cereal and coconut. Drop by teaspoonfuls onto waxed paper; shape into clusters with hands. Refrigerate until firm, about 30 minutes.

Peanut Clusters

About 2 dozen clusters

 1   *cup sugar*
⅓   *cup evaporated milk*
¼   *cup margarine or butter*

¼   *cup crunchy peanut butter*
½   *teaspoon vanilla*
 2   *cups oats*
½   *cup Spanish peanuts*
½   *cup semisweet chocolate chips*

1. Mix sugar, milk and margarine in 2-quart casserole. Microwave uncovered on high (100%) to boiling, 2 to 3 minutes.

2. Stir in peanut butter and vanilla until blended. Stir in oats, peanuts and chocolate chips. Drop by tablespoonfuls onto waxed paper. (If mixture becomes too stiff, stir in 1 or 2 drops milk.) Refrigerate until firm, about 30 minutes.

Date-Pecan Cereal Squares

About 2 dozen squares

 1   *package (10 ounces) large*
        marshmallows or 1 package
        (10½ ounces) miniature
        marshmallows (5½ cups)
¼   *cup margarine or butter*
        Dash of salt

 1   *cup chopped dates*
 1   *cup coarsely chopped pecans*
 4   *cups crispy corn puff cereal*

1. Place marshmallows, margarine and salt in 3-quart casserole. Cover tightly and microwave on high (100%) until marshmallows are melted, 2½ to 3½ minutes; stir.

2. Stir in dates and pecans. Fold in cereal until well coated. Press mixture evenly with buttered back of spoon in greased baking pan, 13 × 9 × 2 inches. Let stand at room temperature about 1 hour. Cut into about 2-inch squares.

Microwave marshmallow mixture until melted.

Stir in dates and nuts; fold in cereal until coated.

Press into baking dish. Cut into squares when cooled.

Chocolate Caramel Apples (pictured on page 214)   9 *caramel apples*

9   *medium apples*

1   *package (14 ounces) caramel
    candies (about 48)*
¼   *cup semisweet chocolate chips*
2   *tablespoons water*
½   *teaspoon salt*

1. Remove stems and blossom ends of 9 apples (make sure apples are completely dry). Insert wooden skewer or ice cream stick in stem end of each apple.

2. Place caramels, chocolate chips, water and salt in 4-cup measure. Microwave uncovered on high (100%) 2 minutes; stir. Microwave until caramels can be stirred smooth, 1 to 2 minutes longer. Place 4-cup measure in bowl of hot water to keep caramel sauce warm. Dip each apple into sauce, turning to coat; remove and place on waxed paper. If desired, roll bottoms of apples in chopped peanuts before placing on paper. If mixture thickens, reheat uncovered on high (100%) 30 seconds. Refrigerate apples until coating is firm, about 45 minutes.

Chocolate Caramel Corn Balls   *About 6 popcorn balls*

¼   *cup sugar*
¼   *cup light corn syrup*
2   *tablespoons margarine or butter*
2   *tablespoons cocoa*
1   *teaspoon vanilla*
⅛   *teaspoon salt*

4   *cups popped corn (about ¼ cup
    unpopped)*
½   *cup pecan halves*
¼   *cup blanched almonds*

1. Mix sugar, corn syrup, margarine, cocoa, vanilla and salt in 2-quart casserole. Microwave uncovered on high (100%) to boiling, about 1 minute; stir until smooth. Microwave 30 seconds longer.

2. Mix remaining ingredients; stir into hot mixture. Microwave uncovered on high (100%) 1 minute; stir until coated. Spread on waxed paper. Let cool 30 minutes. Shape into 2¼-inch balls and wrap in plastic wrap or let stand until hardened; break and serve.

Chocolate Caramel Corn Balls

Chocolate-Bourbon Balls (pictured on page 235)

About 2½ dozen candies

½ cup semisweet chocolate chips
2 tablespoons honey

1½ cups finely crushed vanilla
     wafers (about 27)
1 cup ground walnuts
3 tablespoons bourbon whiskey
   Sugar

1. Mix chocolate chips and honey in 1½-quart casserole or bowl. Microwave uncovered on high (100%) until chips can be stirred smooth, 1 to 2 minutes.

2. Stir in vanilla wafers, walnuts and whiskey. Shape into 1-inch balls. Roll balls in sugar. Store in tightly covered container at least 4 days to develop flavor, but no longer than 4 weeks.

Orange-Date Balls (pictured on page 235)

About 5 dozen candies

1 pound chopped dates
½ cup margarine or butter
⅓ cup sugar

1 egg, well beaten
½ teaspoon salt

2 tablespoons orange juice
2 teaspoons grated orange peel
1 teaspoon vanilla
½ cup chopped nuts
½ cup graham cracker crumbs

4 cups toasted whole wheat flake
     cereal
   Finely chopped nuts

1. Mix chopped dates, margarine, and sugar in 3-quart casserole. Cover tightly and microwave on high (100%) 4 minutes.

2. Stir in egg and salt. Cover tightly and microwave on medium high (70%) until mixture is slightly thickened, 3 to 4 minutes.

3. Stir in orange juice, orange peel, vanilla, ½ cup nuts and the cracker crumbs. Let cool 10 minutes.

4. Stir in cereal. Shape into 1-inch balls with buttered hands. Roll balls in finely chopped nuts. Store in refrigerator no longer than 1 week.

Caramel Drops (pictured on page 235)

About 3 dozen candies

1 package (14 ounces) caramel
     candies (about 48)
2 tablespoons water
   Dash of salt

3 cups toasted oat cereal

1. Place caramels, water and salt in 3-quart casserole. Microwave uncovered on high (100%), stirring every minute, until caramels can be stirred smooth, 3 to 4 minutes.

2. Stir in cereal until well coated. Drop by rounded teaspoonfuls onto waxed paper. Refrigerate until firm, about 30 minutes.

Coco-Mocha Drops (pictured at right)

About 4½ dozen candies

1 *package (15.4 ounces) creamy
    white frosting mix*
1 *tablespoon instant coffee*
3 *tablespoons milk*
3 *tablespoons margarine or butter*

2 *cups flaked coconut, toasted
    (page 12)*

1. Mix frosting mix (dry) and instant coffee in 1½-quart casserole; stir in milk and margarine. Microwave uncovered on high (100%) until margarine is melted and mixture can be stirred smooth, 1 to 2 minutes.

2. Stir in coconut. Drop by teaspoonfuls onto waxed paper. Refrigerate until firm, about 1 hour.

Double Chocolate Fudge (pictured at right)

About 2 pounds candy

1 *can (14 ounces) sweetened
    condensed milk*
2 *cups (12 ounces) semisweet
    chocolate chips*
1 *ounce unsweetened chocolate*

1 *teaspoon vanilla*
1½ *cups chopped nuts*

1. Butter baking pan, 8 × 8 × 2 inches. Stir milk and chocolate chips in 2-quart casserole; add chocolate. Microwave uncovered on high (100%) 1 minute; stir. Microwave until chocolate is melted and mixture can be stirred smooth, about 2 minutes longer.

2. Stir in vanilla and nuts. Spread mixture evenly in pan. Refrigerate until firm. Cut into 1-inch squares.

Raisin-Rum Fudge

About 1½ pounds candy

1 *package (15.4 ounces) creamy
    white frosting mix*
  Dash of salt
¼ *cup milk*
2 *tablespoons margarine or butter*

¾ *teaspoon rum flavoring*
½ *cup golden raisins*
½ *cup semisweet chocolate chips,
    melted (page 12)*

1. Line bottom and sides of loaf pan, 9 × 5 × 3 inches, with waxed paper. Mix frosting mix (dry) and salt in 2-quart casserole; stir in milk and margarine. Microwave uncovered on high (100%) until margarine is melted and mixture can be stirred smooth, 1 to 2 minutes.

2. Stir in flavoring and raisins. Spread evenly in pan. Spread with melted chocolate. Refrigerate until chocolate is firm, about 1 hour. Lift out candy and cut into 1-inch squares.

Note: Individual paper bonbon cups, available at specialty shops and some supermarkets, can be used to make about 2½ dozen individual candies.

*Top row shows all kinds of candies.
Left to right, top row: Orange-Date Balls (page 233),
Coco-Mocha Drops (above), Chocolate Bourbon Balls (page 233),
Double Chocolate Fudge (above), Caramel Drops (page 233).*

Instant Coffee

For each serving, mix ¾ to 1 cup water and 1 teaspoon instant coffee in microwave-proof Irish coffee mug or cup. Microwave uncovered on high (100%) until hot, 1½ to 2½ minutes; stir.

Instant Irish Coffee: For each serving, stir 2 tablespoons Irish whiskey and 1 to 2 teaspoons sugar into each mug of hot coffee. Top with spoonful of whipped topping.

Chocolate Espresso

4 servings (about ½ cup each)

¼ *cup water*
1 *tablespoon sugar*
  Dash of salt
½ *ounce unsweetened chocolate*

1 *cup hot espresso or double-*
    strength coffee
¾ *cup milk*
  About ¼ cup whipped topping
  Grated orange peel

1. Stir water, sugar and salt in 4-cup measure; add chocolate. Microwave uncovered on high (100%) until chocolate is melted, 2 to 3 minutes.

2. Stir in coffee and milk. Microwave uncovered on high (100%) until hot, 2 to 3 minutes. Beat with hand beater until smooth. Top each serving with spoonful of whipped topping; sprinkle with orange peel.

Note: Chocolate Espresso and other beverages can be served, but never microwaved or reheated, in metal liners as shown below.

Chocolate Espresso

Spiced Mocha Drink (pictured on page 1)   4 *servings (about ⅔ cup each)*

¾ *cup hot water*
¼ *cup sugar*
1 *tablespoon plus 2 teaspoons*
      instant coffee
½ *teaspoon ground cinnamon*
¼ *teaspoon ground nutmeg*
    Dash of salt
1½ *ounces unsweetened chocolate*

2 *cups milk*
⅓ *cup whipped topping*

1. Stir water, sugar, coffee, cinnamon, nutmeg and salt in 4-cup measure. Add chocolate. Microwave uncovered on high (100%) 2 minutes; stir. Microwave until chocolate is melted and can be stirred smooth, 1 to 2 minutes longer.

2. Stir in milk. Microwave uncovered on high (100%) until hot, 3 to 4 minutes. Beat until foamy. Top each serving with spoonful of whipped topping.

Hot Cocoa Drink   5 *servings (about ⅔ cup each)*

3 *tablespoons sugar*
3 *tablespoons cocoa*
⅛ *teaspoon salt*
¾ *cup hot water*

2¼ *cups milk*
¼ *teaspoon vanilla (if desired)*

1. Mix sugar, cocoa and salt in 4-cup measure. Stir in water. Microwave uncovered on high (100%) to boiling, 1 to 2 minutes.

2. Stir in milk. Microwave uncovered on high (100%) until hot but do not boil, 3 to 4 minutes. Stir in vanilla.

Wassail (pictured on page 255)   10 *servings (½ cup each)*

3 *cups dry red wine*
2 *cups apple juice*
¼ *to ⅓ cup packed brown sugar*
1 *teaspoon ground cinnamon*
½ *teaspoon ground nutmeg*
½ *teaspoon ground ginger*
10 *whole cloves*
    Apple wedges

Mix all ingredients except apple wedges in 2-quart measure. Cover tightly and microwave on high (100%) 5 minutes; stir. Cover and microwave to boiling, 6 to 8 minutes longer. Garnish each serving with apple wedge.

Mulled Tomato Juice (pictured on page 214)   6 *servings (about ½ cup each)*

3 *cups tomato juice*
1 *teaspoon Worcestershire sauce*
¼ *teaspoon salt*
¼ *teaspoon celery salt*
⅛ *teaspoon oregano leaves*
3 *to 4 drops red pepper sauce*

Mix all ingredients in 4-cup measure. Microwave uncovered on high (100%) until hot, 4 to 6 minutes. Serve in small cups or mugs. Garnish with celery sticks or green onions if desired.

Weekend Brunch for Four

Zesty Beef Cocktail
(opposite)

Eggs in Vegetable Wreath
(below)

Date-Nut Muffins
(page 168)
with Orange Sauce
(opposite)

Coffee

Several Hours Before:
☐ Microwave Orange Sauce and Date-Nut Muffins. Cover and reserve Orange Sauce and 8 of the muffins. (Wrap, label and freeze remaining muffins if desired.)
☐ Prepare vegetables for Eggs in Vegetable Wreath but do not microwave.

About 5 Minutes Before Appetizer:
☐ Microwave Zesty Beef Cocktail. Pour, garnish with carrot curls and serve.

About 25 Minutes Before Main Course:
☐ Prepare coffee.
☐ Microwave Eggs in Vegetable Wreath; cover to keep warm.
☐ Heat Orange Sauce covered on high (100%) until hot, 2 to 3 minutes; stir.
☐ Heat Date-Nut Muffins uncovered on medium (50%) until warm, about 1 minute.

Serve Brunch.

Eggs in Vegetable Wreath

4 servings

2   *medium green peppers, sliced*
2   *small onions, sliced*
1   *small clove garlic, finely chopped*
½   *teaspoon salt*
½   *teaspoon dried basil leaves*

2   *medium tomatoes, cut into wedges*

8   *eggs*
½   *cup dairy sour cream*
½   *cup shredded Cheddar cheese*
      (about 2 ounces)
1   *teaspoon salt*
¼   *teaspoon pepper*

1. Mix green pepper, onion, garlic, ½ teaspoon salt and the basil in 2-quart casserole. Cover tightly and microwave on high (100%) 3 minutes; stir. Cover and microwave until green pepper is crisp-tender, 2 to 4 minutes longer.

2. Stir in tomatoes. Cover tightly and microwave on high (100%) until tomatoes are hot, 2 to 3 minutes; drain. Arrange vegetables around edge of platter; cover to keep warm.

3. Mix eggs, sour cream, cheese, 1 teaspoon salt and the pepper in same casserole. Microwave uncovered on high (100%), stirring every 2 minutes, until eggs are soft and almost set, 6 to 8 minutes. (Eggs will continue to cook while standing.) Mound scrambled eggs in center of vegetables.

Pictured on previous page: Summer Ham Dinner for Six

Zesty Beef Cocktail

4 servings (about ¾ cup each)

2 cans (10½ ounces each) condensed
     beef broth
1 cup water
2 to 3 teaspoons horseradish
   Carrot curls

Mix beef broth, water and horseradish in 4-cup measure. Microwave uncovered on high (100%) until hot, 4 to 6 minutes. Serve in small cups or mugs. Garnish with carrot curls.

Orange Sauce for Muffins

About ¾ cup sauce

¼ cup sugar
1 tablespoon cornstarch
1 tablespoon grated orange peel
¾ cup orange juice

Mix sugar and cornstarch in 4-cup measure. Stir in orange peel and juice. Microwave uncovered on high (100%) 1 minute; stir. Microwave to boiling, 1 to 1½ minutes longer.

SALLY: © 1960 United Feature Syndicate, Inc.

Weekend Brunch for Four

Soup Supper for Four

Cauliflower-Pepper Soup
(opposite)

Tomato-Cottage Cheese Salads

Brown Bread
(page 173)

Butterscotch Apple Sundaes
(below)

Coffee

One Day Before:
- ☐ Microwave Brown Bread. Wrap cooled loaves and reserve 1 loaf. (Wrap, label and freeze 1 loaf for another time if desired.)

Several Hours Before:
- ☐ Slice 1 loaf Brown Bread. Cut each slice into halves; spread with margarine. Arrange in circle on serving plate. Cover tightly and reserve.
- ☐ Microwave apples for Butterscotch Apple Sundaes; let cool. Cover tightly.

About 1 Hour Before:
- ☐ Microwave Cauliflower-Pepper Soup except — do not add wine, chopped green pepper or paprika.
- ☐ Prepare salads. Refrigerate until serving time.

About 15 Minutes Before:
- ☐ Prepare coffee.
- ☐ Add ¼ cup wine to Cauliflower-Pepper Soup. Cover tightly and microwave on medium-high (70%) 3 minutes; stir. Microwave until soup is hot, 2 to 4 minutes longer. Sprinkle ¼ cup chopped green pepper and paprika over soup.
- ☐ Heat Brown Bread covered on medium (50%) until warm, 1 to 2 minutes.
- ☐ Set out salads.

Serve Main Course.

About 5 Minutes Before Dessert:
- ☐ Microwave apples covered on high (100%) for Butterscotch Apple Sundaes until warm, 2 to 3 minutes. Serve over ice cream.

Butterscotch Apple Sundaes

6 servings

6   *medium cooking apples (such as Rome Beauty, Greening, Starr, Jersey Red), cut into eighths*
⅓   *cup packed brown sugar*
3   *tablespoons margarine or butter*
3   *tablespoons water*
    Cinnamon or vanilla ice cream

Place all ingredients except ice cream in 2-quart casserole. Cover tightly and microwave on high (100%) 4 minutes; stir. Cover and microwave until apples are almost tender when pierced with fork, 4 to 6 minutes longer; stir. Cover and let stand 5 minutes. Serve over ice cream.

Cauliflower-Pepper Soup

4 *servings (about 1 cup each)*

1	*cup ½-inch flowerets cauliflower (about ¼ pound)*
2	*tablespoons margarine or butter*
1	*cup hot water*
6	*ounces pasteurized process cheese loaf cut into ½-inch cubes*
½	*cup half-and-half*
1	*teaspoon instant chicken bouillon*
	Dash of ground nutmeg
	Dash of ground allspice
¼	*cup dry white wine*
¼	*cup finely chopped green pepper*
	Paprika

1. Place cauliflower and margarine in 2-quart casserole. Cover tightly and microwave on high (100%) until crisp-tender, about 2 minutes.

2. Stir in water, cheese, half-and-half, bouillon, nutmeg and allspice. Cover tightly and microwave on medium-high (70%) 3 minutes.

3. Stir in wine. Cover tightly and microwave until soup is hot, 2 to 4 minutes. Sprinkle green pepper and paprika over soup.

Italian-Style Dinner for Eight

Zucchini Soup
(page 217)
with Croutons
(below)

Beef-Wine Spaghetti
(page 23)

Tossed Mushroom-Spinach Salad

Garlic Bread
(opposite)

Chocolate-Almond Brownies
(page 204)

Spumoni Ice Cream

One Day Before:
- ☐ Microwave Chocolate-Almond Brownies. Cover and reserve until serving time.
- ☐ Microwave Beef-Wine Spaghetti except — do not cook spaghetti. Refrigerate sauce.
- ☐ Microwave Croutons; reserve.

Several Hours Before:
- ☐ Microwave Zucchini Soup except — omit sour cream. Cover tightly and refrigerate.
- ☐ Assemble Garlic Bread. Wrap in plastic wrap. Do not microwave.
- ☐ Prepare salad but do not add dressing. Cover and refrigerate.
- ☐ Cook 1 pound spaghetti as directed on package; drain. Toss with 2 tablespoons margarine. Cover tightly and reserve.

About 10 Minutes Before Guests Arrive:
- ☐ Heat Zucchini Soup covered on high (100%) until hot, 6 to 8 minutes; stir. Pour into cups; sprinkle with Croutons and serve.

About 25 Minutes Before Main Course:
- ☐ Heat sauce for Beef-Wine Spaghetti covered on high (100%) 5 minutes; stir. Cover and microwave until hot, 7 to 9 minutes longer.
- ☐ Heat spaghetti covered on high (100%) until hot, 3 to 4 minutes.
- ☐ Set out Parmesan cheese.

About 5 Minutes Before Main Course:
- ☐ Unwrap 1 loaf Garlic Bread. Microwave as directed in Step 3. Microwave remaining loaf as needed.
- ☐ Toss salad with dressing.

Serve Dinner and Dessert.

Croutons

About 1 cup

2 *tablespoons margarine or butter*

½ *teaspoon parsley flakes*
⅛ *teaspoon garlic salt*
⅛ *teaspoon paprika*
2 *cups ½-inch bread cubes*
    (about 2 slices bread)

1. Place margarine in baking dish, 8 × 8 × 2 inches. Microwave uncovered on high (100%) until melted, 15 to 30 seconds.

2. Stir in parsley flakes, garlic salt and paprika. Add bread cubes and mix to coat. Microwave uncovered on high (100%), stirring every minute, until golden brown and crisp, 3½ to 4½ minutes. Let cool.

Garlic Bread

20 to 24 one-inch slices

1. Place ½ cup margarine or butter in small bowl. Microwave uncovered on medium-low (30%) until softened, 30 to 45 seconds.

2. Finely chop 1 clove garlic; stir in margarine. Spread over top and sides of 20 to 24 one-inch slices Italian or French bread (1-pound loaf). Reassemble slices to make 2 loaves.

3. Place 1 loaf at a time in paper napkin-lined basket or on dinner plate. Cover with paper towel and microwave on medium (50%) 1 minute; rotate basket ½ turn. Microwave until warm, 1 to 1½ minutes longer.

The day before, microwave the brownies; cover and reserve until serving time.

Then microwave spaghetti sauce, but not spaghetti. Cover tightly and refrigerate.

Microwave Croutons for salad. Cover and reserve at room temperature.

Hours before, cook the spaghetti. Drain, add the margarine and cover.

Microwave soup to reheat at last minute for appetizer. Assemble Garlic Bread.

Five minutes before dinner, heat pasta and sauce. Unwrap bread and microwave.

Autumn Pork Roast Dinner for Eight

Herbed Pork Roast
(page 39)

Cheese-Scalloped Potatoes
(opposite)

**Tossed Green Salad
with Croutons**
(page 244)

Celery-Carrot-Pickle Relish
(below)

Coffee-Peach Mallow
(opposite)

Coffee

Several Days Before:
- ☐ Prepare Coffee-Peach Mallow except for topping and peaches. Wrap, label and freeze until serving time.

One Day Before:
- ☐ Microwave Celery-Carrot-Pickle Relish. Cover and refrigerate until serving time.
- ☐ Microwave Croutons; reserve.

Several Hours Before:
- ☐ Mix ingredients for salad but do not add dressing or croutons. Cover and refrigerate.
- ☐ Prepare topping and peaches for Coffee-Peach Mallow. Cover and refrigerate topping and peaches separately.
- ☐ Microwave Cheese-Scalloped Potatoes; reserve uncovered.

About 1 Hour Before:
- ☐ Microwave Herbed Pork Roast. Cover gravy and keep warm.
- ☐ Prepare coffee.
- ☐ While carving roast, heat scalloped potatoes on high (100%) until hot, 2 to 3 minutes.
- ☐ Set out Celery-Carrot-Pickle Relish.
- ☐ Toss salad. Sprinkle with croutons.
- ☐ Heat gravy covered on high (100%) until hot, if necessary, about 1 minute; stir.

Serve Main Course and Dessert.

Celery-Carrot-Pickle Relish

8 servings

2 *cups ¼-inch diagonal slices celery
(about 4 medium stalks)*
2 *jars (16 ounces each) whole
carrots (reserve liquid
from 1 jar)*
6 *whole cloves*
½ *teaspoon salt*

1 *medium onion, sliced*
1 *cup watermelon pickles*

1. Mix celery, reserved carrot liquid, cloves and salt in 2-quart bowl or casserole. Cover tightly and microwave on high (100%) until celery is crisp-tender, 4 to 6 minutes.

2. Stir in carrots, onion and pickles. Cover tightly and microwave on high (100%) until hot, 3 to 5 minutes; stir. Serve hot or cold.

Cheese-Scalloped Potatoes

8 *servings*

¾ *cup milk*
1 *can (10¾ ounces) cream of*
  chicken soup
4 *cups ⅛-inch slices potatoes*
  (about 4 medium)
1 *cup shredded Cheddar cheese*
¼ *cup chopped onion*
½ *teaspoon salt*
⅛ *teaspoon pepper*

Gradually stir milk into soup in 2-quart cassrole. Stir in remaining ingredients. Cover tightly and microwave on high (100%) 10 minutes; stir. Cover and microwave until potatoes are tender, 10 to 15 minutes longer; stir. Sprinkle with Parmesan cheese if desired.

Coffee-Peach Mallow

9 *servings*

3 *cups miniature marshmallows*
½ *cup water*
1 *to 2 tablespoons instant coffee*
½ *teaspoon ground nutmeg*

1 *cup chilled whipping cream*

½ *cup chilled whipping cream*
2 *tablespoons packed brown sugar*
½ *teaspoon vanilla*
1 *cup sliced peaches*

1. Mix marshmallows, water, coffee and nutmeg in 3-quart casserole. Cover tightly and microwave on high (100%), stirring every minute, until smooth, 3 to 4 minutes; stir. Refrigerate until mixture mounds slightly when dropped from spoon, about 20 minutes.

2. Beat 1 cup cream until stiff. Fold marshmallow mixture into cream. Pour into baking pan, $8 \times 8 \times 2$ inches; freeze until firm, about 3 hours.

3. Beat ½ cup cream, the brown sugar and vanilla until stiff. Top each serving with cream and peaches.

Autumn Pork Roast Dinner for Eight

Summer Ham Dinner for Six (pictured on page 238)

Fruit Soup
(*page* 218)

Glazed Ham with Corn Relish
(*page* 40)

Cheesy Vegetables
(*opposite*)

Baking Powder Biscuits
(*page* 164)

Brownie Nut Cupcakes
(*opposite*)

Iced Tea

Several Days Before:
☐ Prepare Corn Relish. Cover and refrigerate until serving time.

Several Hours Before:
☐ Microwave Fruit Soup. Cover and refrigerate until serving time.
☐ Microwave Glazed Ham; let cool and slice. Arrange slices in circle on serving plate. Cover tightly and refrigerate.
☐ Prepare water, salt and vegetables as directed for Cheesy Vegetables but do not microwave. Cover and refrigerate.
☐ Microwave Brownie Nut Cupcakes. Cover and reserve until serving time.
☐ Prepare Baking Powder Biscuits and arrange on 1 plate (not 2 as directed). Do not microwave. Cover loosely and refrigerate.

Just Before Guests Arrive:
☐ Set out Fruit Soup.

About 25 Minutes Before Main Course:
☐ Microwave Cheesy Vegetables. Cover.
☐ Heat plate of ham covered on high (100%) until hot, 4 to 5 minutes.
☐ Prepare Iced Tea.
☐ Set out Corn Relish.
☐ Arrange Baking Powder Biscuits in circle as directed. Microwave 1 plate uncovered on high (100%) 1 minute; rotate plate ½ turn. Microwave until no longer doughy, 1 to 2 minutes longer. Let stand 1 minute. Microwave second plate as needed.

Serve Main Course and Dessert.

Planning Microwave Menus

Use your plan-ahead skills! Include foods that can be microwaved a day or two ahead of time, then refrigerated or frozen. Add foods with longer built-in standing times — whole chicken and some roasts. This allows you time to microwave other foods. Take advantage of the high heat retention in many foods, if covered. This can help you dovetail microwave tasks. Think about foods that can be partially prepared ahead of time and quickly finished — or completely cooked and reheated — such as pasta. And don't forget porous foods that can be microwaved at the last minute. For safety's sake, don't allow hot or cold foods to remain at room temperature more than 2 hours; bacteria thrive on lukewarm food.

Cheesy Vegetables

6 to 8 servings

¼ cup water
½ teaspoon salt
1 package (10 ounces) frozen green beans
1½ cups ¼-inch diagonal slices carrots (about 3 medium)

2 cups small flowerets cauliflower
¼ cup chopped onion

2 tablespoons margarine or butter
2 tablespoons all-purpose flour
½ teaspoon salt
⅛ teaspoon pepper

Milk
2 tablespoons grated Parmesan cheese
Paprika

1. Place water, salt, beans and carrots in 1½-quart casserole. Cover tightly and microwave on high (100%) 5 minutes.

2. Stir in cauliflower and onion. Cover tightly and microwave on high (100%) until tender, 7 to 9 minutes. Drain vegetables; reserve liquid. Let stand covered while preparing sauce.

3. Place margarine in 4-cup measure. Microwave uncovered on high (100%) until margarine is melted, 15 to 30 seconds. Stir in flour, salt and pepper.

4. Add enough milk to reserved vegetable liquid to measure 1 cup. Gradually stir liquid into flour mixture. Microwave uncovered on high (100%) until thickened and bubbly, stirring every minute, 3 to 4 minutes. Pour sauce over vegetables. Sprinkle with cheese and paprika.

Brownie Nut Cupcakes

About 1½ dozen cupcakes

1 cup milk
½ cup cocoa
½ cup shortening

1½ cups all-purpose flour
1 cup sugar
1 teaspoon baking powder
½ teaspoon baking soda
1 egg
½ cup semisweet chocolate chips
½ cup chopped walnuts

1. Place paper liners in 6 muffin cups, 2½ × 1¼ inches, or 6-ounce custard cups. Arrange cups in circle on 12-inch plate.

2. Mix milk and cocoa in 2½-quart bowl; add shortening. Microwave uncovered on high (100%) 2 minutes; stir until shortening is melted.

3. Stir in flour, sugar, baking powder, baking soda and egg. Add chocolate chips and walnuts; mix until smooth. (Mixture will be thick.) Fill muffin cups half full. Sprinkle with additional chocolate chips and walnuts if desired. Microwave uncovered on high (100%) 1 minute; rotate plate ¼ turn. Microwave until wooden pick inserted in center comes out clean, 1 to 2 minutes longer. (Parts of cupcakes will appear moist, but will continue to cook while standing.) Let stand 1 minute; remove to rack. Repeat 2 times with remaining batter and additional cupcake liners.

Chicken Dinner for Six (pictured on back cover)

Chicken with Stuffing
(page 59)
and Giblet Gravy
(opposite)

Cranberry Relish
(below)

**Squash with Peppers
and Tomatoes**
(below)

Hard Rolls

Coconut Pineapple
(opposite)

*Note: Giblet Gravy is reprinted
opposite for easy reference.*

Several Hours Before:
- ☐ Microwave Giblets. Cover and refrigerate chopped giblets and broth separately.
- ☐ Microwave Cranberry Relish. Cover and refrigerate until serving time.
- ☐ Prepare vegetables for Squash with Peppers and Tomatoes but do not microwave.
- ☐ Microwave Coconut Pineapple except — do not sprinkle with coconut. Refrigerate fruit and coconut separately.

About 1 Hour Before:
- ☐ Prepare and microwave chicken.
- ☐ During standing time for chicken, microwave Squash with Peppers and Tomatoes. Cover to keep warm.
- ☐ Microwave Giblet Gravy.
- ☐ Set out Cranberry Relish and rolls.

Serve Main Course.

Just Before Serving Dessert:
- ☐ Sprinkle fruit with coconut and serve.

Squash with Peppers and Tomatoes

6 servings

1 cup ¼-inch slices celery
½ medium green pepper, cut into ¼-inch strips
1 small onion, sliced
1 tablespoon margarine or butter
½ teaspoon salt
½ teaspoon ground ginger

1½ cups 1-inch slices yellow summer squash (about ½ pound)
2 tomatoes, cut into eighths

1. Mix celery, green pepper, onion, margarine, salt and ginger in 1½-quart casserole. Cover tightly and microwave on high (100%) 3 minutes.

2. Stir in squash. Cover tightly and microwave until vegetables are crisp-tender, 2 to 4 minutes. Stir in tomatoes. Cover tightly and microwave on high (100%) until tomatoes are heated through, 2 to 3 minutes longer.

Cranberry Relish

About 2 cups

3 cups cranberries (¾ pound)
1¼ to 1⅓ cups sugar
½ cup water
Grated peel of 1 orange

Mix all ingredients in 3-quart casserole. Cover tightly and microwave on high (100%) 5 minutes; stir. Cover tightly and microwave on medium (50%) to boiling, 5 to 7 minutes. Cover and refrigerate at least 3 hours.

Coconut Pineapple

6 *to* 8 *servings*

⅓ cup coconut
1 teaspoon margarine or butter

4 cups pineapple chunks,
      (about 1 medium)
1 can (11 ounces) mandarin
      orange segments, drained
⅓ cup packed brown sugar
¼ cup rum
2 tablespoons margarine or butter

1. Place coconut and margarine in 2-cup measure. Microwave uncovered on high (100%), stirring every 15 seconds, until lightly browned, 2 to 2½ minutes. (Watch carefully after first brown flakes appear. Coconut continues to brown after cooking.)

2. Mix pineapple, oranges, brown sugar, rum and margarine in 1½-quart casserole. Cover tightly; microwave on high (100%) until bubbly, 4 to 6 minutes; stir. Sprinkle with coconut. Serve warm or cold.

Giblet Gravy

About 1 cup

2 tablespoons drippings
2 tablespoons flour

1 cup broth from giblets
    Salt and pepper

1. Place chicken on platter; keep warm while preparing gravy. Pour 2 tablespoons drippings in 4-cup measure. (Measure accurately because too little fat makes gravy lumpy.) Stir in flour. Microwave uncovered on high (100%) until bubbly, about 1 minute.

2. Stir in broth from giblets. Microwave uncovered on high (100%), stirring every minute, until thickened, 2 to 3 minutes. Stir in giblets; sprinkle with salt and pepper. Stir in few drops bottled brown bouquet sauce if desired.

Chicken Dinner for Six

Festive Fish Dinner for Five

Madrilene with Wine
(opposite)

Fish Fillets with Grapes
(page 101)

Artichoke Hearts with Peas
(below)

Cheesy French Bread
(page 182)

Sour Cream Spice Cake
(opposite)

Orange Sherbet

Several Hours Before:
- ☐ Microwave Sour Cream Spice Cake. Cover and reserve until serving time.
- ☐ Assemble Cheesy French Bread. Wrap in plastic wrap.
- ☐ Prepare onions, fish, wine and lemon juice in baking dish for Fish Fillets with Grapes but do not microwave. Cover and refrigerate.

About 10 Minutes Before Guests Arrive:
- ☐ Microwave Madrilene with Wine. Pour in punch cups and serve.

About 30 Minutes Before Dinner:
- ☐ Microwave Artichoke Hearts with Peas but do not stir in lemon juice. Cover and reserve.

About 20 Minutes Before:
- ☐ Microwave Fish Fillets with Grapes. Cover to keep warm.
- ☐ Unwrap Cheesy French Bread. Place in napkin-lined basket. Cover with paper towel and microwave on medium (50%) 1 minute; rotate basket ½ turn. Microwave until cheese starts to melt, 1 to 1½ minutes longer.
- ☐ Heat Artichoke Hearts with Peas covered on high (100%) until hot, 1 to 2 minutes. Stir in lemon juice.

Serve Main Course and Dessert.

Artichoke Hearts with Peas

5 or 6 servings

¼ cup water
1 teaspoon salt
1 package (9 ounces) frozen artichoke hearts, broken apart
2 packages (10 ounces each) frozen green peas, broken apart
2 tablespoons margarine or butter
1 jar (3½ ounces) cocktail onions, drained (if desired)
1 jar (2 ounces) sliced pimiento, drained

2 tablespoons lemon juice

1. Mix water, salt, artichoke hearts and peas in 2-quart casserole. Cover tightly and microwave on high (100%) 8 minutes; stir. Cover and microwave until peas are crisp-tender, 6 to 9 minutes longer; drain. Stir in margarine, onions and pimiento.

2. Just before serving, stir in lemon juice.

Festive Fish Dinner for Five

Madrilene with Wine

5 *servings (about ⅔ cup each)*

Pour 2 cans (13 ounces each) red madrilene (consommé) into 4-cup measure. Cover tightly and microwave on high (100%) to boiling, 6 to 8 minutes. Stir in ¼ cup dry red wine.

Sour Cream Spice Cake

One 8-inch square cake

1	*cup all-purpose flour*
¾	*cup packed brown sugar*
1½	*teaspoons pumpkin pie spice*
¾	*teaspoon baking soda*
½	*teaspoon baking powder*
¼	*teaspoon salt*
⅔	*cup dairy sour cream*
¼	*cup shortening*
¼	*cup water*
1	*egg*
¾	*cup raisins*
1	*tablespoon sugar*
¼	*teaspoon pumpkin pie spice*

1. Mix flour, brown sugar, 1½ teaspoons pumpkin pie spice, baking soda, baking powder, salt, sour cream, shortening, water and egg in 3½-quart bowl. Beat on low speed, scraping bowl constantly, 30 seconds. Beat on high speed, scraping bowl occasionally, 3 minutes. Stir in raisins. Spread in baking dish, 8 × 8 × 2 inches.

2. Mix sugar and ¼ teaspoon pumpkin pie spice; sprinkle on cake. Elevate on inverted 9-inch pie plate in microwave. Microwave uncovered on medium (50%) 4 minutes; rotate baking dish ½ turn.

3. Microwave on high (100%) until cake begins to pull away from side of dish, 5 to 6 minutes longer. (Parts of cake will appear moist but will continue to cook while standing.) Let cool on heatproof surface (do not use rack). Serve with orange sherbet if desired.

Holiday Snacks for Six

Wassail
(page 237)

Party Cheese Log
(page 222)

Gingered Nuts
(below)

Granola
(opposite)

**Brandied Butterscotch Fondue
with Dippers**
(below)

Coffee

One Day Before:
- ☐ Prepare Party Cheese Log. Refrigerate until serving time.
- ☐ Microwave Granola. Reserve at room temperature until serving time.

Several Hours Before:
- ☐ Mix ingredients for Wassail but do not microwave until 20 minutes before party.
- ☐ Prepare Brandied Butterscotch Fondue but do not microwave and do not add brandy. Prepare Dippers for fondue. Cover and reserve until serving time.

About 20 Minutes Before:
- ☐ Prepare coffee.
- ☐ Microwave Brandied Butterscotch Fondue.
- ☐ Microwave Wassail.
- ☐ Microwave Gingered Nuts.
- ☐ Set out Cheese Log and Dippers.

Serve the Snacks.

Brandied Butterscotch Fondue

6 to 8 servings

1   *package (14 ounces) caramel
        candies (about 48)*
⅓   *cup whipping cream*
½   *teaspoon salt*
¼   *cup brandy*

*Dippers (pineapple chunks,
    banana slices, seedless
    grapes, cake cubes)*

1. Place caramels, cream and salt in 4-cup measure. Microwave uncovered on high (100%) 2 minutes; stir. Microwave until caramels can be stirred smooth, 1 to 2 minutes longer. Stir in brandy.

2. Pour into fondue pot or chafing dish to keep warm. Serve with Dippers.

Gingered Nuts

1 cup snack

1   *cup pecan or walnut halves*
½   *teaspoon salt*
½   *teaspoon ground ginger*
1   *tablespoon margarine or butter*

Place nuts in 1-quart casserole. Sprinkle with salt and ginger; dot with margarine. Microwave uncovered on high (100%) until toasted, 2 to 3 minutes; stir. Drain on paper towels. Serve warm.

Granola

About 4 cups snack

1 cup oats
½ cup sunflower seed kernels
½ cup flaked coconut
¼ cup sesame seed
1 tablespoon wheat germ
⅓ cup honey
¼ cup vegetable oil
1 teaspoon vanilla
¼ teaspoon salt

¼ cup raisins

1. Mix oats, sunflower kernels, coconut, sesame seed and wheat germ in 2-quart casserole. Mix honey, oil, vanilla and salt. Pour over oat mixture; stir well. Microwave uncovered on high (100%) stirring every 2 minutes, until toasted, 4 to 6 minutes.

2. Stir in raisins. Let cool about 1 hour. Break granola into pieces. Store in tightly covered container no longer than 1 week.

Holiday Snacks for Six

Walkabout Snacks for Six

Rumaki
(opposite)

Tiny Coconut-Chutney Meatballs
(page 224)

Curried Cereal Snack
(below)

Cheese Bread
(page 85)

Apricot-Fig Compote
(opposite)

Coffee

One Day Before:
☐ Prepare Curried Cereal Snack. Reserve until serving time.
☐ Microwave Tiny Coconut-Chutney Meatballs. Stir meatballs into sauce but do not microwave. Cover tightly and refrigerate.

Several Hours Before:
☐ Prepare Rumaki but do not microwave. Cover and refrigerate.
☐ Microwave Cheese Bread. Let cool, wrap and reserve.
☐ Microwave Apricot-Fig Compote. Cover and refrigerate fruit and topping separately.

About 20 Minutes Before:
☐ Prepare coffee.
☐ Heat Meatballs on high (100%) until hot, 4 to 6 minutes. Pour into chafing dish or fondue pot to keep warm.
☐ Microwave Rumaki.
☐ Unwrap Cheese Bread. Cover loosely and heat on medium (50%) until warm, 1 to 2 minutes. Slice.
☐ Set out Apricot-Fig Compote in bowls. Serve topping separately.

Serve the Snacks.

Curried Cereal Snack

About 8 cups snack

⅓ cup margarine or butter
1 tablespoon Worcestershire sauce
½ to 1 teaspoon curry powder

1 cup slivered almonds

1½ cups raisins
4 cups crispy corn puff cereal
2 cups oyster crackers

1. Place margarine, Worcestershire sauce and curry powder in 3-quart casserole. Microwave uncovered on high (100%) until margarine is melted, 45 to 60 seconds; stir.

2. Mix in almonds. Microwave uncovered on high (100%), stirring every minute, until hot and bubbly, 1 to 2 minutes.

3. Stir in raisins, cereal and oyster crackers; microwave uncovered on high (100%) until hot, about 2 minutes. Let stand at room temperature until cool, about 30 minutes.

Rumaki

12 appetizers

6 *chicken livers, cut into halves*
4 *water chestnuts, cut into thirds*
⅓ *cup bottled Teriyaki sauce*

6 *slices bacon, cut into halves*
   Brown sugar

1. Place chicken livers and water chestnuts in bowl. Pour on sauce. Refrigerate at least 1 hour; drain.

2. Wrap a piece of liver and a piece of water chestnut in each bacon piece. Secure with wooden pick; sprinkle with about ½ teaspoon brown sugar. Arrange in circle on microwave rack in baking dish or 9-inch pie plate. Cover with waxed paper and microwave on high (100%) 4 minutes; rotate baking dish ¼ turn. Microwave until bacon is crisp, 4 to 6 minutes longer. Drain on paper towel.

Apricot-Fig Compote

6 to 8 servings

1½ *cups dried apricots, apples,*
        peaches, pears or prunes
¾ *cup dried figs*
3 *cups water*
½ *cup raisins*
2 *tablespoons honey*
2 *tablespoons lemon juice*

   Lemon Whipped Cream (right)

1. Cut apricots and figs into bite-size pieces. Place apricots, figs, water and raisins in 2-quart casserole. Cover tightly and microwave on high (100%) 5 minutes; stir. Cover and microwave until almost tender when pierced with fork, 4 to 6 minutes longer. Stir in honey and lemon juice. Cover and let stand 30 minutes.

2. Serve fruit with slotted spoon. Top with Lemon Whipped Cream and, if desired, sliced almonds.

Lemon Whipped Cream
Beat ½ cup chilled whipping cream, 1 tablespoon sugar and 1 teaspoon grated lemon peel until stiff.

Walkabout Snacks for Six

After-Skating Snacks for Six

Cranberry Punch
(below)

Chicken-Pineapple Kabobs
(opposite)

Cheese Fondue with Dippers
(below)

Double Chocolate Fudge
(page 234)
and/or Coconut Chews
(page 205)

Coffee

One Day Before:
- ☐ Microwave Double Chocolate Fudge and Coconut Chews. Cover and reserve until serving time.

Several Hours Before:
- ☐ Complete Steps 1 and 2 of Chicken-Pineapple Kabobs. Arrange kabobs in baking dish but do not microwave. Cover and refrigerate kabobs. Cover and reserve Peanut Sauce.
- ☐ Mix ingredients for Cranberry Punch but do not microwave.
- ☐ Prepare Dippers for Cheese Fondue. Cover and reserve.

About 20 Minutes Before:
- ☐ Microwave Cranberry Punch. Cover.
- ☐ Microwave Cheese Fondue Dip. Set out dippers and bamboo skewers around Fondue.
- ☐ Microwave Chicken Kabobs. To heat Peanut Sauce for Kabobs, microwave uncovered on medium (50%) until warm, ½ to 1 minute; stir.
- ☐ Prepare coffee.
- ☐ Set out fudge and cookies.

Serve the Snacks.

Cranberry Punch

6 servings (about ¾ cup each)

2 cups cranberry juice cocktail
2 cups dry white or red wine
1 cup orange juice
2 tablespoons lemon juice
1 stick cinnamon
½ teaspoon grated orange peel
3 whole cloves

Mix all ingredients in 2-quart casserole. Cover tightly and microwave on high (100%) until punch is hot, 8 to 10 minutes.

Cheese Fondue

About 1¾ cups

2 cups shredded sharp process American cheese
4 to 6 drops red pepper sauce
⅓ cup dry white wine
   Dippers (raw vegetable strips and rye bread cubes)

Place cheese, red pepper sauce and wine in 1-quart casserole. Microwave uncovered on high (100%) until cheese is melted, 1 to 2 minutes; stir until smooth. Pour into fondue pot or chafing dish to keep warm. Serve with Dippers.

Chicken-Pineapple Kabobs

6 or 7 appetizers

1 *whole chicken breast (1 to 1¼ pounds)*
2 *tablespoons soy sauce*
1½ *teaspoons vegetable oil*
½ *teaspoon sugar*
¼ *teaspoon ground ginger*
1 *small clove garlic, crushed*

Peanut Sauce (below)
1 *can (8 ounces) pineapple chunks, drained*

1. Remove bones and skin from chicken breast. For ease in cutting, partially freeze chicken. Cut chicken into ¾-inch pieces. Mix chicken, soy sauce, vegetable oil, sugar, ginger and garlic in glass bowl. Cover and refrigerate 10 minutes.

2. Prepare Peanut Sauce. Remove chicken from marinade; reserve marinade. Thread 2 or 3 chicken pieces alternately with pineapple chunks on each of 6 or 7 bamboo skewers, 6 inches long. Brush chicken with reserved marinade.

3. Arrange skewers in baking dish, 12 × 7½ × 2 inches or on 12-inch round platter. Brush with marinade. Cover with waxed paper and microwave on high (100%) until chicken is done, 4 to 6 minutes. Serve with Peanut Sauce.

Peanut Sauce

2 *tablespoons finely chopped onion*
1 *teaspoon vegetable oil*

¼ *cup peanut butter*
¼ *cup water*
1 *teaspoon lemon juice*

1. Place onion and vegetable oil in 2-cup measure. Microwave uncovered on high (100%) 1 minute.

2. Stir in remaining ingredients. Microwave uncovered on medium (50%) until mixture can be stirred smooth, about 1 minute.

After-Skating Snacks for Six

THE PLAN~AHEADS

Beef Rolls

4 servings

½ *pound bulk pork sausage*

1 *cup soft bread crumbs (about 2 slices bread)*
¼ *cup chopped celery*
2 *tablespoons finely chopped onion*
⅛ *teaspoon ground sage*
⅛ *teaspoon dried basil leaves*
4 *beef cubed steaks (3 to 4 ounces each)*

1 *can (10¾ ounces) condensed tomato soup*
2 *tablespoons water*
⅛ *teaspoon dried basil leaves*

About 3 cups Hot Cooked Rice (page 185)

1. Crumble sausage into 2-quart casserole. Cover loosely and microwave on high (100%) 2 minutes; break up and stir. Cover and microwave until no pink remains, 1 to 2 minutes longer; drain.

2. Mix in bread crumbs, celery, onion, sage and ⅛ teaspoon basil. Spread about ½ cup sausage mixture evenly onto each beef cubed steak. Roll up, beginning at short side; secure with wooden picks.

3. Place beef rolls in 2-quart casserole. Mix soup, water and ⅛ teaspoon basil; pour over beef rolls. (To serve immediately, see below.) Cover tightly and refrigerate no longer than 24 hours.

4. **About 1 hour before serving, remove beef rolls from refrigerator.** Microwave covered on medium (50%) 20 minutes; rearrange beef rolls. Cover and microwave until tender, 13 to 18 minutes longer. Let stand 5 minutes. Serve beef rolls on rice; pour sauce over beef rolls.

To Serve Immediately: Decrease first cooking time in Step 4 to 15 minutes and second cooking time to 10 to 15 minutes.

To plan ahead, prepare but do not microwave Beef Rolls and sauce. Cover and refrigerate up to 24 hours.

About one hour before serving, microwave Beef Rolls until tender, rearranging once. Let stand 5 minutes.

Serve Beef Rolls over hot cooked rice. Spoon the sauce from casserole over the Beef Rolls and rice.

Pictured on previous page: Creamy Cheese and Cranberry Pie, Broccoli-Chinese Cabbage Medley, Little Salmon Casseroles, Sherried Chicken

Beef Kabobs

6 *servings*

1½	*pound beef boneless top loin or sirloin steak, cut into 1-inch cubes*
¼	*cup soy sauce*
1	*small fresh pineapple*, cut into pieces*
36	*fresh mushroom caps*
1	*large green pepper, cut into 1-inch pieces*
1	*cup honey*
2	*teaspoons dry mustard*
1	*teaspoon ground cloves*

1. Toss beef cubes with soy sauce.

2. Alternate meat, pineapple and vegetables on eighteen 8-inch bamboo skewers. (To serve immediately, see below.) Cover kabobs with plastic wrap and refrigerate no longer than 24 hours.

3. **About 15 minutes before serving, remove kabobs from refrigerator.** Place 6 skewers on microwave rack in baking dish.

4. Mix honey, mustard and cloves in 2-cup measure. Microwave uncovered on medium-high (70%) until warm, about 1 minute.

5. Brush kabobs with honey mixture. Microwave uncovered on medium-high (70%) 6 minutes; turn over and rearrange skewers. Brush with honey mixture. Microwave until beef is almost done, 4 to 7 minutes longer; keep warm. Repeat with remaining kabobs. Brush with any remaining honey mixture just before serving. Garnish each skewer with a cherry tomato if desired.

To Microwave Immediately: Decrease first cooking time in Step 5 to 4 minutes and second cooking time to 3 to 6 minutes.

* 1 can (20 ounces) pineapple chunks, drained, can be substituted for the fresh pineapple.

Beef in Squash Halves

4 servings

2   medium acorn squash (about 1
       pound each)

1   pound ground beef
2   cups chopped tart apples (about
       2 medium)
¼   cup raisins
1½ teaspoons salt
½   teaspoon ground nutmeg

4   teaspoons sugar
2   tablespoons margarine or butter,
       melted (page 11)

1. Microwave squash as directed on page 156. Remove stems and cut thin slice from pointed ends if necessary to prevent tipping.

2. Crumble ground beef into 2-quart casserole. Cover loosely and microwave on high (100%) 3 minutes; break up and stir. Cover and microwave until very little pink remains, 2 to 3 minutes longer; drain. Stir in apples, raisins, salt and nutmeg.

3. Turn squash halves cut sides up. Scoop pulp from shells, leaving a ¼-inch thick wall in each. Stir into meat mixture and pile into shells. Sprinkle 1 teaspoon sugar over each shell; drizzle shells with margarine. (To serve immediately, see below.) Cover tightly and refrigerate no longer than 24 hours.

4. **About 15 minutes before serving, remove squash from refrigerator.** Microwave covered on high (100%) until hot, 10 to 12 minutes. Uncover and let stand 3 minutes.

To Serve Immediately: Decrease cooking time in Step 4 to 7 to 9 minutes.

To plan ahead, cook squash. Scoop out pulp, leaving ¼-inch wall in each squash.

Mix squash with filling; fill shells. Add sugar and margarine; refrigerate.

To serve, microwave covered 10 to 12 minutes. Uncover; let stand 3 minutes.

Pork Cubes with Noodles

4 servings

1 - *pound pork boneless shoulder,
    cut into ¾-inch pieces*

¾   *cup water*
2   *tablespoons vinegar*
2   *cloves garlic, finely chopped*
1   *teaspoon salt*
1   *teaspoon bottled brown bouquet
    sauce*
½   *teaspoon ground cumin*

2   *tablespoons water*
1   *tablespoon all-purpose flour*
¼   *cup sliced pitted ripe olives*
3   *cups hot cooked noodles*

1. Place pork in 1½-quart casserole. Cover tightly and microwave on medium (50%), stirring every 3 minutes, until no pink remains, 9 to 11 minutes; drain.

2. Stir in ¾ cup water, the vinegar, garlic, salt, bouquet sauce and cumin. Cover tightly and microwave on medium (50%), stirring every 3 minutes, until pork is tender, 28 to 30 minutes. (To serve immediately, see below.) Cover tightly; refrigerate up to 48 hours.

3. **About 10 minutes before serving, remove pork cubes from refrigerator.** Microwave covered on high (100%) 2 minutes.

4. Shake 2 tablespoons water and the flour in tightly covered container. Stir into pork. Cover tightly and microwave on high (100%) until thickened, 2 minutes. Stir in olives. Serve over noodles.

To Serve Immediately: Omit Step 3.

Sherried Chicken (pictured on page 260)

6 servings

6   *small chicken breast halves*
2   *tablespoons margarine or butter,
    melted (page 11)*
    Paprika

1   *can (10¾ ounces) condensed
    cream of chicken soup*
½   *cup half-and-half*
⅓   *cup dry sherry or dry white wine*
1   *can (8 ounces) water chestnuts,
    drained and sliced*
1   *can (4 ounces) mushroom stems
    and pieces, drained*

1   *cup sliced seedless green grapes*

1. Arrange chicken breast halves skin sides up with thickest parts to outside in baking dish, 12 × 7½ × 2 inches. Pour margarine over chicken; generously sprinkle with paprika. Cover with waxed paper and microwave on high (100%) 10 minutes; rotate dish ½ turn. Microwave until thickest parts of chicken are done, 6 to 10 minutes longer; drain.

2. Mix remaining ingredients except grapes; spoon on chicken. (To serve immediately, see below.) Cover tightly; refrigerate no longer than 24 hours.

3. **About 30 minutes before serving, remove chicken from refrigerator.** Microwave covered on high (100%) 10 minutes; rotate baking dish ½ turn. Microwave until chicken is hot, 10 to 13 minutes longer. Sprinkle with grapes. Cover and let stand 5 minutes. Garnish with parsley if desired.

To Serve Immediately: Decrease first cooking time in Step 3 to 5 minutes; second time to 5 to 7 minutes.

Fish Fillets with Stuffing

5 or 6 servings

½ cup chopped onion (about 1
    medium)
2 tablespoons margarine or butter
1 cup soft bread crumbs (about 2
    slices bread)
¼ cup snipped parsley
1 teaspoon salt
¼ teaspoon ground nutmeg
1 egg, slightly beaten

1 pound fresh or frozen
    (defrosted) fish fillets,
    cut into serving pieces
1 tablespoon margarine or butter,
    melted (page 11)
1½ teaspoons vinegar
    Paprika

    Snipped parsley

1. Place onion and margarine in 1-quart casserole. Microwave uncovered on high (100%) until onion is crisp-tender, about 2 minutes. Stir in bread crumbs, ¼ cup parsley, the salt, nutmeg and egg.

2. Spread stuffing evenly over fish fillets. Roll up fish fillets; fasten with wooden picks. Arrange seam sides down in circle in round baking dish, 8 × 1½ inches. Mix 1 tablespoon melted margarine and vinegar; drizzle over fish. Sprinkle with paprika. (To serve immediately, see below.) Cover fish with waxed paper and refrigerate no longer than 24 hours.

3. **About 10 minutes before serving, remove fish from refrigerator.** Microwave covered on high (100%) 4 minutes; rotate baking dish ½ turn. Microwave until fish flakes easily with fork, 3 to 5 minutes longer. Garnish with parsley.

To Serve Immediately: Decrease first cooking time in Step 3 to 2 minutes and second cooking time to 2 to 4 minutes.

Tuna-Noodle Casserole

4 servings

¼ cup finely chopped onion
    (about 1 small)
1 small clove garlic, finely chopped

4 ounces uncooked egg noodles
    (about 2¼ cups), cooked
    and drained
1 can (6½ ounces) tuna, drained
¾ cup creamed cottage cheese
½ cup dairy sour cream
¼ cup sliced pimiento-stuffed olives
½ to 1 teaspoon Worcestershire
    sauce
¼ teaspoon salt
    Dash of cayenne red pepper

½ cup shredded Cheddar cheese
    (about 2 ounces)

1. Place onion and garlic in 1½-quart casserole. Cover tightly and microwave on high (100%) until onion is crisp-tender, 1 to 2 minutes.

2. Mix in remaining ingredients except Cheddar cheese. (To serve immediately, see below.) Cover tightly and refrigerate no longer than 24 hours.

3. **About 15 minutes before serving, remove casserole from refrigerator.** Microwave covered on high (100%) 5 minutes; stir. Cover and microwave until hot, 3 to 5 minutes longer. Sprinkle with cheese. Let stand 5 minutes.

To Serve Immediately: Decrease first cooking time in Step 3 to 4 minutes.

Salmon-Noodle Casserole: Substitute 1 can (7¾ ounces) salmon for the tuna.

Raclette

Raclette

12   *slices bacon*
1½   *pounds new potatoes (10 to 14 small) cooked, (page 152) and drained*

12   *ounces Muenster, Swiss or raclette cheese, cut into twelve 1-inch cubes*
 1   *jar (8 ounces) midget dill pickles*
 1   *jar (5 ounces) pickled cocktail onions, drained*

1. Layer ⅓ of bacon between paper towels on 10-inch plate. Repeat 2 times. Microwave on high (100%) 3 minutes; rotate plate ½ turn. Microwave until almost crisp, 3 to 4 minutes longer; drain. Roll up; fasten with wooden picks. (Can be served immediately. Omit Steps 2 and 3.) Cover and refrigerate bacon, potatoes and cheese cubes no longer than 24 hours.

2. **About 15 minutes before serving, remove bacon, potatoes and cheese cubes from refrigerator.** Microwave potatoes covered on high (100%) 3 minutes; stir. Microwave until hot, 3 to 4 minutes longer.

3. Cover bacon with paper towel and microwave on high (100%) until hot, about 1 minute.

4. Divide bacon, potatoes and cheese cubes among 4 luncheon plates, arranging as pictured above. Cover plates with waxed paper. Microwave 2 at a time until cheese is melted, 1½ to 2½ minutes. Serve with pickles and onions. (Bacon, potatoes and pickles are swirled in the melted cheese.)

Savory Cabbage

4 to 6 servings

6 cups coarsely shredded cabbage
    (about 1 pound)
⅓ cup milk

1 tablespoon margarine or butter
½ teaspoon salt
¼ teaspoon dried oregano leaves
    Dash of pepper
    Grated Parmesan cheese

1. Place cabbage and milk in 2-quart casserole. (To serve immediately; see below.) Cover tightly and refrigerate no longer than 24 hours.

2. **About 15 minutes before serving, remove cabbage from refrigerator.** Microwave covered on high (100%) 7 minutes; stir. Cover and microwave until crisp-tender, 4 to 6 minutes longer.

3. Stir in margarine, salt, oregano and pepper. Serve with cheese.

To Serve Immediately: Decrease first cooking time in Step 2 to 5 minutes.

To plan ahead, shred the cabbage; add milk. Cover; refrigerate up to 24 hours.

Fifteen minutes before serving time, microwave until cabbage is crisp-tender.

Stir in margarine, salt, oregano and pepper. Sprinkle with Parmesan cheese.

Broccoli-Chinese Cabbage Medley (pictured on page 261)   6 servings

4 cups sliced Chinese or celery
    cabbage (about 1 pound)
3 cups small (1-inch) flowerets
    broccoli (about 1 pound)
1 can (8 ounces) water chestnuts,
    drained and sliced
2 medium onions, sliced
2 tablespoons water
1 tablespoon vegetable oil
½ teaspoon salt

1 tablespoon soy sauce

1. Mix all ingredients except soy sauce in 2-quart casserole. (To serve immediately, see below.) Cover tightly and refrigerate no longer than 24 hours.

2. **About 15 minutes before serving, remove broccoli and cabbage from refrigerator.** Microwave covered on high (100%) 5 minutes; stir. Cover and microwave until hot, 5 to 7 minutes longer; drain. Toss with soy sauce. Serve with additional soy sauce.

To Serve Immediately: Decrease first cooking time in Step 2 to 4 minutes and second cooking time to 4 to 6 minutes.

Creamy Cheese and Cranberry Pie (pictured on page 260) *One 9-inch pie*

Cranberry Topping (below)

¼ *cup margarine or butter*
1¼ *cups graham cracker crumbs*
    (about 16 squares)
2 *tablespoons sugar*

2 *packages (8 ounces each) cream*
    cheese, softened (page 13)
2 *eggs*
¾ *cup sugar*
1 *tablespoon grated orange peel*
2 *teaspoons vanilla*

1 *cup dairy sour cream*
2 *tablespoons sugar*
2 *teaspoons vanilla*

1. Prepare Cranberry Topping. Let cool. (Can be served immediately.) Cover tightly and refrigerate no longer than 1 week.

2. Place margarine in 9-inch pie plate. Microwave on high (100%) until melted, 30 to 45 seconds. Stir in crumbs and 2 tablespoons sugar with fork. Press mixture firmly and evenly on bottom and side of pie plate. Microwave uncovered on high (100%) 1 minute; rotate pie plate ½ turn. Microwave until set, about 1 minute longer.

3. Place cream cheese, eggs, ¾ cup sugar, the orange peel and 2 teaspoons vanilla in 2½-quart bowl. Beat on high speed until smooth, about 2 minutes. Microwave uncovered on medium (50%), stirring every 2 minutes, until hot and thickened, 8 to 9 minutes. Pour into crust.

4. Mix sour cream, 2 tablespoons sugar and 2 teaspoons vanilla; spread carefully over filling. Refrigerate until cold, about 2 hours. (Can be served at this time.) Cover and refrigerate no longer than 3 days.

5. **At serving time, remove pie and Cranberry Topping from refrigerator. Spoon the topping over wedges of pie.**

Cranberry Topping
Mix ½ cup sugar, ½ cup corn syrup and 2 cups cranberries in 1-quart casserole. Cover tightly and microwave on high (100%) 4 minutes; stir. Cover and microwave until sugar is dissolved and mixture boils, 2 to 3 minutes longer.

To plan ahead, cook topping; refrigerate up to 1 week.

Microwave pie up to 3 days ahead of time; refrigerate.

At serving time, spoon topping on wedges of pie.

Spicy Tomato Meatballs

4 servings

1   *pound ground beef*
½   *cup dry bread crumbs*
¼   *cup water*
¼   *cup shredded Cheddar cheese*
¼   *cup chopped onion*
    (about 1 small)
1   *tablespoon finely chopped green*
    chilies
1   *egg*
1   *teaspoon salt*
¼   *teaspoon pepper*

    Tomato Sauce (below)

1. Mix all ingredients except Tomato Sauce. Shape mixture by teaspoonfuls into 1-inch balls. Arrange in baking dish, 12 × 7½ × 2 inches, or on 12-inch plate. Cover loosely and microwave on high (100%) 3 minutes; rearrange meatballs. Cover and microwave until no longer pink inside, 3 to 5 minutes longer; drain. (To serve meatballs immediately, see below.)

2. Freeze meatballs uncovered 15 minutes so they will separate easily. Place partially frozen meatballs in 1-quart freezer container. Cover, label and return to freezer. Freeze no longer than 2 months.

3. **About 20 minutes before serving, remove meatballs from freezer.**

4. Prepare Tomato Sauce. Gently stir meatballs into sauce until coated. Cover tightly and microwave on high (100%), stirring every 5 minutes, until hot and bubbly, 12 to 15 minutes.

To Serve Immediately: Decrease cooking time with Tomato Sauce in Step 4 to 4 to 6 minutes.

Tomato Sauce

1   *can (8 ounces) tomato sauce*
¾   *cup finely chopped tomato*
    (about 1 medium)
2   *cloves garlic, finely chopped*
1   *tablespoon lemon juice*
⅛   *teaspoon ground cumin*
⅛   *teaspoon salt*

Mix all ingredients in 1½-quart casserole.

To plan ahead, freeze the cooked meatballs 15 minutes for easy separation.

Place meatballs in 1-quart freezer container. Freeze up to 2 months.

To serve, mix sauce, add frozen meatballs; heat through and serve.

Cheesy Potatoes

4 servings

| 4 | medium baking potatoes |

⅓ to ½ cup milk
¼ cup margarine or butter, softened
    (page 11)
½ teaspoon salt
    Dash of pepper
¼ cup shredded Cheddar cheese
    (if desired)

1. Prepare and microwave whole potatoes as directed on page 153.

2. Cut thin slice from top of each potato; scoop out inside leaving thin shell. Mash potatoes until no lumps remain. Add small amounts of milk, beating after each addition. (Amount of milk needed to make potatoes smooth and fluffy depends on kind of potatoes.) Add margarine, salt and pepper; beat vigorously until potatoes are light and fluffy. Stir in cheese. Fill potato shells with mashed potatoes. (To serve immediately, see below.) Freeze uncovered 15 minutes. Place in freezer container. Cover, label and return to freezer. Freeze no longer than 2 months.

3. **About 15 minutes before serving, remove Cheesy Potatoes from freezer.** Arrange in circle on 10-inch plate. Cover loosely and microwave on high (100%) 5 minutes; rotate plate ¼ turn. Microwave until hot, 4 to 6 minutes longer. Sprinkle with imitation bacon and snipped chives if desired.

To Serve Immediately: Arrange potatoes in circle on 10-inch plate. Decrease first cooking time in Step 3 to 2 minutes. Continue as directed.

Steamed Molasses Puddings

8 to 10 servings

1 *egg*
2 *tablespoons shortening*
½ *cup boiling water*
1⅓ *cups all-purpose flour*
½ *cup molasses*
2 *tablespoons sugar*
1 *teaspoon baking soda*
¼ *teaspoon salt*

Honey Sauce (below)

1. Beat egg in 1½-quart bowl on high speed until very thick and lemon colored, about 5 minutes. Stir shortening into boiling water until shortening is melted. Beat shortening mixture, flour, molasses, sugar, baking soda and salt into egg on low speed.

2. Pour ½ of batter (about 1 cup) into greased 2-cup measure. Cover tightly and microwave on medium (50%) 3 minutes; rotate measure ½ turn. Microwave until wooden skewer inserted in center of pudding comes out clean and pudding pulls away from sides of measure, about 2 minutes longer. Let stand 5 minutes; unmold. Repeat with remaining batter. (Can be served warm immediately with Honey Sauce.) Wrap each loaf tightly in plastic freezer wrap. Label and freeze no longer than 3 months.

3. **About 10 minutes before serving, remove Steamed Molasses Puddings from freezer.** (Do not remove plastic wrap.)

4. Prepare Honey Sauce.

5. Microwave wrapped loaves on medium (50%) 1 minute; turn loaves over. Microwave until warm, 1 to 2 minutes longer. Let stand 3 minutes. Slice and serve with Honey Sauce.

Honey Sauce

½ *cup packed brown sugar*
¼ *cup honey*
¼ *cup margarine or butter*
2 *tablespoons brandy or rum*

Mix sugar, honey and margarine in 4-cup measure. Microwave uncovered on high (100%) 2 minutes; stir. Microwave until sugar is dissolved, 1 to 2 minutes longer. Let cool 5 minutes; stir in brandy.

Microwave puddings one at a time, using 2-cup measure.

To plan ahead, freeze the puddings up to 2 months.

To serve, microwave sauce; heat and slice puddings.

Peach Pie with Raspberry Sauce

One 9-inch pie

9 *inch Two-crust Pastry (page* 206)

½ *cup sugar*
2 *tablespoons cornstarch*
1 *can (29 ounces) plus 1 can (17 ounces) peach slices, drained (reserve ¼ cup syrup)*

1 *package (10 ounces) frozen raspberries, defrosted and drained (reserve ½ cup syrup for Raspberry Sauce)*
1 *tablespoon margarine or butter*

Raspberry Sauce (below)
Vanilla ice cream

1. Prepare pastry.

2. Mix sugar, cornstarch and reserved peach syrup in 4-cup measure. Microwave uncovered on high (100%), stirring every minute, until thickened and boiling, 3 to 4 minutes. Pour mixture over peaches.

3. Cover and refrigerate reserved raspberry syrup no longer than 1 week. Spread raspberries evenly in pastry-lined pie plate; cover with peach mixture. Dot with margarine. Cover with top crust that has slits cut in it; seal and flute. Microwave uncovered on high (100%) until filling begins to bubble through slits in crust, 10 to 12 minutes.

4. Transfer pie to conventional oven (do not pre-heat). Bake at 450° until crust is brown and flaky, 12 to 18 minutes. Let cool until barely warm, about 2 hours. (Can be served immediately with ice cream and Raspberry Sauce.) Freeze uncovered until completely frozen, at least 3 hours. Wrap, label and return to freezer. Freeze no longer than 1 week.

5. **About 8 hours before serving, remove pie from freezer.** Remove wrap. Let stand at room temperature until defrosted.

6. Prepare Raspberry Sauce.

7. To reheat pie, microwave uncovered on medium (50%) 5 minutes; rotate pie plate ½ turn. Microwave until warm in center, 2 to 4 minutes longer. Serve pie with ice cream and Raspberry Sauce.

Raspberry Sauce
Mix 1 tablespoon cornstarch and ¼ cup currant jelly in 2-cup measure; gradually stir in reserved raspberry syrup. Microwave uncovered on high (100%), stirring every minute, until thickened, 2 to 3 minutes. Let cool.

Individual Meatloaves

6 servings

1½ *pounds ground beef*
1 *cup soft bread crumbs (about 2 slices bread)*
¾ *cup milk*
¼ *cup chopped onion (about 1 small)*
1 *egg*
1 *tablespoon Worcestershire sauce*
1 *teaspoon salt*
½ *teaspoon dry mustard*
¼ *teaspoon pepper*
¼ *teaspoon ground sage*
Barbecue sauce

Mix all ingredients except barbecue sauce. Divide mixture into 6 parts; shape into loaves. Arrange on microwave rack in baking dish, 12 × 7½ × 2 inches. Spread each loaf with about 1 teaspoon barbecue sauce. Cover with waxed paper and microwave on high (100%) 5 minutes; rotate baking dish ½ turn. Microwave until meatloaves are almost done, 7 to 9 minutes longer. Let stand covered 3 minutes. Spread with additional barbecue sauce if desired.

To Plan Ahead for One to Six: Before microwaving, cover and refrigerate no longer than 24 hours. At serving time, cover with waxed paper and microwave on high (100%) as directed in Timetable. Let stand 3 minutes.

TIMETABLE

Servings	1	2	3*	4*	5*	6*
Utensil	16-oz. casserole		Microwave rack in baking dish, 12 × 7½ × 2″			
Minutes	3½ to 3	5 to 7	7 to 9	9 to 11	12 to 14	14 to 16

*Rotate ½ turn after ½ time.

Pancake Reheats for One or More

Pancakes need surface cooking for a golden, lacey crust, but you can refrigerate or freeze any extras for a quick microwave breakfast another time. Spread the pancakes with a thin layer of margarine or butter to help them heat evenly. Wrap in packets of two or four. Label and freeze no longer than 3 months or refrigerate no longer than 48 hours.

Microwave Reheat Directions

Medium (50%) Power

Pancakes	Room Temperature	Frozen
2	1 to 1½ minutes	2 to 3 minutes
4	2 to 3 minutes	3 to 4 minutes

Unwrap pancakes and place stack on plate. Cover loosely with plastic wrap to microwave. Serve pancakes with Quick Maple-Flavored Syrup, page 187.

Individual Meatloaves, servings for four

Beef and Biscuit Casseroles

4 servings

1 *pound ground beef*
½ *cup chopped onion (about 1 medium)*
¼ *cup chopped green pepper*

1 *can (8 ounces) tomato sauce*
1 *can (4½ ounces) chopped pitted ripe olives*
2 *tablespoons water*
1 *teaspoon salt*
1 *teaspoon chili powder*

Biscuit Topping (below)
Chili powder

1. Crumble ground beef into 2-quart casserole; add onion and green pepper. Cover loosely and microwave on high (100%) 3 minutes; break up and stir. Cover and microwave until very little pink remains in beef, 2 to 3 minutes longer; drain.

2. Stir in tomato sauce, olives, water, salt and 1 teaspoon chili powder. Cover tightly and microwave on high (100%) until hot and bubbly, 4 to 6 minutes. Divide beef mixture among 4 individual baking dishes or 10-ounce custard cups. Arrange dishes in circle on 12-inch plate.

3. Prepare Biscuit Topping; drop dough by teaspoonfuls onto beef mixtures. Sprinkle with chili powder. Microwave uncovered on high (100%) 2 minutes; rotate plate ½ turn. Microwave until biscuits are no longer doughy, 2 to 4 minutes longer.

Biscuit Topping
Stir 1 cup buttermilk baking mix, ⅓ cup cold water and ¼ cup shredded Cheddar cheese until soft dough forms; beat vigorously 20 strokes.

To Reheat for One to Four: After microwaving, cover and refrigerate no longer than 24 hours. At serving time, cover with paper towel and microwave on medium-high (70%) as directed in Timetable.

TIMETABLE

Servings	1	2	3*	4*
Minutes	2 to 3	3 to 5	6 to 8	8 to 10

*Arrange dishes in circle on 12-inch plate; rotate ½ turn after ½ time.

Microwaving for One or More

These plan-ahead recipes could be the answer to frantic, fragmented mealtimes in some families. The secret? Prepare servings for the family in individual portions — then refrigerate. Take out as many as you need, when you need them, and microwave or reheat (depending on the recipe) according to the time chart.

Potato-Topped Frankfurters

5 servings

Instant mashed potatoes (enough for 4 servings)
2 *tablespoons parsley flakes*
1 *tablespoon instant minced onion*
½ *teaspoon dry mustard*
1 *pound frankfurters (about 10)*
Paprika
¼ *cup shredded cheese*

Microwave potatoes as directed on package. Stir in parsley, onion and mustard. Cut frankfurters lengthwise, being careful not to cut completely through. Place cut side up in baking dish, 12 × 7½ × 2 inches. Spread about 3 tablespoons potato mixture on each frankfurter. Sprinkle with paprika and cheese. Cover with waxed paper and microwave on medium-high (70%) 3 minutes; rotate baking dish ½ turn. Microwave until hot, 3 to 4 minutes longer.

To Plan Ahead for One to Five: Before microwaving frankfurters, cover and refrigerate no longer than 24 hours. At serving time, cover with waxed paper. Microwave 1 and 2 servings on high (100%) and 3 to 5 servings on medium-high (70%) as directed in Timetable.

TIMETABLE

Servings (2 frankfurters)	1	2	3*	4*	5*
Minutes	1 to 1½	2½ to 3½	4 to 6	6 to 8	8 to 10

*Rotate dish after ½ the time. Let stand 3 minutes before serving.

Serve Potato-Topped Frankfurters right away or reheat 1 serving or more as needed.

To prepare for either use, microwave mashed potatoes and stir in seasonings.

Sprinkle potatoes in franks with paprika and cheese. Cover; microwave or refrigerate.

Quick Chicken Pies

4 servings

1 *can (10¾ ounces) condensed
  cream of chicken soup*
1 *can (8½ ounces) green peas,
  drained*
1 *can (5 ounces) boned chicken,
  broken into chunks*
1 *can (4 ounces) mushroom stems
  and pieces*
¼ *cup chopped celery*
¼ *teaspoon poultry seasoning*

1 *cup buttermilk baking mix*
⅓ *cup milk*
¼ *cup broken pecans
  Paprika*

1. Mix soup, peas, chicken, mushrooms (with liquid), celery and poultry seasoning in 1½-quart casserole. Cover tightly and microwave on high (100%) until hot and bubbly, 3 to 4 minutes.

2. Stir baking mix, milk and pecans until soft dough forms; beat vigorously 20 strokes. Spoon chicken mixture into 4 individual dishes or 10-ounce custard cups; top each with ¼ of the biscuit dough. Sprinkle with paprika. Arrange dishes in circle on 12-inch plate. Microwave uncovered on high (100%) 2 minutes; rotate each casserole ½ turn. Microwave until biscuits are no longer doughy, 2 to 4 minutes longer.

To Reheat for One to Four: After microwaving, cover and refrigerate no longer than 24 hours. At serving time, cover with waxed paper and microwave on medium-high (70%) as directed in Timetable.

TIMETABLE

Servings	1	2	3*	4*
Minutes	2 to 3	3 to 5	6 to 8	8 to 10

*Rearrange after ½ the time.

Little Salmon Casseroles (pictured on page 261)

4 servings

1 *can (15½ ounces) salmon,*
   drained and flaked
1 *egg, slightly beaten*
2 *tablespoons milk*
½ *teaspoon salt*
   Dash of pepper

⅔ *cup chopped celery*
2 *tablespoons chopped onion*
3 *tablespoons margarine or butter*

2 *cups soft bread crumbs (about 4*
   slices bread)
⅓ *cup milk*
½ *teaspoon ground sage*

4 *slices process American cheese*
4 *green pepper rings*

1. Mix salmon, egg, 2 tablespoons milk, the salt and pepper. Press lightly on bottoms and about halfway up sides of 4 individual baking dishes or 10-ounce custard cups.

2. Place celery, onion and margarine in 1½-quart casserole. Cover tightly and microwave on high (100%) 2 minutes; stir. Cover and microwave until vegetables are crisp-tender, 1 to 2 minutes longer.

3. Stir in bread crumbs, ⅓ cup milk and the sage. Spoon into center of each baking dish, pressing lightly to make celery mixture level with salmon mixture. Arrange dishes in circle on 12-inch plate. Microwave uncovered on medium-high (70%) until hot, 7 to 9 minutes.

4. Top each dish with cheese and green pepper ring; rotate dishes ½ turn. Microwave until cheese is melted, 1 to 1½ minutes longer.

To Plan Ahead for One to Four: After filling casseroles, cover and refrigerate no longer than 24 hours. At serving time, microwave uncovered on medium-high (70%) as directed in Timetable.

TIMETABLE

Servings	1	2	3	4
Minutes	3½ to 4½	4 to 6	8 to 10	9 to 11

Note: After microwaving go back to Step 4, continue as directed.

Reheating Casseroles and Vegetables in the Microwave

Casseroles and vegetables reheat well. Cover for fastest heating and stir once or twice. Casseroles that can't be stirred benefit by a cover and a standing time. If the casserole contains delicate foods such as eggs, cheese or large chunks of meat, a lower power setting will help avoid overcooking.

A microwave thermometer to see whether foods are hot enough in the center is a good investment. If using a conventional thermometer, use it after microwaving.

Meat and poultry should be sliced thinly or in uniform pieces, then covered with gravy or a sauce and covered loosely.

Rosy Apples, servings for two

Rosy Apples

4 *apples*

Core 4 large baking apples. Pare skin on top half of each apple in petal design if desired; place upright in individual baking dish or 10-ounce custard cup. Fill center of each with 1 tablespoon cinnamon candies and top with about 1 tablespoon packed brown sugar, pushing firmly into core. Microwave uncovered on high (100%) until tender when pierced with fork, 4 to 6 minutes. Serve with cream.

TIMETABLE

Servings	1	2	3*	4*
Minutes	2½ to 3½	3 to 4	3½ to 5½	4 to 6

Note: Size and variety of apples will influence microwave time.

*Rotate dishes ½ turn after ½ time.

Hot Orange Cider

6 servings (about ¾ cup each)

Mix 4½ cups apple cider, 2 tablespoons grenadine syrup, 1¼ teaspoons grated orange peel and ⅛ teaspoon crushed anise seed in 1½-quart casserole. Cover tightly and microwave on high (100%) until hot, 6 to 8 minutes; stir. Stir in 2 tablespoons brandy if desired.

To Serve One to Five: For each serving, allow ¾ cup cider, 1 teaspoon grenadine syrup, ¼ teaspoon grated orange peel and a dash of anise seed. Microwave uncovered on high (100%) as directed in Timetable. Add 2 teaspoons brandy if desired.

TIMETABLE

Servings	1	2	4	5
Minutes	1 to 2	2 to 3	4 to 6	5 to 7

Spiced Tea

1 cup mix

½ cup orange-flavored instant
   breakfast drink
½ cup instant tea
¼ cup sugar
¼ cup lemonade flavor drink mix
¼ teaspoon ground cinnamon
⅛ teaspoon ground cloves

Mix all ingredients; store in tightly covered container at room temperature.

To Serve One to Six: For each serving, stir 2 to 3 teaspoons mix into ¾ cup water in cup or mug. Microwave uncovered on high (100%) until hot, as directed in Timetable. Stir and serve.

TIMETABLE

Servings	1	2	4*	6*
Minutes	1 to 2	2 to 3	4 to 5	6 to 8

*Arrange cups in circle on 12-inch plate; rotate ½ turn after ½ time.

INDEX